Library of
Davidson College

THE DIPLOMATIC RECORD 1989-1990

Published in cooperation with the

INSTITUTE FOR THE STUDY OF DIPLOMACY

School of Foreign Service, Georgetown University

An integral part of the Georgetown University School of Foreign Service, the **Institute for the Study of Diplomacy** concentrates on the processes of diplomacy. Through its research and publication programs, the Institute seeks to improve diplomatic skills and broaden public understanding of diplomacy.

Advisory Committee

Miguel Gonzalez Avelar
Mexico City, Mexico

Anthony T. Bryan
Trinidad and Tobago

Andrea G. Mochi Onory diSaluzzo
Rome, Italy

Peter F. Dunkley
Washington, DC

Allan E. Goodman
Washington, DC

Brandon Grove
Washington, DC

A.N.D. Haksar
New Delhi, India

J. Bryan Hehir
Washington, DC

Gary Hufbauer
Washington, DC

Peter F. Krogh
Washington, DC

Robert Lieber
Washington, DC

Christopher Maule
Ottawa, Canada

Theodore Moran
Washington, DC

John Muzhar
Jakarta, Indonesia

Thereza Marie Machado Quintella
Brasilia, Brazil

Jeswald W. Salacuse
Medford, MA

Editorial Staff

David D. Newsom
Editor

Jean C. Newsom
Associate Editor

Charles Dolgas
Production Coordinator

Michael Snyder
Production Assistant

James Bjork   Alexander Espinosa   Thomas Evans   Taylor Fain   Richard Gold
Research Assistants

THE DIPLOMATIC RECORD 1989-1990

edited by
David D. Newsom
INSTITUTE FOR THE STUDY OF DIPLOMACY

WESTVIEW PRESS
Boulder • San Francisco • Oxford

The Diplomatic Record

All rights reserved. No part of this publication may be reproduced or transmitted in any form or by any means, electronic or mechanical, including photocopy, recording, or any information storage and retrieval system, without permission in writing from the publisher.

Copyright © 1991 by Westview Press, Inc.

Published in 1991 in the United States of America by Westview Press, Inc., 5500 Central Avenue, Boulder, Colorado 80301, and in the United Kingdom by Westview Press, 36 Lonsdale Road, Summertown, Oxford OX2 7EW

Library of Congress ISSN: 1052-0309
ISBN: 0-8133-1142-X

Printed and bound in the United States of America

∞ The paper in this publication meets the requirements of the American National Standard for Permanence of Paper for Printed Library Materials Z39.48-1984.

10 9 8 7 6 5 4 3 2 1

Contents

Editor's Note ix

About the Editor and Authors xi

ESSAYS

1 What Works in Diplomacy?
David D. Newsom and Allan E. Goodman 3

2 Peacemaking in Southern Africa: The Namibia-Angola Settlement of 1988
Chester A. Crocker 9

3 The Afghanistan Negotiations
Riaz Mohammad Khan 35

4 The INF Treaty in Perspective
Leo Reddy 57

5 US-Soviet Bilateral Relations Since Reykjavik
John M. Evans 77

6 Ending the Iran-Iraq War
Sohrab C. Sobhani 89

7 The Negotiations on a Chemical Weapons Ban in 1989
Barend ter Haar 115

8 International Negotiations on Environmental Issues:
   The Year Ahead
   Andrew D. Sens 133

 9 Ozone Diplomacy
   Richard Elliot Benedick 141

10 Antarctic Treaty Diplomacy: Problems, Prospects,
   and Policy Implications
   Christopher C. Joyner 155

DEPARTMENTS

Looking Ahead: Diplomatic Challenges of 1991 183

The Governance of Diplomacy: Recent Developments
Harold E. Horan 189

Diplomatic Chronology 193

List of Acronyms and Abbreviations 229

Bibliography 233

Index 237

Editor's Note

With this inaugural issue, the Institute for the Study of Diplomacy of Georgetown University and Westview Press are pleased to introduce *The Diplomatic Record*. In a world of ferment where diplomacy vies with conflict, we intend to bring you annual highlights of the world of the diplomats, their accomplishments, their continuing efforts, and the changing circumstances of their profession.

In this as in future issues, we begin with essays on recently concluded diplomatic negotiations both by practitioners involved in the action and by scholars who have combined research with detailed discussions with the participants. Then follow summaries of significant continuing negotiations, accompanied by a review of developments in the governance of diplomacy, a chronology, and a bibliography of recent works on diplomacy.

This project is supported by a generous grant from the Harriman Foundation, through the active interest of Pamela Harriman. It is highly appropriate that a publication dedicated to a greater understanding of diplomacy should be associated with the name of Averell Harriman, one of America's distinguished diplomats.

Other donors made possible the research and writing of individual authors. Support was received from the J. Howard Pew Freedom Trust, the Earhart Foundation, the United States Institute of Peace, the H.J. Heinz Company Foundation, the John Thomas Smith Memorial Foundation, the Chevron Corporation, and Mobil Oil.

In the production of *The Diplomatic Record* we are indebted also to the editorial advisory committee. This committee draws not only on the faculty of the School of Foreign Service of Georgetown University but also on the worldwide network of deans and directors of schools and academies of diplomacy around the world. Their support and advice will make this publication truly international.

Editor's Note

When undertaking a work of this kind, an editor is conscious both of opportunities and of limitations. Opportunities are present in the progress made in the resolution of regional and global conflicts. Limitations are present in space restrictions that prevent as full an account as might be warranted and reduce the number of documents that can be cited. An additional factor is the lead, or production, time that precludes reference to the most up-to-date developments in a dynamic, unpredictable field. Nevertheless, we present this initial issue with a confidence that within these limitations we have assembled a survey of some of the significant accomplishments of recent diplomacy that will be of value to scholars, practitioners, and general readers who, in the search for peace and freedom, look to the skill of the diplomat.

David D. Newsom

About the Editor and Authors

Richard Elliot Benedick, as deputy assistant secretary of state for environment, health, and natural resources, was the chief US negotiator for the Vienna Convention on the Protection of the Ozone Layer and the Montreal Protocol on Substances That Deplete the Ozone Layer. He is currently on assignment from the State Department as senior fellow of the Conservation Foundation and World Wildlife Fund in Washington, DC.

Chester A. Crocker, Ph.D., Landegger distinguished research professor at the School of Foreign Service, was assistant secretary of state for African affairs from 1981 to 1989. He was the principal US negotiator in the protracted diplomacy leading to the Namibia-Angola settlement of 1988.

John M. Evans is coordinator for the Conference on European Security and Cooperation in the Department of State.

Allan E. Goodman, Ph.D., is associate dean of the School of Foreign Service and director of the Master of Science in Foreign Service Program.

Harold E. Horan, director of programs at the Institute for the Study of Diplomacy, was formerly US ambassador to Malawi, deputy assistant secretary of state for African affairs, and staff member of the National Security Council.

Christopher C. Joyner, Ph.D., is professor of political science at George Washington University.

Riaz Mohammad Khan, a member of Pakistan's Foreign Service, holds the rank of director general. He participated in all of the Geneva rounds of the negotiations on Afghanistan from 1982 to 1988 as a member of the Pakistan delegation.

David D. Newsom is director of the Institute for the Study of Diplomacy, former US ambassador to Libya, Indonesia, and the Philippines, former under secretary of state for political affairs (1978-1981), and the author of numerous books and articles.

Leo Reddy was the State Department representative on the US delegation to the INF negotiations in Geneva, March 1985-December 1987, after which he served as director of the State Department's Treaty Ratification Task Force until the Senate gave its advice and consent in May 1988.

Andrew D. Sens is director of the Office of Environmental Protection in the Department of State.

Sohrab C. Sobhani, Ph.D., professor of international relations at Georgetown University, specializes in US national security concerns in the Middle East.

Barend ter Haar is an officer in the Netherlands Foreign Service. He is currently a diplomatic associate of the Institute for the Study of Diplomacy.

THE DIPLOMATIC RECORD 1989-1990

ESSAYS

1

What Works in Diplomacy?

David D. Newsom and Allan E. Goodman

THE DECADE OF THE 1980S saw a resurgence of the use of diplomatic negotiations to bring about the cessation of conflict and a lessening of tensions between the world's superpowers. Within the space of two years, agreements were signed that resulted in the withdrawal of Soviet troops from Afghanistan, a cease-fire between Iraq and Iran, and, in parallel, the withdrawal of Cuban troops from Angola and the independence of Namibia. Although these agreements left serious problems in the respective regions unresolved, each represented a triumph of the intricate art of diplomacy and a renewal of faith in the ability of the international community to find alternatives to conflict and confrontation. In 1989, Nigeria's Joseph Garba, president of the United Nations General Assembly, characterized this period as representing a "new and constructive spirit in world politics."[1]

What accounts for this upsurge in the use and effectiveness of negotiation as a tool of conflict resolution? What does recent experience say about the necessary conditions for effective diplomacy? First, it suggests that bringing adversaries together to resolve their differences requires extensive, patient groundwork. Diplomacy is too often narrowly defined as negotiation. It should be seen more broadly as interaction between the diverse political systems of the world's nation-states in which their representatives advance national interests and, where possible, seek to find areas of mutuality in those interests with other states. Diplomacy is a constant, not an intermittent, effort, a fact that is easily forgotten because the popular image of diplomacy is that which captures headlines—peace conferences and summits, walks-in-the-woods between high-level representatives of adversaries, statesmen gathered around conference tables debating the future of the international economic order. What is often overlooked is that diplomacy consists mainly of day-to-day contacts that take place between officials of one government and those of another. It takes place at many levels in international affairs and involves not only professional diplomats, but also officials of many other government agencies who have an increasing stake in the nation's international relationships and whose policy initiatives are affected by them. Similarly, executives in the private sector are discovering that successful diplomacy can contribute substantially to the effectiveness of their enterprises.

As three of the essays in this volume make clear, the recently acclaimed agreements could not have been reached without years spent patiently seeking those elements of common ground that might ultimately bring protagonists to the table. In the case of Afghanistan, the signing of the agreement was preceded by more than eight years of discussions under the auspices of the United Nations. The cease-fire between Iraq and Iran may have come about through the mutual exhaustion of the belligerents, but without prior efforts of mediators reaching a basis for an accord, it would have been far more difficult to achieve. The diplomacy that resulted in the agreement on Angola and Namibia had its roots in a UN resolution enacted ten years before.

The second factor facilitating the work of diplomacy has been the change in the international climate brought about by a relaxation in the confrontation between the United States and the Soviet Union. Strong foreign policy establishments, and able diplomats and wise statesmen willing to rely on them, are necessary for successful diplomacy. But even with their best efforts, diplomatic breakthroughs are difficult, if not impossible, to achieve without some basic changes in the structure and dynamics of international relations of the kind created by the new thinking in Moscow and the response from the West.

For most of this century, international relations have been structured by the rivalries among great military, industrial powers.[2] Although officials and individuals of neutral nations such as Sweden have played significant roles from time to time in the resolution of conflicts, military power has generally been the most reliable indicator of which states could influence international affairs decisively as well as of the tools they would be relying upon to do so. Such power, of course, did not exist in a vacuum from economic realities; poor states could not afford the navies and armies necessary to project power or sustain it over long periods of time.

Since 1945, the effectiveness of diplomacy at practically all levels and on an enormous number of issues has been directly related to the perceived power of the United States and the Soviet Union. Where they determined arms should continue to flow to protagonists, as in the Middle East and Afghanistan, the possibilities of a peaceful resolution of conflict declined. Where they made clear their willingness either to limit support, as in the case of Iran and Iraq, or to participate actively in negotiations, such as in Namibia and Afghanistan, progress could be made.

As instructive as these cases may be, they are far less than precise indicators of the global environment in which diplomacy will take place in the future. At the beginning of the 1990s, unprecedented and unexpected changes in the world made possible new approaches to old questions. At the same time, they also set the stage for aggression—for example, the Iraqi invasion of Kuwait—that neither of the superpowers forecast or desired. The preferences and rivalries between major powers, consequently, may no longer define alignments in international relations, and their interaction may be less and less determinative of what happens in international affairs. Ironically, Soviet Foreign Minister Eduard Shevardnadze was one of the first statesmen to speak openly about this phenomenon when he observed in his ministry's journal on diplomacy that

> the struggle between two opposing systems is no longer a determining tendency of the present-day era. At [this] stage, the ability to build up material wealth at an accelerated rate on the basis of front-ranking science and high-level techniques and technology, and to distribute it fairly, and through joint efforts to restore and protect the resources necessary for mankind's survival acquires decisive importance.[3]

It is more appropriate to use this source rather than to quote a prominent theorist of international affairs, because practitioners in communist as well as democratic systems seem to be ahead of the theorists in grasping that something has changed.

Change is, in fact, occurring in three important dimensions. First, at the systemic level, world politics are less and less shaped by the dynamics of the US-Soviet Union relationship and rivalry. Although détente and balance between the superpowers will remain important prerequisites for international stability—and although tensions in this relationship will always be important to manage, if not avoid—the clear impression is that the 1990s will be shaped by forces, issues, and trends largely independent or out of the range of influence of leaders in Moscow or Washington. Major arms control agreements between and among the nations will lessen the threat of global conflict. Prospects of additional conflict in such regions as the Gulf and Central America are more and more likely to be resolved on a regional level; the same is true of the continuing tensions in the Indo-Pakistan subcontinent. The old ways of doing business will not work as well as they have in the past, and superpowers will be unable to force their preferred solutions to conflicts through unilateral action. Even states that retain huge military establishments and that have the capacity to project power on a global basis will find it increasingly necessary to rely on diplomacy rather than on force to achieve national security and other foreign policy objectives.

Second, at the regional level, the trend toward economic (and to a lesser extent political) integration has also created an atmosphere in which diplomacy and not military power projection seems to be the most effective way to influence events. This is not to say that the motives of states have changed, only that the predominant ways in which leaders seek to achieve their objectives seem to have altered. States of any size still need security and will want to promote national interests; to do this, governments will continue to seek to extend their influence (that is, project power) as far as possible. But the tools used to project such power and even the definition of success in foreign policy may be changing. When governments seek to achieve their purposes with diplomacy and negotiation, they may be more willing to settle for less than they would if they were prepared to wage war.

Measuring these tendencies and shifts is difficult at the micro level. To have access to the thought processes of top decision-makers is not possible, and even if it were they might not reveal that explicit choices were made to settle for less. What can be observed are the venues where statesmen choose to pursue national interests and the instruments that are necessary for success. For example, when addressing issues before the Economic Community in Europe or in the Association of Southeast Asian Nations, regional leaders are finding it increasingly necessary to deal with other states in multilateral forums. Relationships, therefore, must be managed by diplomacy and conflicts resolved largely through negotiation.

Third, the costs of armed conflict seem to be rising, and this may be a reason why so many long-term conflicts have been recently resolved or appear on the verge of ending. Clearly, the United States and the Soviet Union are less and less able or inclined to fund wars in other states over a prolonged period. Ambitious leaders in the Third World also appear to be learning that wars cannot be sustained indefinitely, no matter how widespread popular support for them appears to be.

The more frequent use of diplomacy is, however, no guarantee that the international system can be immunized against war. Many of the wars fought in this century and the last have, in fact, been preceded by periods of intense diplomatic activity aimed at their prevention. Conflict—even on a regional or global scale—can be triggered by the rivalries and actions of relatively small states (Iraq, North Korea, or North Vietnam, for example) or by the threats to stability created by internal divisions and such non-state actors as ethnic or religious fanatics (the murder of Archduke Franz Ferdinand at Sarajevo), guerrilla armies (the contras in Nicaragua), or terrorists.

Finally, in many cases, diplomacy can be an imperfect tool. Major aspects of a conflict might be resolved while others remain unresolved, nourishing the seeds of further conflict. The Camp David accords between Egypt and Israel have not resolved the struggle between Israelis and Palestinians. The internal rivalries in Afghanistan continue to devastate that country. The Iran and Iraq cease-fire is fragile. An internal accord between warring factions in Angola has still not been reached through diplomacy.

To a certain extent, even profound shifts in alignments in the international system may not mean that force will cease to be useful or be considered less useful than diplomacy. What does seem clear is that diplomacy and negotiation are becoming more respected as tools for achieving national interests in the present international system than they were just a few years ago. Most leaders who prefer fighting to negotiating—and who can afford to do so—appear to be waiting longer before using force. Does this mean that they are also trying to achieve their objectives first and primarily through diplomacy? The answer to this question will provide a guide to the circumstances in which the dedication and skills of the diplomat can most effectively be applied in the international system of the 1990s.

Notes

1. Quoted in Paul Lewis, "U.S. Delegate Calls U.N.'s Session 'Constructive'," *New York Times*, December 20, 1989, p. A-3.
2. Paul Kennedy, *The Rise and Fall of Great Powers* (New York: Random House, 1987).
3. *Vestnik Ministerstva Inostrannykh Del SSR*, no. 15 (August 1988), p. 27.

2

Peacemaking in Southern Africa: The Namibia-Angola Settlement of 1988

Chester A. Crocker

WITH THE TREATIES SIGNED by Angola, Cuba, and South Africa at the headquarters of the United Nations in New York on December 22, 1988, and the independence of Namibia that followed, the colonial period in Africa has effectively ended. South Africa's forces have come home after twenty-five years of war beyond its borders. With the completion of the withdrawal of Cuban troops from Angola in 1991, the countries of Southern Africa will be free of foreign troops for the first time since the Napoleonic wars. The agreements changed the geopolitical equation between the South African government and its armed guerrilla opponents, making possible both internal change and transformed relations between Pretoria and its neighbors.

The 1988 settlement has a still broader significance. Doctrines and policies based on violence have been discredited; they have been superceded by moves toward internal reconciliation. Further, they signal the end of Cuba's experiment in African military intervention and coincide with a parallel reappraisal by the Soviet Union of its African interests and policies. Moscow's role as an "observer" in the final phases of the US-mediated Namibia-Angola accords could signal the Soviet Union's desire to be seen as a constructive element in regional conflict resolution.

Above all, the settlement represents the successful implementation of a US initiative. The governments in the region took the hard decisions, but in doing so, they implemented an American blueprint. The US initiative was both realistic and ambitious. It required patience as well as a readiness to use muscle when appropriate and to live with the burdens of temporary unpopularity.

Finally, the negotiations illustrate the effective interaction of great powers and the United Nations. Namibia had long been a UN problem. The implementation of Security Council Resolution 435 (1978) in Namibia's transition to independence demonstrated the unique acceptability of UN instruments, forums, and implementing agencies in highly polarized settings. At the same time, the case underscores the sharp distinction between the roles of peacemaking and the implementation of settlements. This experience suggests that the UN system and the great powers will continue to be dependent on each other in future cases.

The US Decision to Engage: 1981

By 1975, when the United States decided to apply a global strategy to Africa, negative dynamics were already firmly established: Portugal's sudden departure from its African empire left behind one of the messiest and most irresponsible acts of decolonization in the post-1945 period; nationalist military insurgencies directed against colonial or local white authorities erupted in Angola, Mozambique, Rhodesia (Zimbabwe), and Namibia; the Soviets made the unprecedented decision to project their military power into Africa by supporting insurgencies and through Cuban proxies sent to Angola and Ethiopia; and an increasingly isolated, bellicose, and militarily self-sufficient South Africa involved itself in the turmoil beyond its borders.

For the next six years, from 1975 to 1981, the Ford and Carter administrations sought to acquire the capacity for leadership in promoting negotiated solutions and peaceful change in Southern Africa. This necessitated a region-wide vision that embraced the Rhodesian and Namibian conflicts as well as the imperative of an end to apartheid in South Africa.

By 1981, when the Reagan administration entered office, Washington had established effective working relations with the British on Africa and close working ties of its own with the African front line states (FLS) and, to a lesser extent, with the wary South Africans, still deeply scarred by the Western failure to respond to the Soviet/Cuban intervention in Angola.

Washington played a key supporting role to the British in the protracted negotiations leading to the Lancaster House settlement and the independence of Zimbabwe in 1980. At the same time, the US administration took the lead in forming the "Contact Group" with Britain, Canada, the Federal Republic of Germany, and France and, with these allies, shaping a set of

Figure 2.1 Map of Southern Africa

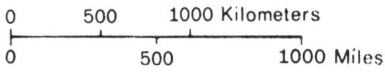

proposals for Namibian independence. These proposals, endorsed by UN Security Council Resolution 435 in September 1978, established a set of complex arrangements for the territory's transition to independence under South African administrative control with simultaneous UN monitoring and supervision. The next two and one-half years were taken up with efforts to gain South African agreement to the implementation of Resolution 435.

Despite the progress made in the 1970s, the Southern African peace process was in trouble at the beginning of the Reagan administration in January 1981. The South Africans, disillusioned with the Angola fiasco and with results of Western diplomacy in Zimbabwe after the victory of Robert Mugabe's Zimbabwe African National Union in the April 1980 election, were increasingly put off by the long history of the UN's pro-South-West African People's Organization (SWAPO) activities and pronouncements regarding Namibia. They began to perceive a pattern in these events. The South African stance on Namibia became increasingly truculent and uncooperative, and Pretoria stepped up its bellicose statements toward its neighbors. On the ground, South African military elements were augmenting clandestine activity in a number of adjacent states, including Angola and Mozambique. Meanwhile, the front line states and SWAPO began to view Pretoria's stalling on Namibia as a test of Western diplomatic manhood. By early 1981, they had resisted Pretoria's provocations to abandon the Western-led peace process and were headed instead toward calling for UN mandatory sanctions to penalize South Africa for its failure to implement the Namibia decolonization plan. The Western nations wanted neither sanctions nor a rupture with the Africans. The Contact Group mediation was caught between increasingly polarized parties that showed every sign of hardening their positions.

Faced with this regional legacy, the incoming Reagan team saw three options: to *continue with the Namibia-only* approach, recognizing its limited prospects but judging that the continuing process could buy time and avoid trouble with allied and African partners; to *downgrade Southern African diplomacy*, thus avoiding the domestic grief visited on previous administrations; or to *restructure the negotiations fundamentally* to incorporate the Angolan factor. Western diplomacy prior to 1981 had carefully avoided addressing the principal negative factor that had prompted Western concern in the mid-1970s: the Soviet-Cuban fait accompli in Angola.

There were reasons why Angola had played no role in Western-led regional diplomacy after 1976. The West had a weak hand—both physically and diplomatically—after the Angola events of 1975-1976. Western efforts to address the question of Cuban troops in Angola, it was argued, would have undercut Angola's cooperation in Namibian diplomacy and led to accusations that the West was more concerned about the communist presence in Angola than about colonialism and racism in South African-ruled Namibia. To many observers in Africa, Europe, and the United States such reasoning made good diplomatic sense. It did not make for sound strategy, however, because the issue of foreign intervention in Angola (both Cuban and South African) had always been uppermost in the thinking of decision-makers in both Luanda and Pretoria. Even prior to 1981, Angolan leaders had recognized the connection between Namibian and Angolan events when they stated that Cubans could leave Angola after Namibia's independence under Resolution 435. On the other side, there were a host of reasons why a narrowly defined Namibia settlement was unattractive to Pretoria. The Cuban presence next door in Angola gave Namibian and South African critics of Resolution 435 further reasons to block a Namibian settlement.

During the Contact Group negotiations prior to 1981, South African officials made no secret of their interest in the issue of the Cuban troops in Angola. The Carter administration had tied the establishment of diplomatic relations with Luanda to Cuban troop withdrawal, but, despite prolonged internal debate over how to handle the Soviet-Cuban factor in Africa, never went beyond that to establish a specific link between Namibia and Angola. As a result, some of the most basic security concerns of both Pretoria and Luanda were never explicitly addressed.

The decision of the Reagan administration to link Namibia and Angola thus represented both continuity and change in Southern African policy. The linkage strategy, by incorporating the Cuban issue, offered two major pluses: a far better chance to nail Pretoria down to a firm commitment on Resolution 435 and an appropriate US response to the extension of the Brezhnev doctrine to the Third World, including Africa. If properly orchestrated, the new US approach would undermine the rationale behind Moscow's heavily militarized African diplomacy and place pressure on Soviet-Cuban-African relations—and on the Angolan regime itself if it became an obstacle to Namibia's independence. At the same time, such an approach had the potential to force decisions in Pretoria: to choose between cooperation or confrontation with the West and between blind exploitation of its regional hegemony or the successful use of that power to solve problems.

Under this strategy, Washington would be asking more than a dozen governments and two isolated guerrilla movements to adapt to and cooperate with a fundamentally restructured negotiation. The new US strategy sought to promote a broadened agenda that recognized the relationship between regional and internal conflict. It looked beyond the region's sharp military and political polarization toward an overarching "common interest" in reduced violence. A skeptic would have been forgiven for wondering, in 1981, why and how all of this would work. The new strategy appeared ambitious; it would require a substantial investment of diplomatic capital, and it contained risks.

Scholars of conflict resolution speak of "ripe moments" for external diplomatic intervention.[1] Measured by such standards, the wars in Southern Africa were not ripe for resolution in 1981. But the absence of ripeness does not tell the external party to do nothing; it can point to obstacles and suggest ways of dealing with them. Washington decided, in its own interest, to mount a regional strategic initiative that would alter the negotiating framework, expand the range of parties and potential trade-offs, and shape a potential alternative to the parties' unilateral options.

Moreover, the Reagan administration was not simply seeking a settlement in Southern Africa; it sought *its* settlement. In this sense, it viewed the Southern African negotiations, which had started back in 1975-1976, as akin to the Middle East peace process. As Harold Saunders has pointed out, there are occasions when the pursuit of negotiated solutions is in itself a strategy not only for regional conflict resolution but also for conflict management and for the pre-negotiations phase of peacemaking until conflict arenas become ripe.[2] The pre-negotiation phase is where most of the action lies, where the basic dies are cast, where the core concepts and principles are defined and legitimized, and where much of the hardest work of the peacemakers actually takes place.

The Negotiations: 1981-1988

The US decisions in early 1981 set the stage for an eight-year Southern African marathon. The United States played multiple roles as alliance leader, directly intervening superpower, third-party mediator, facilitator of indirect communication, source of proposals and compromises, and host/convener of face-to-face meetings. The diplomatic effort went through periods of greater or less activity, but Washington stayed with its essential goals and concepts. Tactics changed in accordance with prevailing conditions and obstacles as the process moved from (a) gaining acceptance of a new agenda that would start with enhancing and nailing down Resolution 435, to (b) legitimizing the linkage concept as the basis for negotiations and persuading the parties to stick to it, to (c) obtaining initial and follow-up proposals on the relationships of Resolution 435 and the Cuban troop withdrawal timetables, to (d) reinforcing the inherent stalemate so that the parties would recognize the cost of unilateral solutions, and (e) getting them to a common table around single texts of documents.

All of this proceeded against a background constantly affected by internal political currents in each country involved and by a changing balance of the military forces in the region. The phases in the prolonged negotiations are summarized in Table 2.1.

When the parties gathered in Geneva in November 1988 after the American electoral victory of George Bush, each side knew exactly where the trade-offs were and what cards could be played. Closure required nearly four days of maneuver as graphs, charts, and numerous illustrative examples were deployed to help resolve what had increasingly become a mathematical/political equation. After final calls to their capitals, delegation heads closed on a 27-month timetable that would remove 66 percent of the 50,000-plus Cuban force during the first year. Champagne toasts signaled that final agreement was near.

Five more weeks were required to complete the drafting of a penultimate Brazzaville protocol, to negotiate a UN verification plan, to agree on a US-proposed joint commission to oversee implementation of the agreements by the signatory parties with US and Soviet participation as observers, and, in consultation with the UN secretary-general, to set a new date for implementation of the package on April 1, 1989. Two more rounds of tripartite meetings in Brazzaville completed the process, producing the Brazzaville Protocol of December 13. Ten days later the parties signed their agreements in a ceremony at UN headquarters chaired by US Secretary of State George P. Shultz and UN Secretary-General Javier Perez de Cuellar.

Why US Diplomacy Succeeded: Key Factors

Eight years of diplomacy conducted against the backdrop of regional war, internal change, and external political dynamics cannot readily be "explained" in terms of causes or replicable hypotheses. Nonetheless, the key factors can be identified. They are discussed here in terms of US

Table 2.1 From Linkage to Leverage: How the Process Worked

Stage I
(April to October 1981)

- Internal Contact Group discussion of Cuban troop-Namibia linkage and intensive consultations with South Africa and the FLS/SWAPO.
- Contact Group tables proposals and launches first mission related to the Namibia issues (Resolution 435).

Stage II
(November 1981 to September 1982)

- Contact Group concludes phased negotiation of all "outstanding issues" related to Resolution 435.
- Agreement reached with FLS, SWAPO, South Africa, and Namibian internal parties on constitutional principles for constituent assembly.
- Agreement reached on necessity of UN Transition Assistance Group (UNTAG) to monitor SWAPO bases in Angola and Zambia.
- Contact Group resolves South African misgivings about UNTAG and "UN impartiality" with "informal understandings."

Stage III
(January 1982 to March 1985)

- Nearly 20 rounds of direct US-Angolan talks on Cuban troop withdrawal (CTW) aimed at establishing US credibility and the legitimacy of linkage.
- Linkage accepted by Angola and forces in southern Angola disengage (1984). Washington tables first negotiating document calling for two-year, front-loaded schedule of CTW to be implemented in tandem with Resolution 435.

Stage IV
(March 1985 to April 1987)

- South Africa delays pull-out from Angola, and Angola does not act against SWAPO violations.
- Angolan offensive against National Union for the Total Independence of Angola (UNITA) defeated by UNITA/South African counteraction (1985).
- US administration adopts limited sanctions against Pretoria (1985).
- South Africa conditionally accepts March 1985 US proposal, creating leverage to obtain

(continues)

Table 2.1 (continued)

Stage IV
(*continued*)

further bids from Angola on CTW timing (Fall 1985).
- US resumes tangible support to UNITA (1986).
- Angola ignores South African offer of "date certain" for Resolution 435 linked to agreement on CTW (1986).
- US Congress initiates further sanctions against South Africa and new sanctions against Angola and other FLS plus colonial Namibia (1986-87).
- Structure of Namibia-Angola negotiation maintained despite mounting frictions and suspicion of US motives in Pretoria and Luanda.

Stage V
(April 1987 to April 1988)

- US-Popular Movement for the Liberation of Angola (MPLA) discussions resume (April 1987).
- US presses Angola to reciprocate South African partial acceptance of March 1985 proposal, and Angola presses United States to offer up bilateral carrots such as an end to US aid to UNITA as "quid" for new MPLA proposal.
- Angola-Cuba approve new CTW timetable, two instead of three years for removal of "southern" Cuba contingent, retaining earlier northern residual for indefinite period. Castro signals that Cuba wishes to enter talks directly.
- UNITA and South Africa smash Soviet-supported Angolan offensive, inflicting huge losses.
- US-Angola discuss conditions for Cuban participation.
- South Africa seeks detailed information about US/MPLA talks.
- Castro sends 15,000 more troops to shore up MPLA defenses and seek political leverage.
- Cuba joins Angola in negotiations and categorically accepts principle of total Cuban withdrawal (January 1988).
- Both sides move to reengage in diplomacy (March 1988).
- US decides parties nearly ready for face-to-face talks, with US mediation (April 1988).

Stage VI
(May 1988 to December 1988)

- First of twelve rounds of face-to-face trilateral discussion with Cuban participation begin in May.

(continues)

Table 2.1 (continued)

Stage VI
(*continued*)

- Scramble for position on ground and for political advantage in talks; direct Cuban-South African Defense Force (SADF) clash at Calueque (June 1988).
- Psychological turning point as parties agree to accept all tabled proposals as "basis for discussion" (Cairo talks, June 1988).
- US assists in hammering out New York Principles, first agreed document of the negotiation, calling for total Cuban withdrawal and implementation of Resolution 435 (mid-July 1988, New York).
- Military commanders of the three armies discuss for first time how to disentangle forces.
- Agreement that linkage specifics between Namibian independence and total Cuban withdrawal would be reflected in a separate bilateral Angolan-Cuban agreement to be signed on same day as tripartite Angola-Cuba-South Africa agreement (early August 1988, Geneva).
- Geneva Protocol spells out specifics and timing of disengagement of military forces in Angola including security measures affecting SWAPO deployments and a Cuban pledge not to attack UNITA's core areas.
- Pretoria proposes CTW timetable of seven months (Geneva).
- Angola-Cuba reiterate their March 1988 CTW timetable of four years.
- Four intensive rounds of negotiation in Brazzaville and New York fail to break the logjam on a compromise CTW timetable; self-imposed November 1 deadline lapses (September-October 1988).
- Delegation heads close on front-loaded twenty-seven-month timetable removing sixty-six percent of the 50,000 Cuban force in the first year (November 1988).
- Penultimate Brazzaville meeting to negotiate UN verification plan and to agree on US-proposed joint commission to oversee implementation of the agreements and to set new date for implementation of package on April 1, 1989.
- Two rounds of tripartite meetings to complete Brazzaville Protocol on December 13.
- Parties sign agreements on December 22, 1988.

diplomatic credibility, the diplomatic leverage of linkage, the regional power equation, the United Nations as a source of legitimacy, timing and deadlines, and the roles of other external actors.

US Credibility. During the first three stages (through March 1985), Washington needed to acquire the credibility to launch a highly complex diplomacy aimed at solving both the Namibia problem and the Cuban issue in Angola. Credibility meant, in the first instance, demonstrating a *balanced commitment* to the pursuit of both goals. To "carry water on both shoulders" required communicating authoritatively to each side the existence of *shared interests* while publicly explaining the strategy to various domestic and external audiences.

Maintaining US credibility through the regional turbulence of the 1980s was a severe challenge. On the one hand, the parties all favored US involvement because they believed in the centrality of the US government (for very different reasons) as an external actor. Closer ties with Washington were high priorities for both Luanda and Pretoria, an incentive for them to cooperate or go through the motions of cooperating. For eight years, Washington carefully resisted requests for bilateral "quids" (or side payments) to advance the talks, but it did nothing to dissuade the parties from believing that their cooperation could improve the climate for bilateral ties.

On the other hand, when the parties clearly were playing double games or pursuing unilateral agendas of their own—as happened on and off through much of the period—Washington had to respond with its own maneuvers. Such responses did not always work. Playing on the suspicions of both sides, US officials inserted themselves into the joint military commission established by the Lusaka accord of 1984. Washington gained invaluable first-hand information on the parties' reciprocal cheating. The US representatives could not prevent it, however, and had to be withdrawn to avoid becoming over-identified with a clearly failed venture.

Diplomatic Leverage. Tactically, the US initiative got off the ground in 1981-1982 because it offered each of the key parties fresh openings to explore and shape both the Namibia and Angola tracks. Each would have new ways to seek the high ground and discredit the other side—or the mediator—and this, no doubt, explains in part why Pretoria was quick to accept the new linkage concept. It also explains Angola's readiness to enter into bilateral talks with Washington in early 1982 in full knowledge that the US agenda was to obtain Cuban troop withdrawal (or CTW, as it came to be known) in the context of a Namibia settlement, a principle that at the time Angola categorically rejected.

An early example of diplomatic leverage is the debate in mid-1981 between the Americans and their Contact Group allies on how to launch the new US-shaped process. Washington needed allies to acquire credibility. The allies needed a continuing Namibian diplomatic process to avert a showdown at the UN, and they needed US leadership to make it credible in Pretoria. Each side got what it most needed—Washington obtained allied help internationally and with the African states, providing the momentum for completion of Stages I and II, and the allies retained a continuing diplomatic process.

From then on, despite endlessly reiterated rejections of linkage, the CTW issue was legitimized as the one remaining issue to be resolved. Ironically, this was confirmed by the UN secretary-general after an August 1983 visit to the region. In a report to the Security Council, he dissociated himself from the link but identified it clearly as South Africa's last condition for implementing Resolution 435. For their part, the allies managed to avoid responsibility for the link, thus freeing themselves to vote and speak out for the unconditional implementation of the resolution. They also obtained US leadership of a visible, if controversial, process in Southern Africa that offered them diplomatic cover. By the time France wearied of this arrangement and suspended its participation in the Contact Group in 1983, it had served its purpose for all concerned. Washington, with quiet help from London, would continue on, having become the indispensable pivot of the region's diplomacy.

Diplomatic leverage of another sort was illustrated after mid-1987 when Castro made his bid officially to join the peace talks. Cuban motives may have included not only the hope of extricating themselves with honor from a failed enterprise, but also gaining some respectability in American eyes as a serious and responsible party with whom business could be done. But the United States gained at least as much from the Cuban gambit: the ability to extract a price for agreeing to Cuban participation (Washington obtained the commitment to total CTW); the ability to play on all three dimensions of the Angolan-Cuban-Soviet triangle for the first time; the acquisition of a competent and highly professional negotiating party that would have an incentive to obtain prompt and coherent action from its often opaque Angolan ally; and the presence of the one party that might be capable of convincing Pretoria that, under certain conditions, the Cubans were prepared to leave Southern Africa.

The Regional Power Equation. As in any negotiation between warring parties, the military balance and the parties' shifting perceptions of their military options played a central role. What made the Namibia-Angola case especially complex was the simultaneous unfolding of three distinct armed conflicts: the bush war of the South African Defense Force (SADF) against SWAPO across the northern Namibian border; the sporadic clash between the SADF and the Cuban-supported Popular Movement for the Liberation of Angola (MPLA) troops as the SADF entered Angola to help the National Union for the Total Independence of Angola (UNITA) or to strike at SWAPO camps; and the continuous UNITA-MPLA civil war waged across the vast Angolan countryside. The US-designed settlement aimed at resolving the first two conflicts and achieving the withdrawal of foreign forces from both Namibia and Angola. The third conflict was beyond the immediate reach of US diplomacy: no external party had the standing or legitimacy to force its mediation upon the Angolan parties, still less to create yet another linkage of the external to the internal Angolan issues. Any attempt by Washington to add this linkage would have blown up the negotiations.

Yet, in practice, the MPLA-UNITA struggle was high on the list of priorities of all parties, as well as of the US mediating team, which openly declared its support for political reconciliation. Each party calculated its moves on the first two conflicts in terms of their potential impact on Angola's civil war. Logically, a resolution of that war would greatly simplify the resolution of the others—termination of the civil war would simultaneously remove a major rationale for both Cuban and South African involvement in Angola's affairs. In reality, however, there was no practical way to terminate the civil war with thousands of foreign troops still engaged on Angolan soil. It would be necessary to approach the problem the other way around: resolution of the external issues would create more favorable conditions in which Angolan brothers could find each other and make peace.

Peacemaking would depend on the existence or creation of perceived stalemates in all three wars. Washington would have to persuade each party that its position—or that of its Angolan ally—was strong enough to run the risk of a settlement. American officials operated throughout the eight-year period on the premise that peace would flow from a perceived stalemate, not from military preponderance or capitulation by one side or another. More important, they operated on the understanding that outright victory was beyond anyone's reach in these conflicts.

The Angolan and Namibian conflicts imposed real financial burdens on the regional parties—and, depending on Angola's ability to earn top dollar for its oil, on Cubans and Soviets as well. Those burdens would only grow if the parties persisted in pursuing unilateral, coercive options. These conflicts could not be "won" by anyone, but they could expand in scope, both geographically and technologically.

Both Cubans and South Africans had hypothetical escalatory options. The logical stalemate would come unstuck if Havana and Luanda expanded the conflict south into Namibia in response to SADF intervention in Angola. This would, however, never become feasible militarily or politically without open-ended Soviet backing: It would cost them the "high ground" as victims of SADF aggression; it would expose them to very high costs as the SADF acquired the advantages of defense-in-depth in territory it had mastered; and it might be the one way of giving South Africa the Western military support it sorely missed.

Pretoria had escalatory options in Angola—to expand its pressure against SWAPO and in support of UNITA—but such action was most unlikely to drive the Soviets and Cubans out; it could, and did, lead to more Cuban troops, not less. Over time, new military stalemates would emerge inside Angola at a higher level of cost and technology. Despite its sophisticated arms industries and undisputed status as regional superpower, South Africa faced a scenario of constraints including the international arms embargo and the absence of military allies. Escalation would run the risk, sooner or later, that the SADF would be sucked into its own Angolan quagmire where it could be matched and bled.[3]

Expanded UNITA operations in large areas of Angola, backed by increased SADF logistic help, by 1984 led to significantly increased Soviet arms deliveries to Luanda and a gradual increase in the number of Cuban troops. Luanda's logistically complex, dry season offensives against UNITA obliged it to mount a conventional defense, diverting resources away from its primary guerrilla strategy. These offensives, however, also set up ideal targets for UNITA counteraction and for SADF air and artillery strikes.

US strategists did not control these military equations. At best, they could endeavor to understand them and share their analysis with the parties in a tactical effort to avoid costly and time-consuming diversions. Washington, however, did have the option of supporting the repeal of the Clark Amendment[4] and providing arms to UNITA. This course was favorably considered in 1981, but the effort failed in Congress. The initial purpose in seeking the repeal had been to acquire the option of aiding

UNITA. Such a move could have been useful in efforts to dilute Pretoria's influence with UNITA or to bolster US diplomatic pressure on the MPLA. When Congress finally acted to repeal in 1985, there was an entirely different context: Soviet military aid to Luanda had expanded dramatically, and a major MPLA offensive was in preparation. Washington quickly exercised the option to channel support to UNITA to bolster its morale and its independence from South Africa and to signal Luanda that the US administration was tiring of its dilatory tactics. The move was also a means of informing Moscow that the United States had the means to raise the price of its escalating arms relationship to Angola.

In the view of those charged with the conduct of African policy, the decision to extend the Reagan doctrine to Angola in 1986 did not represent a change of strategy. Rather, it represented a decision to bolster US diplomacy and adapt it to changing conditions on the ground. It proved to be a good investment. American aid to UNITA did not turn the tide of battle, but it raised the price of battle for Angolan and Cuban pilots and enhanced UNITA's overall battle effectiveness as well as its morale and international standing. The MPLA leadership used the US action in a short-lived effort to discredit US mediation, but it was quietly exploring a return to the table within six months. US and Angolan negotiators resumed official meetings in April 1987, barely a year after Luanda had announced that Washington had forfeited its mediating role. Some of the MPLA's African and Western supporters purported to see the US decision as destroying US credibility. But Luanda, Havana, and Moscow all saw the move, more accurately, as reinforcing a strategic stalemate.

The Asset of UN Legitimacy. Washington's decision in 1981 to retain the UN plan as the basis and pivot for a regional settlement provided indispensable leverage at the launch phase. Without Resolution 435, American diplomats would have lost the leverage to obtain improvements in the plan (for example, the 1982 constitutional principles) and to force the Cuban troop withdrawal issue. Namibia's unique history as de jure UN territory under de facto South African control made this approach necessary even if Washington had wished to start from scratch. Building on the UN plan also dramatically reduced Pretoria's otherwise unlimited room for maneuver.

At subsequent stages, US negotiators gained credibility in Soviet, Cuban, and Angolan eyes when they proposed to frame a package of agreements to be blessed and endorsed by the Security Council. Such an approach was not only "correct" from their perspective; it also contained a suggestion that final agreements would have a vague form of international "guarantee" in the event of South African violations. At an earlier stage, US officials had succeeded in persuading Pretoria that UN procedures could have an advantage for South Africa as well: any UN action acknowledging the CTW issue would give it international standing comparable to the almost scriptural status of Resolution 435. This explained Pretoria's interest in welcoming the UN secretary-general, not traditionally its favorite foreign visitor, in the summer of 1983. His report to the Security Council spoke in pejorative terms of the CTW linkage as "extraneous" and "outside the mandate" of his office.[5] But it shed a brilliant spotlight on the issue and also made clear that South Africa was prepared to implement the UN plan for Namibia if it could be resolved.

All parties could play this game. The Angolan-Cuban decision to propose UN verification of the CTW timetable was aimed consciously at persuading Pretoria of their seriousness. They did so less because of the UN's capability to conduct such verification than because the move would further legitimize CTW as an integral and central element of the overall package of agreements. The UN Verification Mission in Angola (UNAVEM), like the earlier extension of United Nations Transition Assistance Group (UNTAG) mission to include monitoring of SWAPO in Angola, strengthened the mediator's hand in persuading Pretoria that it would get a balanced agreement, not one solely focused on monitoring South African performance.

Timing and Deadlines. Mediators dream about controlling the pace of negotiation and possessing enforceable deadlines, but Southern Africa's wars were deeply rooted, dating back to the 1960s. The ebb and flow of events was primarily regional in origin, not external. Washington did not possess the means to enforce its will. None of the parties depended upon Washington for anything essential except the chance for reduced ostracism and isolation.

The revised structure of the Namibia-Angola process significantly aggravated the problem of timing and deadlines. Because there were two objectives—Resolution 435 and CTW—the process could only ripen when *both* parts were in rough alignment and *both* sides saw the chance for a win-win outcome on *both* tracks. Critics on the right missed this central point when they claimed that US negotiators were not sufficiently tough with the Marxist parties; South Africa, also, had to be ready to compromise.

Critics on the left claimed to perceive US collusion in permitting Pretoria to get away with its failure to implement Resolution 435; this totally overlooked the fact that Angola and its allies had not bitten the bullet on CTW.

Applying time pressure on the parties in these circumstances was a difficult art. Washington attempted it in 1982 and again in 1984, only to drive the parties toward separate talks in which they discussed a separate, partial "détente" that would avoid the basic issues. (The South Africans and the MPLA discussed cooperation in the border areas to reduce SWAPO violence and SADF actions, but the Cubans would have remained and Namibia would have continued under Pretoria's control.) In March 1985, Washington attempted to force the pace by tabling a compromise paper. The South Africans were urged to take quick action to restore their rapidly fading image in the United States and to undercut Soviet-Cuban pressure on the MPLA to play for time. The Angolans were informed of the need for quick action to strengthen the peace party in Pretoria and to prevent the South Africans from abandoning the negotiating track altogether. Some participants claim now to believe that the deal could have been done in 1984-1985. Logically, that may be right, but domestic politics were not ripe in any of the key nations.

US exploitation of the time factor was better in December 1983 when Washington saw through the bravado on both the Angolan and South African teams. Each side had paid a price in the grinding military escalation in southern Angola during 1982-1983. Careful coaching of the sides during December 1983 and January 1984 led directly to the Lusaka disengagement accord—a ripe moment. During the summer of 1985, US diplomats sought to use the mounting American anti-apartheid fervor and the growing public enthusiasm for supporting "freedom fighters" as tools to squeeze the parties toward constructive action. The MPLA, however, was too preoccupied by its disastrous offensive against UNITA to realize that the United States was about to become UNITA's ally. Two months after the imposition of US sanctions by executive order, Pretoria delivered a positive reply to Washington. The South Africans, at the time, however, viewed this as a safe tactical move, because Luanda was most unlikely to reciprocate.

An interesting example of the use of timing and deadlines occurred during the Moscow summit of May 1988. Earlier that month in London, the Cubans had proposed with a rhetorical flourish that September 29—the tenth anniversary of Resolution 435—be accepted as the target date for implementation of a settlement. At Moscow, the United States decided to test the still uncertain Soviet support for an early agreement by proposing US-Soviet endorsement of the Cuban idea. Taken aback by this proposal, the Soviets went along with contained enthusiasm, and a signal was sent from the summit that the two superpowers had added impetus to the process. In Havana, the Cuban distaste for being pushed was matched by delight at this gesture of US respect for their proposal. The other parties were not amused. By mid-1988, the parties were setting—and missing—their own deadlines.

At the very end of the negotiations, a real deadline suddenly emerged: the US election and change of administration. It is impossible to know what would have happened if Bush had lost. One week after his victory, the logjam on the CTW timetable was broken, but, in early December, American diplomats then ran into a set of final hurdles on verification and the scenario for establishing implementation dates. Openly advertising the fact that a new administration would mean a change of personnel and a basic policy review, the US mediators pressed the Angolans, Cubans, and South Africans not to waste years of effort. The agreements were signed ten days later.

Other External Actors. At various points along the way, a wide range of states not party to the peace process played important roles in advancing it.

The African States. The Congo government in Brazzaville extended itself over eighteen months as a champion of a negotiated solution. Excellently positioned as a neighbor of Angola and long-standing friend of the MPLA regime, the Congo used its credibility to help reactivate the US-Angolan talks in 1987 and then to host five tripartite meetings during 1988. By volunteering for this role before it became fashionable, the Congolese leadership earned the respect of all participants. At an earlier stage of the process, Cape Verde and Zambia also played important facilitative roles, using their goodwill and diplomatic resources to press the parties toward common ground. Britain, Egypt, and Switzerland also hosted important diplomatic encounters.

A second African role of major significance in the final year was to encourage and speak out for movement toward national reconciliation in Angola. While this has proven to be a tough challenge, the groundwork laid in 1988 was essential in (a) convincing Pretoria that Africans would not ignore their responsibility to foster internal peace in Angola and (b) persuading the MPLA that acknowledging its internal problem would be both essential and "legitimate" in African eyes. Although their roles varied greatly according to which Angolan party they favored, the governments of Zaire and Congo each played key roles. In addition, Cape Verde, Gabon, Ivory Coast, Morocco, Mozambique, Nigeria, Zambia, and Zimbabwe worked to advance regional thinking on the problem.

African states also played individual roles as intermediaries and negotiating partners of the parties. To illustrate, Mozambique repeatedly opened fresh channels of communication among Luanda, Pretoria, and Washington starting in 1983. At times, Maputo was the principal channel and an invaluable source of ideas and interpretations for US diplomats. Cape Verde played a parallel role throughout the 1980s. These two ex-Portuguese colonies were Washington's best window into the thinking of MPLA and UNITA leaders whom they knew as friends and allies in the anti-colonial struggle.

During 1981-1982, the front line states were indispensable negotiating partners as the Contact Group sought to broker understandings related to Resolution 435. Dealing with the group's emissaries at head of state level, they provided blunt but generally constructive advice and suggestions. More important, they usually delivered SWAPO when the group demonstrated that it could deliver Pretoria. In this sense, the FLS served as an African contact group. Their efforts helped to buffer the diplomacy from the unhelpful intervention of Soviet, Cuban, and radical nonaligned states whose motive was to create a breakdown that would discredit Western diplomacy. The masterful performance of a small group of FLS senior officials during the summer of 1982 made possible the rapid completion of the outstanding Resolution 435 issues. Regrettably, the FLS ceased to function as a group, except as shrill critics of linkage, in the ensuing years. Their absence, however, did not prevent Mozambique, Zambia, and, of course, Angola itself from continuing their separate roles described above.

The Western Allies. Washington's North Atlantic Treaty Organization (NATO) allies played a comparable range of roles in the process. The Contact Group itself functioned as a close-knit team during most of 1981-1982, using a form of man-to-man coverage on the various African parties and South Africa. Like the Americans, the British, Canadians, French, and Germans also had to balance their interests at times, explaining to Pretoria, the FLS, and SWAPO the merits of cooperating with the new approach. US diplomats gained invaluable independent assessments of what the traffic would bear and how to orchestrate the diplomacy of linkage. Allied officials helped reinforce the US message by offering their African interlocutors an unvarnished analysis of Washington political realities.

When the group had completed its work on Resolution 435, it came under growing strains over the linkage issue. France, to no one's surprise, was the first to strike out on its own in an effort to reduce the strain in its African relations and distance itself from the controversy in international forums. The Canadians followed the French lead. These moves did nothing to advance the process and helped foster a false impression of collapse or diplomatic stalemate that only aided the foes of further progress. Nonetheless, useful work was done by the group up to 1984. France's independent channel to Cuba, starting in 1982, may have begun the task of convincing Havana that the African welcome mat for Cuban troops would not be out forever. Allies represented in Luanda helped to fill the empty American diplomatic chair, sometimes alarming the MPLA and sometimes persuading it to take Washington more seriously than it otherwise would have.

For nearly seven years, the British served as Washington's principal channel to the Angolans. British diplomacy was mobilized across Africa, Europe, New York, and Moscow in direct support of the peace process. London had early misgivings as to whether US diplomats understood the region, the inherent ambition of the new approach, and the low odds for success. Soon, however, there developed an outstanding pattern of cooperation, one that served important common interests. Having full relations with Luanda, London chose not to endorse linkage explicitly, but the British provided indispensable support for the overall strategy while pursuing their own interests and tactical preferences.

Unique among US allies, Britain had credibility in both Luanda and Pretoria and knew all the players intimately. This enabled US diplomats constantly to test hypotheses and information, to develop game plans for moving the process along, and to build appropriate nuance into the messages each would pass. By the late 1980s, when Pretoria's Washington links were severely strained, London had acquired special influence there. That influence was used to support South African negotiators as they returned home from each round of meetings to seek a fresh mandate for the next set of decisions. Britain also helped save the settlement in April 1989 when large-scale SWAPO violations of the agreement threatened to derail it. Of all the diplomatic factors that permitted ultimate success, the US-UK working relationship was probably the most important.

The Soviet Factor. Soviet policy toward the Namibia-Angola peace process went through three phases over the 1980s. In the first phase, lasting up to 1986, Moscow generally did its best to obstruct Western efforts. Drawing on the habit of opposing on principle any Western proposal, the Soviets sought to poison the well during the Contact Group's work to prepare Resolution 435 back in 1978. (They backed off in response to FLS-SWAPO support for it.) Three years later, Moscow had switched tactical horses. By 1981-1982, one might have guessed that the Soviets were the most ardent champions of Resolution 435, and they became unalterably opposed to any modifications or enhancements of it. Even more shrill was their opposition to the Namibia-Angola linkage. According to Soviet official statements, the new US approach was nothing less than an attempt to block Resolution 435, to force the capitulation of Angola and its departure from the socialist camp, to join forces with Pretoria in creating a pro-Western security zone, and to reverse the tide of history in Southern Africa.

Behind the scenes, Moscow and its allies worked assiduously to promote these messages and to create an echo chamber of like-minded voices in African media and diplomatic circles. Soviet thinking appears to have been known to the Angolan-Cuban drafters of a February 1982 joint communiqué, which officially endorsed a Namibia-first variety of linkage—the Angolans and Cubans would define a schedule for CTW *after* Namibian independence. Despite these efforts, the process moved ahead over the ensuing months, leading Soviet officials to protest that the Contact Group sought to usurp the prerogatives of the United Nations. Moscow played a lead role in late 1982 in floating the idea of a UN Security Council debate on the CTW linkage, a goal that was realized the following year.

During these years, US and Soviet officials held a series of "informational exchanges" on Southern Africa. US objectives were minimal: to avoid surprises, to probe for constructive openings and offer Moscow a chance to bid, to explain US purposes and indicate how these might serve the interests of both sides. Moscow's objectives appeared to consist mainly of making a record to share with its allies, exploring US logic, acquiring tactical insights, and gaining the visual benefit of superpower consultation. As a result, the exchanges were sterile. US officials were harangued with legalistic debating points. When pressed for better ideas or possible compromises, the Soviet side would simply reiterate its support for the latest Angolan positions. In practice, Moscow had decided not to negotiate directly with Washington but to talk indirectly via Luanda and Havana.

Thus, while vigorously rejecting the concept of linkage or any form of "parallelism," Moscow fully endorsed the 1984 MPLA proposal on partial CTW that was tied to Resolution 435.

Washington assumed that the Soviet Union had substantial leverage with the MPLA. Thousands of Soviet and allied officials were distributed throughout the Angolan government and armed forces, in some cases running and maintaining essential services and sensitive security functions. The arms supply relationship deepened further as deliveries doubled in the first half of the 1980s and the fighting expanded in scope and technology. Given the MPLA's dependence on the Cubans and Soviets, it was logical for US officials to assume that Angolan positions and proposals had been "cleared" in Havana and Moscow, but this assumption could seldom be tested. The three governments met frequently and exuded predictable solidarity. On the other hand, Western diplomats picked up signals of Soviet anxiety about progress in the US-MPLA exchanges as well as of Angolan frustration with the influence of their allies.

A second phase of Soviet policy toward the Namibia-Angola negotiations, from January 1986 to May 1988, witnessed a gradual transition away from classic obstructionism. During much of the period, US officials had the impression that the Soviets were groping for new ideas in regional policy. President Mikhail Gorbachev's declarations, starting in January 1986, in favor of "political solutions" to regional conflicts represented a shift in emphasis away from the language of struggle and confrontation. It did not, at this stage, however, signify reduced opposition to US proposals. Still less did it signify Soviet restraint in the military supply relationship with Luanda.

Despite determined probes, the Soviets had nothing concrete to offer that would advance the process. Publicly, their statements undercut the US-led process and suggested vaguely the need for the UN, the Organization of African Unity, and the Non-Aligned Movement to play larger roles. Privately, Soviet officials discouraged any Angolan cooperation with Washington and criticized UN Secretariat officials for undertaking quiet probes of Luanda's latest thinking on a linkage-based settlement. In April 1986, Soviet diplomats stimulated South African doubts about the continued viability of the US-led process—a line of thinking that was not unwelcome to some in Pretoria who chafed increasingly under US pressure and who were enchanted with the very idea of a direct line to Moscow. In March 1987, Soviet-Cuban-Angolan consultations ratified Luanda's decision to resume direct talks with Washington; but they also witnessed strong

Soviet urging that Luanda mount yet another major offensive against UNITA strongholds to be in a better position for eventual negotiation. Moscow also wanted Luanda to mount its own internal political offensive and thereby preempt UNITA's demand for talks on national reconciliation.

When senior US and Soviet officials met in July 1987, on the eve of the war's largest offensive and a series of fresh Angolan/Cuban political initiatives, the Soviet side declared (inaccurately) that the diplomacy was at a dead end. Moscow expressed interest in fresh thinking as to how US-Soviet cooperation could unblock the process, but it had no concrete proposals except that Washington drop linkage or consider a wholly "new mechanism" for negotiation, a mechanism vaguely described in terms of a large UN role.

The Soviets may or may not have known that Cuban leader Fidel Castro was soon to make his most dramatic bid yet to join the negotiation process or that he and Angolan president Jose Eduardo Dos Santos would soon approve a new CTW timetable, their first significant move on the issue in over two years. What they *did* know was that Soviet arms and advisers were about to support the MPLA's biggest effort yet to achieve a military victory.

Four months later, the Soviet-Angolan offensive, in which Cuban forces played no role, had turned into a SADF-UNITA rout in which thousands of members of the Forces of the Angolan People's Liberation Army (FAPLA) were killed and hundreds of millions of dollars of Soviet hardware were captured or destroyed. The Angolan war had become a humiliating fiasco for Soviet arms, planning, and training. By the end of 1987, Soviet leaders were visibly groping for a coherent policy. They professed to see opportunities for a political settlement, but made no proposals, offered no support to the US-led process, and declined to endorse publicly a settlement entailing both Resolution 435 and CTW. They spoke knowingly of Cuba's recognition that its forces would have to leave Angola, but, in the same breath, they declared that Angola would not be "thrown to the wolves."

It was the Cubans, not the Soviets, who stepped in to shape what can best be described as a chaotic policy vacuum in the ranks of the communist allies. The conditions of late 1987 offered Havana a rare opportunity: the MPLA was on its knees militarily, appealing for a stronger Cuban role; Pretoria, in a characteristic burst of hubris, risked overplaying its hand as UNITA's very public ally; Washington had offered the Cubans a place at the table *if* they would produce proposals for total CTW; and Moscow, whose attention was distracted by Afghanistan and arms control, had just suffered a humiliating setback. Cuban decisions of November 1987 to March 1988 averted a complete collapse of the MPLA military position in the southeast. The arrival and southward deployment of 15,000 fresh Cubans filled the previously empty land and airspace of southwestern Angola, creating a potentially explosive, hair-trigger military balance with the SADF. At the table, the new joint Angolan-Cuban team put forward new proposals, as promised, and urged early, US-chaired, face-to-face talks with Pretoria.

The Soviets, in a March 1988 exchange, side-stepped numerous US suggestions for joint efforts and professed uncertainty as to both their role and their interest in a Namibia-Angola settlement in which "the US gives nothing." Nonetheless, the meeting served to clarify Soviet perceptions of US thinking. Soviet officials urged more regular bilateral discussion and undertook to share the fruits of upcoming exchanges with their allies.

Starting in late April 1988 three in-depth bilateral consultations were held within one month. Moscow had finally given its diplomats a mandate to lend official and public support to a process that was already on a fast track. Low-key side meetings with Soviet officials—self-designated "observers" who kept a discreet distance from the tripartite talks—became a regular feature of the process. Washington had urged that Moscow make appropriate officials available for this purpose and publicly mentioned the Soviet observer role. US-Soviet meetings, both during and between tripartite rounds, graduated from debates about the shape of an acceptable settlement to operational discussion of how the two sides might advance those points agreed upon and how current obstacles could be handled.

By August 1988, at Geneva, the basic turning point in this final phase, US and Soviet officials had settled into a fairly predictable and often useful pattern of exchanges. As the parties labored toward closure on the vital CTW timetable, Soviet officials requested—and received—detailed US briefings on the mediator's priorities and game plans. Washington sought to obtain candid feedback on Angolan-Cuban thinking to elicit suggestions and thus pressure Moscow to accept a measure of responsibility for success and to share enough sensitive detail so that the Soviets could play a confidence-building role with their allies. Equally important, the Soviets welcomed US thinking on whether and how they should talk to the South Africans. American officials strongly encouraged this, and the Moscow-Pretoria dialogue blossomed. This gave the South Africans the benefit of the two superpowers' input as a reality check on Cuban and Angolan motives during the endgame.

US negotiators also persuaded Moscow to drop its advocacy of the Angolan demand that Washington should cease its support for UNITA and to focus on other issues: the key problem of narrowing the gap on CTW timetables and the need to support and legitimize the issue of national reconciliation in Angola. The latter two issues were closely interrelated. MPLA fear of UNITA was directly responsible for its insistence on CTW timetables that had no hope of acceptance by the South Africans. The extent of Soviet influence and pressure on Luanda to bite the bullet on Angolan reconciliation may never be known. Washington, in any case, relied on African leaders to surface the issue because, by doing so, they would make it far easier for Moscow and Havana to follow suit. What is known is that the Cubans, not the Soviets, faced the greatest alliance burdens over the interlinked CTW and reconciliation issues. They wanted a deal and an "honorable exit"—just as Pretoria did. Ultimately, the Cubans prevailed upon their Angolan friends to accept a withdrawal schedule remarkably similar to the one tabled by US mediators in March 1985—and accepted in principle by Pretoria six months later.

The Soviet role in the final phase cannot be understood solely on the basis of the public commentary offered by American and other foreign officials who were quick to salute these novel forms of Soviet behavior. In essence, both the mediation and the solution were of US origin. The Cubans, Angolans, and South Africans took the big decisions. There is no evidence of Soviet arm-twisting of their Marxist allies, though Moscow certainly made clear its general support for a "political solution" and its desire to be perceived as contributing toward one. Moscow, at one level, achieved a visible role and confirmed global status by "free-riding" on an American effort. By placing their imprimatur on a regional settlement whose time had arrived, the Soviets earned some international credit and acted in accordance with the new spirit of US-Soviet relations. At another level, Soviet advice and tactical thinking were at times extremely helpful to harried US diplomats who had to cope day and night with the antics and idiosyncracies of three unusual negotiating parties. With rare exceptions, such as Moscow's India-Pakistan mediation in 1965, Soviet diplomats had little experience in diplomatic problem-solving. But they warmed quickly to their "observer" role, and probably enjoyed it.

In the final analysis, the Soviet record in Southern Africa will be judged both by their readiness to share such burdens and to shed burdens—like the one in Angola—that reflect "old thinking." To date, they have proved more adept at courting erstwhile adversaries in Pretoria than at talking straight to the troubled Angolans. In this regard, it is regrettable that the Soviets did not lean harder on the MPLA to negotiate with UNITA during or immediately after the 1988 settlement. Failure to do so has encouraged MPLA myopia, prolonged Angola's agony, and sustained an old-fashioned Soviet behavior pattern that assures continuing US-Soviet engagement in a wasteful civil war.

Notes

The author conducted research for this chapter while serving as distinguished fellow at the United States Institute of Peace. The views expressed here are the author's alone and do not necessarily reflect the views of the United States Institute of Peace.

1. See the discussion in I. William Zartman, *Ripe for Resolution: Conflict and Intervention in Africa* (New York: Oxford University Press, 1989), Chapter 6.
2. Harold H. Saunders, "The Pre-Negotiation Phase," in Diane B. Bendahmane and John W. McDonald, Jr. (eds.), *International Negotiation: Art and Science* (Washington, DC: Foreign Service Institute, Department of State, 1984), pp. 47-56.
3. For an elaboration of these judgments from a 1981 perspective, see the author's *South Africa's Defense Posture: Coping with Vulnerability*, Washington Papers, Vol. 9, No. 84 (Washington, DC: Center for Strategic and International Studies/Sage Publications, 1981), pp. 84-85, 89-91.
4. An amendment, introduced by Senator Dick Clark (D-Iowa), to the Defense Authorization bill prohibited all but humanitarian aid to UNITA. It was passed over a presidential veto on January 27, 1976.
5. UN secretary-general's report S/15943, published on August 29, 1983.

3

The Afghanistan Negotiations

Riaz Mohammad Khan

THE SPECTACULAR POLITICAL TRANSFORMATION OF Eastern Europe in late 1989 eclipsed the exit of the last Soviet soldier from Afghanistan earlier in the year. That historic development brought to a close the longest post-World War II military engagement by the Soviet Union beyond its borders. The Soviet withdrawal from Afghanistan was completed in accordance with the time schedule laid down in the Geneva accords signed on April 14, 1988, as the culmination of a diplomatic process evolved through United Nations mediation of nearly seven years.[1] (See Table 3.1.)

Political analysts and scholars often debate the circumstances of the Soviet withdrawal. Mostly, they attribute the Soviet decision to the historic transformation of the Soviet outlook and policy under the new Soviet leader, Mikhail Gorbachev, and the resilient armed struggle by Afghans rather than to a diplomatic *coup de maitre*. The question therefore arises: What has been the significance of the diplomatic process?

First, the existence of the UN-sponsored talks and the draft agreements negotiated at Geneva provided Gorbachev with the alternative to pursue a political settlement to extricate the Soviet Union out of the Afghan quagmire. The process offered an honorable way to bring to an end the unpopular military involvement and thus helped to strengthen Gorbachev's political position at home.

Second, the Geneva accords represent the first major success for the United Nations and the first agreement between the United States and the Soviet Union on an important regional issue in many years. Thereafter, in quick succession, a cease-fire was secured in the Gulf, and the Tripartite Agreement on Namibia was signed under the auspices of the United Nations.

Table 3.1 Evolution of the Texts of the Geneva Accords on Afghanistan

Agenda Items (April 1982)

- Withdrawal.
- Noninterference.
- International Guarantees.
- Voluntary Return of Refugees.

Annotated Agenda: Geneva I
(June 1982)

- Consideration of withdrawal in terms of interrelationships with measures under other items.
- Consideration of "measures" to ensure principles of nonintervention and noninterference.
- Discussion on guarantees and identification of guarantors.
- Discussion on conditions and modalities of voluntary return of refugees.

Draft Comprehensive Settlement: Geneva II
(April and June 1983)
Geneva III (August 1984)

- Section I. Interrelationships elaborated as coincidence of dates for implementation of various elements; a blank for time frame for withdrawal; definition of component parts of the comprehensive settlement.
- Section II. Obligations drawn from 1981 UN General Assembly (UNGA) Declaration on Inadmissibility of Interference and Intervention in the Internal Affairs of States. (At Geneva III a draft bilateral agreement based on Section II was proposed to supplement the draft settlement.)
- Section III. Undertakings to respect provisions of Section II. Later scope was broadened by adding expression of support for the settlement.
- Section IV. Conditions for voluntary return; modalities for UN High Commissioner for Refugees (UNHCR) role, etc.

**Draft Instruments:
Geneva IV, V, VI (1985)
Geneva VII A and B (1986)**

- Instrument IV. Discussed and finalized in 1986 on the basis of text of Section I. Legal format and UN monitoring were the last issues to be resolved, leaving time frame to be settled later.
- Instrument I. Draft bilateral agreement on noninterference and nonintervention; Kabul's reservation on "border formulation" revived.
- Instrument II. Draft declaration of guarantees; text finalized and agreed upon in 1985.

(continues)

Table 3.1 (continued)

Draft Instruments: Geneva IV, V, VI (1985) Geneva VII A and B (1986) (*continued*)	Situation Relating to Afghanistan (includes time frame for withdrawal). ▪ Bilateral agreement between Afghanistan and Pakistan on Principles of Mutual Relations, in particular on Noninterference and Nonintervention. ▪ Declaration on International Guarantees. ▪ Bilateral agreement between Afghanistan and Pakistan on the voluntary return of refugees.
▪ Instrument III. Draft bilateral agreement on voluntary return of refugees. The issue of consultation with the refugees remained unresolved until it was dropped in late 1986.	
Geneva Accords (April 14, 1988)	
▪ Agreement on Interrelationships for Settlement of	

Institutionally, the process strengthened the UN secretary-general's role. The experience of addressing the domestic aspects of the Afghan conflict in the later years has given the world organization a new operational flexibility. The Geneva accords can, therefore, be counted among the watershed events that mark the new ease in East-West relations and a promising phase of multilateralism.

Third, the diplomatic process affected the thinking and policies of the major players and had a bearing on the Afghanistan conflict just as the process itself was conditioned by the constantly evolving circumstances of the conflict. For all these reasons, the Geneva negotiations and the accords deserve both more credit and more scholarly attention than they have received so far. This chapter will highlight the salient developments in the negotiations and offer a critical evaluation.

Conflicting Interests and Early Initiatives

The Soviet military intervention in Afghanistan in December 1979 drew overwhelming international censure. A demand for unconditional withdrawal of Soviet troops was made at the specially convened Sixth Emergency Special Session of the UN General Assembly in early January 1980 and was repeated a few weeks later at the first ever Extraordinary Ministerial Meeting of the Organization of the Islamic Conference (OIC). As the initial shock waves subsided, diplomatic initiatives for negotiations began to emerge, motivated by varying political interests.

The first pressures for negotiations sprang from West European concern over the collapse of détente. The European Community (EC)—especially France and the Federal Republic of Germany—did not fully support the US punitive sanctions and the postponement of the ratification of Salt II, the arms control agreement. Nonetheless, the EC shared the US perception that the Soviet action posed a threat to their interests in the sensitive Gulf region. Accordingly, in late February 1980, the EC foreign ministers offered guaranteed neutrality for Afghanistan provided Moscow withdrew its troops.

For the Soviet Union, the primary motive underlying its intervention was to stabilize the government of the People's Democratic Party of Afghanistan (PDPA)—a party with Marxist-Leninist orientation—which was faced with a growing internal revolt. The push for radical socioeconomic reforms by the zealous PDPA leadership, headed by Hafizullah Amin, spawned reaction in a predominantly tribal and religious Afghan society that was traditionally used to minimize control from rulers in Kabul. Ironically, the Soviet military intervention—apparently undertaken to install a more moderate PDPA leader, Babrak Karmal, in Kabul—further spurred the Afghan rebellion.

Throughout the country, disparate anticommunist groups, largely under traditional or fundamentalist religious leadership, became active—Afghans have a well-known history of uniting against foreign invaders. More important, these resistance groups (henceforth referred to as the Afghan Resistance) now received increasing support from outside and developed roots in the growing refugee population in Pakistan and Iran.

Surprised by the tenacity of the widespread Afghan rebellion and the severity of international reaction, Moscow soon developed an interest in negotiations provided these could serve as a means to secure legitimacy for the PDPA government and to isolate the Afghan Resistance. This was the crux of the proposals enunciated by Kabul on May 14, 1980, that envisaged, first, direct bilateral talks between the Democratic Republic of Afghanistan (DRA) and its neighbors, Pakistan and Iran, for negotiating agreements on the normalization of mutual relations—specifically noninterference in each other's internal affairs—and, second, US guarantees of noninterference. The question of withdrawal was treated as an exclusively bilateral matter between Moscow and Kabul to be considered only after noninterference had been fully assured.

Pakistan's opposition to the Soviet intervention and its support for the Resistance were rooted deeply in the mainstream Islamic sentiment of the country and the ideological disposition of President Mohammed Zia ul Haq. Strategically, the Soviet action presented Pakistan with a curious blend of risks and opportunities. It raised legitimate security concerns in Pakistan while offering tempting prospects to augment Pakistan's flagging defense capability through a revitalization of US-Pakistani relations.

The need to contain Soviet hostility, coupled with the domestic compulsion that Pakistan not be found remiss in efforts for a political solution, created an interest in negotiations. This inclination was reinforced by Pakistan's disappointment with the Carter administration's response to its security needs. The Zia government thus embarked on a dual-faceted Afghan policy—providing diplomatic and material support to the Afghan Resistance while actively pursuing a negotiated settlement.

At Pakistan's behest, in May 1980 the OIC set up a three-member Standing Committee, consisting of the foreign ministers of Pakistan and Iran and the OIC secretary-general, to undertake consultations for a comprehensive settlement. The committee attempted to establish a dialogue with the Afghan parties—mainly the Resistance, represented by the Peshawar-based parties—and the PDPA. Kabul and Moscow, however, refused to cooperate because the committee was mandated to deal with the resistance parties, which Kabul-Moscow propaganda viewed as counter-revolutionaries and "bandits."

The internal and external dimensions of the Afghan issue were clearly interrelated, but Soviet rejection of the Afghan opposition elements and Soviet aversion to "internationalizing" the Afghan issue stymied initiatives that were intended to address the two aspects. Moscow indicated some flexibility in early 1981 by suggesting consideration of the external aspect of the Afghan issue in the context of an international conference, proposed by General Secretary Leonid Brezhnev in November 1980, to discuss security of the Gulf. By then, movement among the parties toward UN mediation had already developed.

Prelude to the Geneva Talks

The stalemated OIC initiatives created pressures on Pakistan for fresh diplomatic recourse. At the Thirty-fifth UN General Assembly Session (1980), Agha Shahi, then Pakistan's foreign minister, called for the appointment of a special representative by the UN secretary-general and advocated a political solution that could weave together some elements of Kabul's May 1980 proposals with the principles outlined in the OIC and UN resolutions. Also, in keeping with the precedent set by the OIC Standing Committee, Pakistan accepted the concept of trilateral negotiations involving Pakistan, Iran, and the PDPA representatives under the auspices of the United Nations. This step became the point of departure for a dialogue between Pakistani officials and the Soviet ambassador, Vitaly S. Smirnov, in Islamabad toward the end of 1980 to work out a procedure for UN-sponsored talks.

The Moscow-Islamabad parleys agreed on a mediation role for the UN secretary-general. Accordingly, in February 1981, Javier Perez de Cuellar, a senior Peruvian diplomat who was UN undersecretary-general for political affairs, was nominated as Secretary-General Kurt Waldheim's personal representative to promote peace talks. Iranian refusal to engage in any negotiations that excluded the Afghan Resistance also led Pakistan to accept indirect talks with Kabul. These started in the form of shuttles by Perez de Cuellar to Islamabad and Kabul.

The challenge to Perez de Cuellar during the two shuttles in April and August 1981 was to engage the parties in substantive negotiations. He drafted a four-point agenda for his shuttle diplomacy to include procedures for negotiations, withdrawal, guarantees against intervention, and the return of refugees. He proposed substantive discussion on the refugee issue because it received increasing attention in public statements by the two sides. Kabul, however, wanted direct talks as a prerequisite for negotiations, while Pakistan proposed the inclusion of "self-determination" as a fifth point on the agenda.

By the end of 1981, the positions of the two interlocutors softened. The Babrak Karmal regime relented on its demand for direct talks because the continued absence of negotiations did not serve the regime's need for international recognition. Furthermore, the UN framework suited Kabul because it treated the Kabul government as the sole Afghan interlocutor. On the other hand, Pakistan recognized that Kabul and Moscow would not accept self-determination or any reference to internal political adjustment as part of the agenda. Pakistan's public position had already conceded that Soviet withdrawal would by itself allow the Afghans to determine their political future.

With the election of Perez de Cuellar to head the UN, his mantle was passed to a UN official from Ecuador, Diego Cordovez, who contributed to the negotiations a characteristic vibrant style. In Islamabad, a change in the Foreign Office leadership was made largely because Agha Shahi had differed with the military government's policy of being a conduit of arms for the Resistance. The new Pakistani foreign minister, Sahabzada Yaqub Khan, had little reservation on that score; he looked on the Afghan armed struggle as complementary to diplomacy.

During his first shuttle to the area in April 1982, Cordovez secured an agreement on holding indirect talks at Geneva and on the agenda's four items—withdrawal, noninterference, international guarantees, and voluntary return of refugees. Kabul's acceptance was conditional: first, Kabul insisted on a Pakistani commitment to direct talks at some point and, second, it regarded withdrawal as an exclusively bilateral matter with Moscow. In elaborating the agenda, Cordovez deftly relied on "constructive ambiguity" to avoid objections from the two interlocutors.

The first Geneva round of indirect talks held in June 1982 did not achieve more than an expanded annotation for the agenda. While Pakistanis groped for an equitable, integrated, and comprehensive settlement governed by legally binding arrangements that ensured simultaneous rather than sequential implementation of all aspects, the Afghan position on substance remained anchored in the May 14, 1980, proposals.

The Afghans focused on direct talks, a bilateral agreement with Pakistan on noninterference, and international guarantees limited to noninterference. For them, withdrawal was outside the purview of the UN negotiations. For Pakistani negotiators, their nonrecognition of the Kabul government—formally tied to the January 1980 OIC resolution—ruled out the signing of a bilateral agreement. Pakistan desired a balanced comprehensive settlement that provided for irreversible withdrawal, within a short time frame, and guarantees to cover the entire settlement, including withdrawal. Also, as against an Afghan demand for specific measures on noninterference, Pakistanis wanted this issue to be restricted to a reaffirmation of international principles. The consequent divergences were fundamental and could not be bridged by diplomacy alone.

The external environment was not conducive to progress in the negotiations either. The Geneva indirect talks had begun amid low expectations and in the face of opposition from Iran and the Resistance. Meanwhile, by all indications, the Soviets had become deeply embroiled in Afghanistan, bracing themselves for the long haul. Washington showed little enthusiasm for the negotiations; instead, bipartisan political lobbies had become active in support of Afghan *mujahidin* and in favor of raising the cost of the Soviet transgression. A new US commitment to help Pakistan had been formalized in September 1981 with the signing of a six-year, $3.2-billion package of economic assistance and military sales.

Illusion of Missed Opportunity

In the Soviet Union, the brief interregnum under Yuri Andropov, who succeeded Leonid Brezhnev in November 1982, was marked by heightened optimism that an Afghan settlement might be possible. Andropov's decision to receive Zia ul Haq, when the latter arrived in Moscow to attend Brezhnev's funeral, and Andropov's candid admission of pressure exerted on the Soviet Union by the Afghan conflict impelled Zia to acknowledge "some freshness" in the Soviet attitude.[2] Later in March 1983, Perez de Cuellar and Cordovez returned elated from Moscow where Andropov had restated Soviet difficulties in Afghanistan and personally endorsed UN mediation.

The promising signs quickened the pace of the negotiations. Cordovez scheduled a Geneva round in April and presented a sketchy four-part draft settlement based on the embryonic structure apparent in the annotated agenda. He successfully persuaded Pakistan to engage in discussion of Section II on noninterference, rather than insist on parallel development of all four sections, on the plea that the settlement was of an integrated nature.

At the April 1983 Geneva round, Cordovez placed a whole set of obligations under Section II, drawn from the 1981 UN General Assembly Declaration on Inadmissibility of Nonintervention and Noninterference in the Internal Affairs of States. The ensuing discussion on this section underscored three major problems. First, the Afghans insisted on such specific measures as closing camps and expelling the resistance groups. Cordovez suggested a general formulation, but Pakistan did not want to go beyond the text derived from the UN declaration. Second, the Afghans objected to the phrase on international boundaries borrowed from the declaration. Third, Pakistan had a conceptual difficulty with a provision—introduced by Cordovez in deference to the Soviet-Afghan position—calling for completion of steps for observance of obligations under noninterference before the date of enforcement of the settlement. Pakistan sought a mirror-image provision for withdrawal in an effort to maintain balance.

As Cordovez pushed for an agreement on Section II, the Pakistan side grew anxious over lack of progress in areas of its concern: on withdrawal, the draft text contained barely one sentence providing a blank space for the time frame; the text of guarantees was limited to noninterference; and details for consulting the refugees on conditions of their return remained unaddressed.

Cordovez attempted a shortcut to circumvent problems that blocked progress on the draft text. Using the channel of informal meetings with Yaqub Khan and Stanislav Gavrilov, the Soviet representative, Cordovez promoted the idea that the Soviets offer a time frame in return for Pakistan's acceptance of Section II. He suggested a short recess until June for consultations in the respective capitals. Cordovez thus targeted the time frame and Pakistan's commitment to noninterference as the key issues, which if secured could become the locomotive for a settlement that would generate irresistible political pressures and dwarf the remaining issues of procedure, formats, and substance.

The informal meetings also touched on the internal dimension of the Afghan issue. Cordovez was clearly interested in the conditions under which Pakistan could sign with Kabul a bilateral agreement on noninterference—specifically, whether a change of face at the top could remove Pakistan's reservations. According to Cordovez, Gavrilov had told him that Zia ul Haq had not agreed to a Soviet offer to replace Karmal with the Afghan prime minister, Sultan Ali Kishtmand. Zia ul Haq denied any knowledge of such an offer. Nonetheless, the information, taken at face value, reinforced Pakistani thinking that a settlement at Geneva would follow or coincide with a Soviet-sponsored change to stabilize the government in Kabul.

The April 1983 round was suspended on an upbeat note. Later in May, Cordovez gave an overdrawn assessment to the press that the settlement was "95 percent ready."[3] The Pakistani view was considerably more circumspect, though Yaqub Khan had returned to Islamabad convinced that the negotiations had entered a serious phase. In Islamabad, several high-level meetings, chaired by Zia ul Haq, examined the vexing questions involved and finally decided to approve Section II (on noninterference) and to send Yaqub Khan to consult Riyadh—Saudi Arabia being the chair of the OIC—and the five capitals of the permanent members of the Security Council.

Yaqub Khan found skepticism about Soviet intentions in the capitals he visited before arriving in Moscow, his last stop. Beijing even suggested that guarantees of noninterference should follow withdrawal. In Washington, Secretary of State George P. Shultz disavowed any US intention to bleed the Soviet Union. On specifics, however, Under Secretary of State Lawrence Eagleburger affirmed that guarantees should cover the entire settlement and hinted at legal complications if they were to resemble a treaty. As compared to the somewhat detached US officials, Yaqub Khan was faced with an excited American press, stirred by Cordovez's statement. Given Pakistan's complicity with an expanding US covert operation to assist the resistance, the media doubted Pakistan's interest in a settlement.

Yaqub Khan arrived in Moscow on June 9, 1983, expecting that he would clinch an understanding on time frame and obtain Soviet blessings for a broad-based government in Kabul. The meeting with Andrei Gromyko, the Soviet foreign minister, dashed these hopes. Yaqub Khan's assumption that Moscow had accepted the concept of an equitable comprehensive settlement, which he thought he had developed with Cordovez, turned out to be false. It became even more obvious subsequently, when en route to the airport Soviet Deputy Foreign Minister Georgi Korniyenko sought a few clarifications from Yaqub Khan about Pakistan's stand on textual issues.

At the meeting, Gromyko reportedly likened Pakistan to someone who had given his apartment to bandits to shoot at neighbors and stated that the question of withdrawal of the Soviet contingent would not arise until interference against the Kabul regime ceased and Afghanistan felt fully secure; mere assurances of noninterference were not enough. More important, Gromyko appeared to rule out the inclusion of withdrawal in a UN document and insisted that, "These were Soviet troops, not Afghan or Pakistani." He contended that just as the Soviets had no right to negotiate Pakistani-Afghan differences, Pakistan could not discuss a withdrawal that concerned Moscow and Kabul alone. Gromyko was similarly sensitive to any suggestion pointing to the need for political change in Kabul. The meeting registered one concordant note—the two sides stressed the need for maintaining the momentum of the negotiations.

The exchange in Moscow had sealed the fate of the resumed Geneva round in June 1983. Cordovez was visibly agitated over the receding prospects for a settlement. He put pressure on Pakistan to accept the entire text, including limited scope guarantees. Only such an earnest, he argued, could remove Soviet distrust and enable him to ask the Soviet side to offer a time frame. The Pakistan side, on the other hand, reminded Cordovez of the April understanding—the Soviets would indicate a time frame as a quid pro quo for Pakistan's acceptance of Section II.

Cordovez felt that an opportunity had been missed. This theme later surfaced in press reports, with the responsibility for the impasse ascribed to Pakistan and a hidden US hand. Notwithstanding such speculation, by June 1983 the Soviet position had regressed into the old grooves. A plausible explanation could be found in the first news of the stroke suffered by Andropov. The *London Times* of June 8, 1983, had reported "rapid decline" in Andropov's health. Even had Andropov remained active, it would have taken more than one Geneva round to finalize the settlement. Gorbachev, who picked up Andropov's testament describing Afghanistan "a bleeding wound,"[4] took nearly three years to reach an agreement, despite the fact that by then the draft settlement had been shaped to Soviet liking.

Following the anticlimax of June 1983, the negotiations proceeded at a slow pace, which Cordovez attributed to deterioration in East-West relations. The only significant development in 1984 was Pakistan's decision to unlock its position on signature. This became possible when, in an attempt to accommodate the concerns of the two sides, Cordovez improved the text of the draft comprehensive settlement from Pakistan's viewpoint and simultaneously proposed to supplement it with a draft bilateral agreement on noninterference, based on Section II. At the August 1984 talks, Pakistan offered to sign both documents with Kabul, provided Moscow gave a short time frame.

The Pakistani negotiators had felt that Pakistan was being unjustly criticized for foot-dragging, whereas the Soviets were engaged in a kind of "salami tactics," using every Pakistani concession to raise a new demand. The Pakistani move forced the Afghan-Soviet position to come out in the open. Kabul and Moscow were not prepared to accord legal status to the draft comprehensive settlement because Pakistan could not become a party to an agreement on withdrawal. Similarly, the United States would have no role other than guaranteeing noninterference.

Although the negotiations suffered an eclipse during 1984 and early 1985, this period witnessed a transformation of the military situation when the Resistance matured into an effective guerrilla force. Soviet military tactics also changed, combining military offensives with increased reliance on air power and reprisals against towns and villages harboring the mujahidin. Helicopter gunships (MI24s) and specially trained forces—Spetsnaz—were deployed with considerable effect in counterinsurgency operations. Under pressure, the mujahidin constantly clamored for better arms. Pakistani willingness to allow improved weapons led to a substantial increase in US assistance to the mujahidin by 1985 and, later, to President Ronald Reagan's approval for the delivery of Stingers. When the weapon was introduced in Afghanistan in September 1986, it dramatically altered the military balance in favor of the Resistance.

Advent of Gorbachev

The extent of the extraordinary changes in Soviet policies under Mikhail Gorbachev was not immediately visible, yet his eagerness in opening toward the West and the revival of the US-Soviet summitry following a six-year hiatus were enough to reactivate negotiations on Afghanistan. Between May and December 1985, Cordovez undertook one shuttle to the area and held three rounds of talks at Geneva.

Cordovez divided the draft comprehensive settlement into four separate instruments, structured on the basis of the four corresponding sections. The Afghans had asked that this be done to segregate the issue of withdrawal, but Cordovez assured the Pakistan side that the integrity of the settlement would be preserved. Elaboration of the three instruments dealing with noninterference, guarantees, and return of refugees proved fairly easy, except for a few lingering problems such as Kabul's reservation on the border formulation. On textual issues, Cordovez scored a significant success when he obtained Afghan-Soviet agreement on an expression of support for the entire political settlement in the text of guarantees.

In December 1985, the US State Department conveyed US acceptance of the text of the instrument on guarantees on condition that withdrawal and other issues would be satisfactorily resolved. Cordovez then persuaded the Soviets to withdraw their amendments to the text that they had offered earlier in August. The US initiative was reportedly intended to focus attention directly on the single remaining issue—Soviet refusal to provide a time frame for withdrawal. It was also influenced by the argument that such guarantees were acceptable in view of Pakistan's assertion that the time frame for withdrawal should be based on logistical considerations and therefore should not exceed three to four months.

Discussion of the texts encountered two major obstacles in late 1985. First, the Afghans demanded direct talks for consideration of Instrument IV, dealing with the issue of withdrawal and its interrelationship with the other elements of the settlement. Second, the Soviets could not accept UN monitoring that extended beyond noninterference to cover withdrawal. The Soviet position on the UN role changed toward the end of 1986 and facilitated agreement on monitoring and the establishment of the UN Good Offices Mission in Afghanistan and Pakistan.

The issue of direct talks was dragged into the political arena and debated at the UN General Assembly as well as within Pakistan, where a vocal opposition to Afghan policy was calling for direct talks. Pakistan's suspicion that Kabul sought direct talks only to gain political advantage was reinforced by another development at the December 1985 round of talks.

At Afghan insistence, Cordovez hesitatingly transmitted to the Pakistani side the elements of a draft that the Afghans suggested for Instrument IV. These elements were derived from Kabul's May 1980 proposals, which obviously departed from Pakistan's concept of an equitable settlement. Pakistan, therefore, refused to consider direct talks until all instruments were finalized on the basis of the texts proposed by Cordovez. In April 1986, the Afghan side relented on direct talks. By then the chief protagonist of direct talks, Babrak Karmal, had suffered political decline and was soon replaced by Dr. Najibullah, the chief of Afghan Security (Khad)

The change in Kabul was reckoned among the increasingly clear signals of Moscow's interest in extricating itself from Afghanistan in "the nearest future."[5] Against this background, Kabul's offer at the May 1986 Geneva round of a four-year time frame and the lack of Soviet willingness to pressure Kabul to scale down its offer to a reasonable figure came as a surprise.

The puzzle unraveled when Gorbachev's Vladivostok address on July 28, 1986, foreshadowed a new Soviet approach in its search of an internal political settlement in Afghanistan. Gorbachev supported the creation of "a government with the participation in it of those political forces that found themselves beyond the country's boundaries."[6] According to later analyses, Moscow had undertaken a review of its military involvement in Afghanistan at the Soviet Communist Party Central Committee meeting in October 1985 and took a decision in principle to withdraw Soviet troops at a subsequent Politburo meeting a year later in November 1986. Both occasions were followed by Soviet efforts to encourage the Kabul leadership to seek to compromise with opposition political elements with a view to stabilizing the government in Kabul.

By December 1986, the Soviets had clearly shifted in favor of seeking an internal political reconciliation before undertaking withdrawal, in practical terms linking the two issues. The linkage, Moscow argued, was necessary to prevent bloodshed.

Politics of Reconciliation and Withdrawal

Throughout 1987 the focus of the negotiations kept moving between efforts to finalize the Geneva settlement with an agreed time frame and endeavors to promote an internal political settlement. Najibullah's initiative for "national reconciliation," launched on the last day of 1986, inviting the armed opposition to accept a cease-fire and dialogue was dismissed as a ploy by the seven Peshawar groups, now loosely joined in the "Islamic Unity of Afghan Mujahidin" normally referred to as the Afghan Alliance.[7] The initiative was also flawed by its silence over the crucial issues of power-sharing and the withdrawal of Soviet forces, while its projection remained steeped in offensive revolutionary rhetoric.

Moscow dispatched its deputy foreign minister, Anatoly Kovalyev, to Islamabad to seek Pakistan's endorsement of Najibullah's offer. Yaqub Khan, instead, put forward a counterproposal for an interim government with representatives acceptable to the contending Afghan parties and headed by a neutral personality. Kovalyev (and, later, Soviet Foreign Minister Eduard Shevardnadze) rejected the proposal, arguing that the replacement of the established PDPA government with a new political arrangement was inconceivable. Pakistan developed a counter argument: if in the Soviet assessment the PDPA government was effective, Moscow should not hesitate to offer a short time frame and as Yaqub Khan put it, let the "chips fall where they might."

At the March 1987 round of talks, Cordovez had expected to clinch a settlement on the basis of a one-year time frame. He believed that Pakistan and the United States could not resist political pressures generated by a Soviet offer of such timing. At Geneva, Yaqub Khan was clearly moving in that direction. In response to two successively reduced Afghan offers, he had raised Pakistan's acceptance to seven months. The Afghans, however, refused to reduce further their offer of eighteen months and called off the round.

Failure to bridge the gap on the time frame convinced Cordovez that the Soviets were serious about linkage and impelled him to address the internal dimension of the issue by initiating "second-track" negotiations. Conscious of Kabul's sensitivities, Cordovez defined his second track as supplementary to efforts for national reconciliation; he added that it needed to be synchronized with the Geneva track. Specifically, he asked Pakistan to persuade the majority of the Peshawar-based leaders to accept an interim arrangement under the former king, Mohammed Zahir Shah, and, thereafter, Cordovez would try to gain Soviet acquiescence. Later, in September 1987, Cordovez proposed a scenario paper that envisaged an assembly—comprised of representatives of the PDPA, the Resistance, and prominent Afghan émigrés—to agree to an interim political arrangement on the basis of already identified principles.

Efforts of the Pakistan Foreign Office to activate the second track or elicit an initiative aimed at political compromise from the Alliance, ran aground for several reasons. First, the militarily strong, fundamentalist components of the Alliance, who enjoyed patronage from the Pakistan Interservices Intelligence Agency (ISI), firmly rejected any role for Zahir Shah, and, instead, spoke of an interim government of the mujahidin. Second, deep ideological and political divisions prevented a political consensus within the Alliance. Third, the ISI suspected the moves for a political compromise—such as those being pushed by the Foreign Office—particularly at a time when the ISI attached paramount importance to maintaining the momentum of the impressive military victories scored by the Resistance. Finally, the struggle for power between Zia ul Haq and Mohammed Khan Junejo, who became prime minister following February 1985 elections in Pakistan, resulted in a loss of focus for Pakistan's Afghan policy as well as the coordination necessary to adjust it to changing political and military circumstances.

Frustrated by the lack of a positive response from either Moscow or the Alliance to the idea of a neutral interim government, the Pakistan Foreign Office tilted toward its long-standing position calling for a short time frame. It now argued that the time frame could become a catalyst for the Afghan parties to forge a political consensus. The military assessment that the PDPA regime would collapse without Soviet props reinforced this stance. The Americans maintained a similar position in their contacts with the Soviets.

Meanwhile, Cordovez wavered between his two tracks in the hope of making an advance in either direction. Optimism was high for settling the time frame when, after resisting for nearly four months, Kabul suddenly asked for the convening of Geneva talks in early September. Curiously, however, and despite indications of Moscow's willingness to withdraw within one year, Kabul stalled at sixteen months as against Pakistan's proposal for eight months. The gap between the two positions had narrowed and conceivably was bridgeable.

Either for genuine reasons or to gain time to pursue the military option, Zia ul Haq became interested in promoting an internal political settlement. In late October, he conveyed to Moscow, through the informal channel of American industrialist Armand Hammer, a proposal predicated on Soviet agreement to the convening of a jirga in Pakistan with PDPA participation and a role for Zahir Shah.[8] Subsequently, in November, Zia ul Haq publicly endorsed the idea of a tripartite interim political arrangement with the PDPA as one of the segments.

Zia ul Haq had acted late. By October-November 1987, the Soviets were already in the process of dropping linkage between withdrawal and an internal settlement. First indications had come during a September meeting between Shevardnadze and Yaqub Khan in New York. Later at the December Washington summit, Gorbachev publicly announced Soviet acceptance of a twelve-month time frame, provided there was simultaneous agreement on a cut-off of aid to the Resistance.[9] Linkage was thus abandoned, and Moscow was now ready for the Geneva settlement that was to emerge several months later.

The Final Phase

For some time following Yaqub Khan's exit from office in October 1987, there was growing unhappiness in Islamabad over Pakistan's concessions, which had stretched the time frame beyond the three-to-four months deemed justifiable for logistical requirements. Gorbachev's statement in Washington heightened controversy over cutting off supplies to the mujahidin and was bitterly opposed by Washington's conservative lobbies. Both the Pakistan Foreign Office and the US State Department now agreed on the need to rectify the perceived imbalance in the existing texts by introducing safeguards. The centerpiece of the concept was symmetry in the treatment of the contending Afghan factions with regard to cutoffs of supplies.

Zia ul Haq felt outmaneuvered by the Washington summit and pursued with determination the objective of an interim government. He asked Cordovez to reactivate the second track when the latter undertook a shuttle in January 1988. Zia ul Haq even declared that Pakistan would be unwilling to sign the settlement with the Najibullah government, but the second track could not take off. First, the hardliners within the Afghan Alliance rejected any proposal based on dialogue with the PDPA or PDPA participation in any political arrangement. Second, in view of the growing pressures exerted on Pakistan by the Afghan conflict, Prime Minister Junejo supported an early settlement on the basis of agreements negotiated at Geneva with added safeguards. The Americans favored such a defensible settlement and conceded that establishment of an interim government was "desirable," but they were skeptical that it would be brought about within a reasonably short time.[10]

On February 8, 1988, Gorbachev reduced the time frame to ten months, agreed to front-loading of withdrawal, and set a deadline of March 15 for signing the settlement. This foreclosed options for Pakistan. In a stormy meeting with Soviet Deputy Foreign Minister Yuli Vorontsov, who arrived in Islamabad the next day, Zia ul Haq pressed for delaying Geneva in an effort to permit an acceptable internal political settlement to emerge. He argued that this was necessary to prevent bloodshed and to ensure the return of refugees. Vorontsov did not relent. He recapitulated the arguments Pakistan had invoked over the years to underscore the central importance of withdrawal and dismissed the demand for an internal settlement as "tactical." The Soviets reportedly thought Zia ul Haq was simply stalling.

An Alliance proposal for a transitional government offered in late February under Pakistani pressure was lost in the heightened international expectations focused on Geneva. Some observers believe it could have had an impact had it been made a few months earlier.

Pakistan could not have retreated from Geneva without loss of international credibility. Consultations with allies confirmed this view. Prime Minister Junejo, therefore, approved Cordovez's suggestion to hold the final round on March 2 and braced himself to mobilize domestic support in favor of signing. In a high-profile move, he invited the leaders of all major political parties for consultations. The conclusion was foregone, as summed up in the remarks of the chairperson of the Pakistan People's Party, Benazir Bhutto, who urged efforts on behalf of the Resistance, but not at the expense of an agreement on Soviet troop withdrawal.

At Geneva, statements by Pakistan's chief delegate, Minister of State Zain Noorani, were a chronicle of a retreat from the demand for an interim government. In the end, Pakistan's demand was reduced to a statement—

made by Cordovez prior to the signing of the Geneva accords—reflecting an understanding on the continuation of efforts for the formation of a broad-based government to be decided by all Afghan political elements. Ironically, following withdrawal, Moscow was the first to invoke UN intercession for restoration of peace in Afghanistan.

The principal hindrance to a settlement in this final round was the issue of symmetry, technically to be decided between the two guarantor states. The United States proposed "negative symmetry" calling for a "time-bound" moratorium on supplies to all Afghan factions. The proposal, first taken up in Moscow before the March 15 deadline, was rejected by Shevardnadze when he visited Washington on March 22-23. The Soviets argued that the arms supply relationship between the Soviet Union and Afghanistan was sanctified by intergovernmental treaties dating back to 1921.

As the prospects for an understanding on symmetry receded, the Soviets pressed Pakistan at Geneva to proceed with the settlement without the American guarantee. Pakistan's refusal drew a sharp reaction from Shevardnadze at Sofia, where he attacked Pakistan's position and alluded to undefined "consequences" for Soviet-Pakistan relations if the Soviet troops were to withdraw without a Geneva settlement.[11] Moscow clearly wanted the settlement to put a gloss of international good behavior on its decision to withdraw from Afghanistan.

At the suggestion of the Pakistani leadership, Shultz eventually proposed to Shevardnadze an understanding on "positive symmetry" on the basis of a continuation of arms supplies to all Afghan factions. Moscow acquiesced, as became apparent when Junejo received a message from Shevardnadze, who had arrived in Kabul on April 4, 1988, seeking Pakistan's cooperation for resolving the question of the border formulation that Shevardnadze described as the last remaining obstacle.

The tacit agreement on positive symmetry rests on public statements by Pakistan and the United States and a confidential exchange of communications between the two guarantors prior to the signing of the accords. Essentially, the American statement and the confidential communication assert a US right to provide military assistance to Afghan factions should the Soviet Union continue such assistance to the faction it supports. The Soviet response provided an ambiguous acquiescence in the American assertion. Publicly, Pakistan has invoked the understanding on symmetry to defend its decision to sign the accords, but it has refrained from doing so in its formal exchanges with the United Nations.

Epilogue

The character of the conflict inside Afghanistan has been deeply transformed as a result of Soviet withdrawal. The Najibullah government has displayed unexpected staying power, even considering the massive Soviet military and financial resources (estimated at $250 million per month) made available to it during most of the post-withdrawal period. On the other hand, persisting rivalries within the Resistance have come into full view. Now the Najibullah regime is one among several Afghan factions locked in a military conflict that persists, though at a comparatively lower intensity than in the past.

The prospects for a political consensus in Afghanistan have narrowed mainly because of the failure of the Resistance to develop a credible political profile. Political power remains fragmented in Afghanistan following the dissolution of the traditional power structures during the decade-long conflict.

The Afghan Interim Government (AIG), established in February 1989 by an Afghan *shura* (assembly) convened near Islamabad, has not been able to assume the role of a broad coalition of the Resistance. The principal reasons why a more effective and representative AIG has not emerged include, first, the failure of the seven Peshawar-based parties to submerge their differences and accommodate other Afghan groups within the AIG and, second, Islamabad's inability to provide political direction because Pakistani politics was itself undergoing a radical transition. Furthermore, the competing influences of Iran and Saudi Arabia have compounded the search for consensus among the members of the heterogeneous Afghan Resistance.

The AIG suffered an early setback in its attempt—in the shape of the March 1989 Jallalabad offensive—to establish a foothold in Afghanistan. Controversy surrounds this abortive operation. Some observers blame it on an ill-advised Pakistani-American push and reported interruption in the supply of US arms to the mujahidin. Nonetheless, reasons appear to be more political than military. The lack of coordination among mujahidin commanders and their inability to synchronize tactical attacks in other areas are clearly linked to the paucity of support for the AIG among local commanders.

As the military and political stalemate continues, a persistent question has been how outside powers can help the Afghan factions to move toward peace and political consolidation. The positions of the principal protagonists, however, remain divergent and do not promise an early political breakthrough.

Moscow insists, as before, on a cease-fire and intra-Afghan dialogue for a government of reconciliation in which the PDPA would retain a substantial role. Najibullah has also proposed a cease-fire and UN-supervised elections but rejected the suggestion of his stepping down to facilitate such elections. The stigma against the PDPA remains potent. Neither the Afghan émigrés nor any of the resistance groups have, so far, accepted overtures for a dialogue with Najibullah. Local resistance commanders also reject a cease-fire because it could result in the demobilization of the irregular mujahidin fighters while leaving the Soviet-supplied Kabul army intact under Najibullah's control. Purges within the PDPA of the rival Khalq component in late 1989 and the coup attempt by Defense Minister General Shahnawaz Tanai in March 1990 also reveal that Najibullah remains vulnerable internally.

The post-withdrawal Pakistani and American positions have largely kept to staying the course—support for the AIG and the demand for Najibullah's removal as a precondition for movement toward a political settlement. Disillusionment with the AIG has gradually led to a review of the US position, as evident in the offer reportedly made by Secretary of State James Baker in February 1990 in Moscow proposing Najibullah's removal as part of a "phased transition process."[12] The new position foreshadows shifting currents in US policy. Because US strategic interests appear to have been served by the Soviet withdrawal, questions are being raised in Washington over the rationale of continuing US involvement in the conflict to support Afghan factions known to be fundamentalist.

The Benazir Bhutto government, on the other hand, fears a conservative backlash and is in no position to make concessions or dilute support for the Afghan mujahidin. Barring an unexpected change in Kabul, Pakistan's hopes for an internal Afghan settlement rest on the emergence of a galvanized AIG as a result of a new Afghan shura or elections.

UN diplomacy has continued, though now under the UN secretary-general's personal direction—Cordovez resigned in August 1988 to become Ecuador's foreign minister. The United Nations seeks, first, a stronger role for itself, endorsed by outside powers and, second, a political consensus among the Afghan parties for a political arrangement, interim or otherwise. On specifics, it has attempted to develop an agreed panel of prominent Afghans, possibly technocrats, who could facilitate a settlement through UN-sponsored elections or a shura. The Zahir Shah option still attracts attention, but its prospects remain as narrow as before.

The package proposal offered by Gorbachev at the United Nations in

December 1988 indicated for the first time Soviet willingness to accept a mutual halt in arms supplies linked to a cease-fire, negotiations among Afghan parties, and an international conference on Afghanistan. This has revived debate on negative symmetry. The proponents of the idea point to the futility of prolonging the military stalemate and argue that a cooling-off period in Afghanistan is necessary to allow Afghan political factions to find an internal balance.

Internationally, there is broad support for a political settlement that could lead to a peaceful, stable, nonaligned Afghanistan. But an agreed practical approach toward this objective remains elusive. An unconditional US-Soviet understanding on negative symmetry and a stronger UN role could serve as a cutting edge. A larger peace effort would have to involve Pakistan, Iran, and Saudi Arabia. Success, however, would depend on the emergence of a viable and dynamic coalition of the fragmented Afghan political forces, one that isolates elements of extremism and attracts support from a majority of the important segments of the Afghan population.

Notes

1. UN press release SG/1860, April 14, 1988: The Geneva Accords for the Settlement of the Situation Relating to Afghanistan, signed by Afghanistan and Pakistan, and by the Union of Soviet Socialist Republics and the United States as States-Guarantors.
2. *New York Times*, November 21, 1982, p. 8.
3. *Pakistan Times* (Rawalpindi), May 12, 1983.
4. Foreign Broadcast Information Service (FBIS)-USSR, February 26, 1986, p. O-31.
5. FBIS-USSR, February 26, 1986, p. O-31.
6. FBIS-USSR, July 29, 1986, pp. R-19-20.
7. *Kabul New Times*, January 3, 1987; see also UN Document A/42/83-S/18564, January 7, 1987.
8. The Islamic fundamentalist parties within the Afghan Alliance, as well as many mujahidin groups operating inside Afghanistan, preferred the nomenclature *shura* for representation assemblies instead of the traditional Afghan concept of *jirga* for such assemblies. This bias was reinforced as pro-Zahir Shah elements proposed from time to time the convening of a *loya jirga* (grand assembly) to secure a role for the former Afghan king.
9. *Washington Post*, December 11, 1987, p. A-33.
10. *New York Times*, February 23, 1988, p. I-6.
11. TASS, Sofia, Shevardnadze interview, 0818 GMT, March 31, 1988.
12. *New York Times*, February 9, 1990, p. I-9.

4

The INF Treaty in Perspective

Leo Reddy

THE GUESTS ARRIVING AT THE White House on the morning of December 8, 1987, walked briskly from their cars. It was a breezy, chilly day. The invigorating air added to the sense of expectation. Everyone was in good spirits as they entered the East Room.

The Soviet retinue was large; this gathering was a major event in General Secretary Mikhail Gorbachev's first state visit to Washington. Raisa Gorbachev and Nancy Reagan sat in the middle of the front row. They were flanked by senior diplomatic and military advisers of the US and Soviet governments who greeted each other with considerable camaraderie. Leaders from the US Congress were present. The White House Press Corps was well represented. TV cameras were banked up in the back of the room.

Also arriving were members of the US and Soviet Intermediate Nuclear Forces (INF) delegations who had negotiated the "Treaty Between the United States of America and the Union of Soviet Socialist Republics on the Elimination of Their Intermediate-Range and Shorter-Range Missiles." Each page of the treaty, which had just been completed in a photo finish of round-the-clock negotiations in Geneva, had been initialed only the night before by the chief US INF negotiator, Ambassador Maynard W. Glitman, and the chief Soviet INF negotiator, Ambassador Alexei A. Obukhov, on a special US Air Force flight from Geneva.

As soon as the guests were seated, the doors at the front of the East Room opened, revealing a long corridor. President Ronald Reagan and General Secretary Gorbachev walked alone down this corridor and took their seats at the long mahogany table which stood at the front of the room. Each made relatively brief, good-humored speeches. They signed both the Russian and English versions of the treaty, which had been bound in heavy leather covers, and exchanged pens.

Tucking their respective copies of the signed treaty under their arms, the two leaders smiled and shook hands with a sweeping exuberance that brought the guests to their feet in an enthusiastic round of applause. Cameras whirred.

The picture of that robust handclasp appeared on TV news around the world that evening and many times since. Whatever their views of the merits of the INF Treaty, all who watched that scene knew they were witnessing an historic event, a major turning point in US-Soviet relations that appeared to symbolize the end of the Cold War between the two military superpowers.

This event also symbolized the central meaning of the treaty itself, its political significance, and the deep personal involvement of Reagan and Gorbachev. The treaty became a metaphor for the political controversies that swirled around East-West relations in the 1980s: the internal political pressures on North Atlantic Treaty Organization (NATO) governments that accompanied the deployment of US Pershing II and ground-launched cruise missiles in Europe; the ability of the alliance to withstand overt military and political pressure from the Soviet Union; the debate over how and whether to "help" a reform-minded, new Soviet leader; the split within the West over whether arms control negotiations should be used merely as a "process" to placate public opinion or as a vehicle to conclude actual agreements; and the concerns in Asia that US foreign policy had become too Eurocentric.

The treaty also became caught up in US domestic politics. Differences between progressive and conservative views within Washington over INF negotiating strategy were a mirror-image of the perennial, often ideological altercation within the body politic over how to deal with Soviet communism. Underlying this argument was a more profound struggle over the allocation of national resources, with some believing that continued high investment in military programs to thwart Soviet military power was indispensable to national security, and others wanting to divert greater resources to domestic economic and social uses. In the background stood another political issue well understood by Americans: the sharing of power between the executive and legislative branches of government, an issue that surfaced with a vengeance during the treaty ratification process in the US Senate.

As a result of this wholesale politicization, INF negotiations were, from the very outset, largely open negotiations performed with high drama on a public stage. Options vetted in the Washington interagency process were routinely leaked, as different factions within the government tried to gain public support for their position. Positions of various allied governments on key issues were generally well known outside the chambers of the North Atlantic Council in Brussels, the inner sanctum of confidential alliance consultations. Major moves by either side in the negotiations were often announced to the public before they were formally proposed at the negotiating table in Geneva. Even in Geneva, each side routinely held a press backgrounder shortly after making a new proposal in the talks. It was also a time when US and allied governments learned, painfully, that Gorbachev not only understood "public diplomacy" and image-making, but was besting them at this, their own, game.

The overarching political dimension of the negotiations also pervaded the internal discussions within the interagency community in Washington and the US delegation. Although the specific topics for discussion were usually military or technical in nature, consideration of those issues was rarely free of deep-seated differences between agencies over how to manage US-Soviet relations. As a result, discourse over seemingly obscure points could quickly become rancorous—especially if the discussion involved even the suggestion of a change in the US position to move the negotiations forward. "Technical" details in the treaty could—and often did—become political both during the treaty negotiations and the ratification debate.

The ultimate expression of the INF Treaty as a political instrument became its critical importance to the political futures of both Gorbachev and Reagan—and of George Bush. This is not to say that the treaty is significant only in political terms and not also in military terms. Although not of the same magnitude militarily as a strategic arms reduction accord, the INF agreement, when fully implemented, will nonetheless eliminate all US and Soviet ground-launched missiles with ranges between 500 and 5,500 kilometers (300 to 3,400 miles). Even though these forces represent well under 10 percent of the nuclear arsenals of the two superpowers, this treaty represents the first time the United States and the Soviet Union have agreed to reduce rather than merely to limit their nuclear forces. An unprecedented regime of on-site inspection and comprehensive data exchange embodied in the treaty promises to increase mutual confidence and reduce the risks of military miscalculation.

Yet, understanding the full significance of the INF Treaty requires grasping its political dimensions. They are what give the treaty its raison d'être and historic significance. Therefore, in an effort to put the INF Treaty in perspective, this chapter focuses primarily on the interaction between the process of negotiations and contemporary political dynamics. The politics of the INF negotiations were marked by continuous testing—of the strength of collective security commitments, of the courage and resolve of government leaders, of Gorbachev's ability to bring the Soviet military into line, of Reagan's willingness to override the opposition of Republican conservatives to an arms control deal with the Soviets.

Origins of the Negotiations

The process of testing began in 1977, when the Soviets started replacing aging SS-4s and SS-5s with SS-20 missiles. This new missile was far more capable than its predecessors. A triple-warhead, road-mobile, solid-fuel system with a range of nearly 5,000 kilometers, the SS-20 was more accurate and practically invulnerable to attack.

West German Chancellor Helmut Schmidt, in a highly-publicized speech in London late in 1977, raised the alarm over this threatening weapon system, warning that, "in Europe this magnifies the significance of the disparities between East and West as regards nuclear tactical and conventional forces."[1] As a Western response, Schmidt called for either a negotiated reduction of forces or for a vigorous INF buildup by NATO.

Many in Washington did not share Schmidt's concern over the SS-20, viewing it as a routine modernization program. But there was no mistaking his political message: he was elevating the SS-20 deployment to the level of a Soviet politico-military challenge requiring a staunch NATO—and especially US—response. Partly as a result of Schmidt's political challenge and partly because the US military perceived this as an opportunity to deploy a new generation of US intermediate-range missiles, Washington decided to mount a military response.

Both the United States and its allies recognized, however, that US deployment of INF missiles in Europe would encounter stiff resistance from left-of-center parties and pacifist groups in Western Europe. Building on Schmidt's two alternatives, NATO decided to pursue both a deployment path and a negotiating path in NATO's "two-track" decision of December 1979. This opened the way to US and NATO military authorities to develop a plan to deploy 464 US ground-launched cruise missiles (GLCMs) with a range of 2,500 kilometers and 108 Pershing II ballistic missiles with a range of 1,800 kilometers. This NATO decision also set the stage for political ferment that nearly toppled friendly allied governments.

An Alliance Under Pressure

In 1981, the combination of President Reagan's hard-line anticommunist views and former president Jimmy Carter's repeated warning in the 1980 presidential campaign that Reagan would lead the nation into a dangerous military course aroused fears in Europe over an escalation of East-West tension. Reagan's proclivity to engage in tough anti-Soviet rhetoric and the tendency of Secretary of Defense Caspar Weinberger and Secretary of State Alexander Haig to speculate publicly on warfighting scenarios in Europe—including the notion of a winnable nuclear war—added to those fears.

Public opinion polls in Europe at the time reflected growing opposition to US missile deployments. Many Europeans were concerned that these deployments would increase the risks of a nuclear exchange. Others believed that the Reagan administration was seeking a pretext for nuclear war-fighting in Europe.

As a result of this rising tide of discontent, pressure grew within the alliance to begin work on the negotiating track. The year was drawing to a close with no appearance of serious interest within the Reagan administration in arms control negotiations. The administration appeared to be concentrating its energies exclusively on the largest military buildup in the nation's peacetime history—of which INF developments in Europe were only one element.

Somewhat belatedly, the president tried to respond to European apprehensions by outlining a comprehensive position on arms control at the National Press Club in Washington on November 18, 1981. As the centerpiece of his presentation, Reagan announced his famous "zero-zero" proposal: the United States would refrain from deploying new INF missiles in Europe if the Soviet Union would dismantle its existing INF force of 250 SS-20 missiles and 350 SS-4 and SS-5 missiles.

The fact that the president had finally come out with a comprehensive policy on arms control was greeted with considerable relief and gave hope to European publics that the INF negotiating track would have some actual substance. Public opinion in both Europe and America reacted positively to the fact that the president was sending his negotiators to Geneva with something in hand. Reagan's proposal that a whole class of nuclear missiles be eliminated and thus "substantially reduce the dread threat of nuclear war which hangs over the people of Europe"[2] struck a responsive note with pacifist groups.

Knowledgeable observers were aware that President Reagan had enunciated a position that was patently nonnegotiable. Leonid Brezhnev and Andrey Gromyko would have scant interest in a situation in which they would scrap the entire deployed Soviet INF missile force in return for a US commitment not to deploy a nonexistent US INF missile force. For a time, however, the president had appeared to calm jitters in Europe. In the bargain he had inadvertently demonstrated that public opinion does not distinguish between negotiable and nonnegotiable proposals in arms control. *Any* proposal is welcome, theatrical or real, if it appears to add stimulus to the negotiations. This lesson became more important as the negotiations wore on.

In any case, the favorable public reception for zero-zero was especially good news for the leaders of the five NATO countries that had agreed to serve as the "basing" countries for US INF deployments: Belgium, the Federal Republic of Germany (FRG), Great Britain, Italy, and the Netherlands. INF deployments had already become a burning political issue in all of these countries, and opposition groups to US deployments were numerous and well organized.

On November 30, 1981, US-Soviet negotiations on INF began in Geneva, with Paul Nitze as the chief US representative and Yuli Kvitsinsky as the chief Soviet representative. The fact that Nitze was a distinguished American with long experience in national security affairs helped to bolster public confidence in the talks.

That same day, November 30, Ambassador Nitze tabled the zero-zero plan as a formal US proposal in Geneva. The Soviet delegation responded with a counterproposal that dramatized the gulf between the positions of the two sides. The Soviets proposed that NATO reduce its INF forces, missiles, and aircraft to 300, leaving this as the INF ceiling for both sides in Europe. This position was also plausible publicly, because it called for equality between NATO and the Soviet Union in intermediate-range nuclear forces in Europe.

Again, however, knowledgeable observers recognized that this approach would be wholly unacceptable to the United States and NATO. First, in

The INF Treaty in Perspective

discussing NATO forces, the Soviets were referring to the nuclear forces of Great Britain and France, who were not even represented at the talks in Geneva. If Britain and France were to accept the Soviet proposal, their forces alone would meet the collective ceiling of 300 missiles and aircraft. In other words, acceptance of the Soviet proposal would have automatically excluded any US INF deployments in Europe and curtailed existing deployments of US dual-capable aircraft, including those based on carriers stationed in the seas around Europe. Moreover, the Soviet proposal would not affect SS-20s based in the Asian territory of the Soviet Union.

These observers would have missed the critical point. The Soviet proposal—like the US proposal—was not advanced with any serious expectation that it would include elements acceptable to the other side. Rather, it was designed explicitly for its public appeal and its divisiveness in Europe. The argument that the Soviet Union faced a threat from three Western nuclear powers and should thus enjoy parity with them collectively would sound reasonable to Western opinion. The targeting of allied nuclear forces in this proposal underlined the Soviet intention to focus on public opinion in Western Europe and to exacerbate internal divisions within Europe. Both Britain and France were engaged in significant, and costly, nuclear force modernization programs that were controversial within their own countries.

Predictably, given the incompatible positions of the two sides, the talks wore on inconclusively. As the climate of US-Soviet relations worsened and public opinion became restive with the ostensible lack of progress in Geneva, Nitze and Kvitsinsky attempted to break the deadlock. During a renowned walk in the woods in the Jura Mountains above the Swiss town of Nyon, the two worked out a comprehensive approach under which the United States and the Soviet Union would have had equal numbers of INF launchers and aircraft, and the Soviets would freeze SS-20 deployments in Asia.

This was a classic example of two experienced, respected negotiators working on the margins of formal sessions to hammer out an informal compromise package that involved significant concessions from both sides. Under the "walk in the woods" formula, the Soviet Union would have to reduce its existing SS-20 force from about 250 to 75, to cease further SS-20 deployments in its Asian territory, limit its intermediate-range nuclear-capable bombers, and drop its demand for inclusion of British and French nuclear forces in the agreement. For its part, the United States would replace the zero-zero approach with limited deployments by each side, forego means to deploy the Pershing II, and reduce the number of its land-based, dual-capable aircraft stationed in Europe.

This was a workmanlike solution, which would have left both sides with their essential political and military interests in the matter intact. It was also a bold solution, precipitating the two governments toward a denouement more rapidly than either had anticipated. This promising gambit by Nitze and Kvitsinsky fizzled, however, within a few months.

In Washington, Nitze was criticized for offering this formula to his counterpart without instructions, for abandoning Pershing II deployments, and for including aircraft. More important, the domestic politics and timing of this solution were all wrong. A stunning diplomatic breakthrough on INF in mid-1982 would precipitate a resurgence of détente, undermining the rationale for the massive US military buildup and changing the administration's priorities. Especially given the fact that the administration was pursuing a hard line rhetorically against the Soviets at that time, a sudden rush to an arms control agreement would be deeply divisive within the Republican Party.

Although US officials are not privy to Moscow's deliberations on this matter, subsequent events made it clear that Moscow essentially decided to postpone a diplomatic solution, which would require major concessions on their part, and to fight out this issue on the streets of Europe in a battle for public opinion. Moscow must have calculated that a better course would be to allow the debate in the West over US INF deployments to fester. At best, public opposition to stationing Pershing II and ground-launched cruise missiles would be so intense that the Americans would be blocked from making these deployments altogether—and conservative governments, especially in Britain and the FRG, might fall in the bargain. At least, US deployments would be plagued by public protest at each step of the way and, even if INF missile modernization in Europe succeeded, a precedent of political upheaval would be established that would deter future modernization programs of this kind.

If these were Moscow's calculations, they were nearly correct. While the Soviets in Geneva rejected any negotiated outcome in 1982-83, massive protests broke out all over Europe, and the future of the governments in the five allied basing countries did, in fact, appear to hang in the balance at times. Nonetheless, government leaders held the line, the alliance maintained its cohesion, and US INF deployments began in November 1983. Ambassador Kvitsinsky led his delegation out of the INF talks on November 23.

This entire episode is a case study in the close interaction between politics, military power, and diplomacy. If the United States had had its preference, it would have preferred to modernize its INF forces in Europe as a routine military activity without the encumbrances of a negotiating track. One could argue that a "dual track" approach, by promising negotiations prior to deploying a weapon system, has proven an unwise precedent that will forever impede needed force modernization.

In the case of INF deployments, however, allied leaders in Europe correctly sensed that this track was vital to their own political requirements. Had the United States rejected negotiations and attempted to deploy Pershing IIs and GLCMs without this political cover, the vigorous public opposition to deployments would probably have succeeded in blocking them. This would not only have undermined incumbent governments in London, Bonn, The Hague, Brussels, and Rome, it could also have unraveled the postwar collective security system in Europe.

For both Washington and Moscow, therefore, the negotiations were a political necessity, but not necessarily a forum for resolving the INF issue. The overarching US requirement was to proceed with INF modernization, and Moscow estimated that it could prevent those deployments politically without resorting to cutbacks in the SS-20 program. What sustained the negotiations, in addition to the ingenuity of the negotiators themselves, was the need for both sides to demonstrate seriousness of purpose to public opinion. This required the periodic exchange of proposals, each accompanied by public fanfare. Yet, with the exception of the remarkable walk in the woods formula, the proposals from both sides were half measures that did not reflect the underlying reality.

The reality was that the United States simply did not have negotiating leverage because it had no weapon systems to trade off against proposed Soviet reductions. And the political climate seemed to be running in the Soviets' favor. There was little actual inducement for the Soviet Union to give something for nothing, especially when they stood to gain mightily both in military and political terms if deep fissures within NATO over nuclear modernization blocked US deployments.

This Soviet game plan bore some fruit from the Soviet standpoint. The missile deployment issue did create deep scars in NATO at the time. The United States was left appearing to public opinion as the aggressor, while the Soviet Union was unencumbered by any arms control agreement to postpone its own SS-20 deployments. Certainly the political groundwork was laid for blocking future generations of new US nuclear weapon systems in Europe.

From the political perspective, however, the Soviets sacrificed some of these hard-won gains when they walked out of Geneva, a maladroit step that created greater sympathy for the United States and NATO. The Soviets compounded this error by walking out of the negotiations on conventional force reductions in Vienna as well—even though they quickly rejoined those talks in January 1984.

By the time the Soviets returned to the negotiating table in Geneva in March 1985, they were relieved to be back. Their effort to block US INF deployments through political and public pressure had failed. They were now facing a qualitatively different situation, however. Conservative governments in Western Europe had strengthened their position, partly because of their steadfastness over the INF issue. Public opinion had come to accept the Pershing II and GLCM deployments, which were proceeding inexorably and on time. Washington was also pleased to be back at the negotiating table—especially now that it had real negotiating leverage.

A New Soviet Leader Makes the Difference

Although the Soviets returned to Geneva more prepared to bargain on INF, they retained their penchant for striking positions designed to appeal to public opinion in the West and to create fissures within the alliance. Their public villain in 1985, however, was no longer INF deployments, but a new target, "Star Wars," President Reagan's Strategic Defense Initiative (SDI) program. SDI had stirred a major controversy in the United States, where many questioned its feasibility, desirability, and cost, and also in Europe, where the program reinforced the impression of a trigger-happy president fixed on military-technology solutions to world problems.

The Soviets were determined to subordinate their strategic objectives in Geneva to an all-out effort to block the SDI program. When US Secretary of State George P. Shultz and Soviet Foreign Minister Gromyko met early in 1985 to work out the terms of reference for the arms control negotiations, Gromyko insisted on a close interrelationship between the negotiations on defense and space (D&S) issues, which would focus on SDI, the negotiations on INF, and on strategic arms reductions (START). This interrelationship would give the Soviets leverage to link progress on INF and START to progress on SDI issues in the D&S talks.

Shultz reluctantly agreed to this infelicitous arrangement as the price for resuming the arms control process. All three negotiations were placed under a single umbrella, the Nuclear and Space Talks (NST). Ambassador Max M. Kampelman served both as head of the overall NST delegation and the D&S delegation, with Soviet veteran negotiator on strategic arms, Viktor Karpov, as his counterpart heading the Soviet NST delegation. The US INF delegation within this framework was headed by Ambassador Glitman, who had served as Ambassador Nitze's deputy in the 1981-1983 INF talks, and the Soviet delegation was led by Ambassador Obukhov, a senior Soviet arms control expert.

This Soviet concentration on the SDI program was reinforced by the new general secretary of the Communist Party, Mikhail Gorbachev, soon after he assumed power in March 1985. Vociferous opposition to the US SDI program marked Gorbachev's earliest statements on foreign and defense policy. In the early rounds in Geneva, the Soviets echoed Gorbachev, trying among other things to minimize the frequency of START and INF meetings and to maximize the number of meetings of the overall NST delegation, which had no independent substantive area for negotiation.

This Soviet posturing on SDI, both publicly and at the negotiating table, effectively stalled any progress on INF in the first six months of the Geneva talks. Both sides were essentially repeating positions held over from the 1981-1983 INF talks. In the meantime, Gorbachev was gaining substantial mileage from his public incantations against Star Wars. Public opinion polls in Western Europe began to show even at that early stage in Gorbachev's incumbency that publics viewed him as "more of a man of peace" than the US president.

Gorbachev's associates were quick to build upon this favorable public image of their new leader. They began to hold press conferences in Moscow where hitherto anonymous Soviet military figures took questions and answers. *Glasnost* suddenly made news from the Soviet Union more abundant and credible. The Soviet leader displayed his charisma and self-confidence in more open exchanges with the press and with visiting officials. He also made clear that he would play a direct, personal role in arms control matters.

Typically, the first break in the Soviet INF position came from Gorbachev personally and was enunciated in public before taking the form of a formal, written proposal in Geneva. In October 1985, in his first visit to the West in his new capacity, Gorbachev traveled to Great Britain and France. His interlocutors were impressed with his candor, constructiveness, and pragmatic approach to problem solving. They were also impressed with how well he was received by public opinion.

The most striking thing about these visits to London and Paris, however, was that Gorbachev used them to change the Soviet position on British and French nuclear forces in INF. He stated publicly that they were "off the ledger" in the INF negotiations. To INF-watchers, this was a dramatic change in the Soviet position. The inclusion of third-country nuclear forces in the INF agreement was more than a question of principle, it was an article of faith in the Soviet position in the 1981-1983 talks. Gorbachev was also signaling that from the potpourri of arms control possibilities—strategic, defense and space, conventional, chemical, nonproliferation, nuclear testing—INF was the most promising area in which to test the waters.

In what became customary in Geneva, the US delegation waited to see when the Soviet delegation would put one of Gorbachev's publicly stated positions on the negotiating table as a formal Soviet proposal. Starting with the Soviet position on British and French nuclear forces, the time gap was often considerable. The US delegation pressed the Soviet delegation daily for some indication of a formal change in the Soviet position on this issue. Because Gorbachev's ability to sustain his power was potentially tenuous in those early days, there was much speculation on the US side over the meaning of these delays. Was Gorbachev having difficulty gaining Politburo support for moves on arms control? Was there an Old Guard in the Foreign Ministry loyal to Gromyko that was resisting change? Were Soviet military leaders dragging their feet? Was the military supporting Gorbachev or opposing him? When, some weeks after Gorbachev's public statements in Great Britain and France, the Soviet delegation did alter its position on third-country nuclear forces, there was a sense that this important move on the Soviet side was linked to internal shakeups in both the Foreign Ministry and the General Staff.

Whatever was happening behind the scenes, the United States was interested in exploring the limits of Gorbachev's flexibility. It responded to Gorbachev's move on British and French nuclear forces with a proposal for an "interim" INF agreement—something short of zero-zero. The United States proposed a limit of 140 Pershing II and GLCM launchers and reductions of Soviet SS-20 missile launchers in Europe to the same number.

The idea of an interim agreement seemed to catch hold. In November 1985, President Reagan and General Secretary Gorbachev met for the first time in Geneva. Their communiqué included a commitment to progress on arms control, including "the idea of an interim agreement."[3]

Yet something more profound had happened at the Geneva summit. Ronald Reagan and Mikhail Gorbachev discovered that they could communicate and could understand each other's political agendas. It was that discovery that opened the path to the INF Treaty.

The Political Imperatives of Reagan and Gorbachev

From the time of his earliest pronouncements on *perestroika*, Gorbachev took the position that reductions in Soviet military expenditures were central to his economic reforms. He and his followers had clearly concluded that the Soviet economy was in dire straits and that extraordinary measures were required to reverse its fortunes. He made clear that sweeping reforms of the Communist Party and the government bureaucracy were needed concomitants of change. He also moved swiftly to place his own appointees in charge of the armed forces.

In promulgating both glasnost and perestroika, Gorbachev presented himself as a reformer. His survival in power would depend upon the success of these reforms. They were not achievable, however, without much improved relations with the West, particularly the United States. In the absence of sweeping arms control agreements with the United States, he could not justify reducing the Soviet armed forces by amounts large enough to affect the overall Soviet economy. Without the personal prestige and influence that derive from playing the role of a well-liked and respected world statesman, Gorbachev would have less leverage in securing his power base at home. He was also less likely to obtain critical technology, commerce, and credits from the West as long as the Soviet Union was overtly threatening its neighbors with nuclear weapons.

A major arms control agreement, especially if it involved nuclear weapons and could be the basis for frequent meetings with US leaders, would be well tailored to satisfy all of Gorbachev's objectives. He was quite aware of the strong resistance in some quarters in the United States to reducing defense spending or to concluding an arms control agreement with Moscow. The best way to accelerate progress would be a series of bold moves on the arms control front that would capture the imagination of Western publics and add pressure on Washington to be responsive.

Any arms control agreement with the United States would meet Gorbachev's political desiderata. As the public reaction to the zero-zero option had demonstrated, the public does not make nice distinctions between arms control plans. Most people are pleased to see any kind of movement on nuclear arms control. Gorbachev could have chosen to focus on INF for any number of reasons: progress there would appeal to popular opinion both in Europe and the United States; INF was less organically linked to SDI than was START and thus could be split off more easily for separate consideration; INF was relatively less complex than START and could thus be advanced more rapidly; it was easier to pressure the United States through its allies for progress in INF than it was in START, where allied interests were not as directly involved; the substantive positions of the sides were closer together in INF than in other arms control fields; and the Soviet military would need to be asked for fewer sacrifices to achieve an INF agreement than they would for a strategic or conventional force reductions agreement. The fusion between Gorbachev's political imperatives and an INF Treaty was thus plain to see.

The political imperatives underlying President Reagan's quest for an arms control agreement with the new Soviet leader were less dramatic than in the case of Gorbachev, but were quite tangible nonetheless. In 1985, concern was growing in the nation over the burgeoning federal budget deficit, which was soaring over the $200 billion mark. Defense spending was contributing heavily to that deficit. The president had established national priorities in his first administration—a major defense buildup accompanied by a cut in taxes—which could be financed only through strong economic growth. Yet an unexpected recession in 1981 reduced expected federal revenues and plunged the Reagan presidency into a position of indebtedness from which it would never recover.

Indeed, the Reagan defense boom was over by 1985; defense spending had tapered off and was starting a gradual decline as a percentage of gross national product (GNP). The choices for reducing the deficit were limited and politically unattractive to the White House: raise taxes, cut domestic programs further, or reverse the defense buildup. Pressures were growing in Congress to single out the defense budget to bear the greatest burden. For example, the Gramm-Rudman-Hollings Budget Deficit Reduction Act required that the Pentagon bear 50 percent of the balance needed to reach prescribed annual deficit reduction targets.

The savings accruing from an INF agreement would be insignificant in this context, but would shield the president and his party against charges that they had endorsed runaway defense spending in flagrant disregard of budgetary realities. They could argue that the main rationale for the defense buildup—to restore America's military strength in order to bring the Soviets to the negotiation table—had been successful. In other words, the strategy of negotiating from positions of strength had worked. (Indeed, this is precisely the way then-Vice President Bush used the INF Treaty in his successful campaign for the presidency. The treaty nailed down the peace plank for the Republican Party.)

If an arms control success could illustrate the validity of the "peace through strength" thesis, then that same thesis could be applied to other areas as well. It would be imprudent, for example, to cut back unilaterally on strategic modernizations programs or on the SDI program until a START agreement were concluded—or on the next generation of tanks or tactical fighters until a conventional accord had been reached. Thus, a successful INF agreement could simultaneously placate criticism that the administration was not serious about arms control and preserve the rationale for continuing with the essential elements of the president's military buildup program, including SDI.

On a more subjective level, a skeptic could argue that the 1986 Iran-contra affair[4] strengthened the president's interest in arms control, primarily to divert public attention; however, it is difficult to establish any clear cause-and-effect relationship in this case. Another explanation of the president's growing interest in INF was that he was becoming increasingly conscious of his historical legacy and wanted to be remembered as a man of peace.

There was also the practical consideration that the INF negotiations were simply advancing more rapidly in Geneva than the START and D&S talks. President Reagan, like Gorbachev, might also have calculated that an INF Treaty would be less controversial among his military advisers than an agreement on substantially reducing strategic nuclear arms. Certainly it would have been more difficult to gain Senate ratification of a START Treaty than an INF Treaty, and there was a greater risk that a more complex START agreement would not be completed before the end of his administration.

Nonetheless, there is a strong case to be made that, although an INF agreement was important for NATO solidarity and did reduce an entire class of nuclear missiles, it would have been more fitting—and more courageous—for Reagan to choose a START agreement either together with or ahead of an INF agreement. After all, the Soviet medium-range missiles eliminated under the INF Treaty cannot reach US territory. A START agreement would have done more to make the American populace somewhat less exposed to Soviet strategic nuclear capabilities and possibly have reduced the cost of strategic modernization.

In any case, it was unnecessary politically for Reagan to choose the more hazardous path of preferring a START agreement over an INF agreement. As events bore out, the INF Treaty more than satisfied his and his party's political requirements. After the INF Treaty was signed with suitable fanfare, neither American public opinion nor trained observers picked up on the obvious point that a START agreement would have made a more direct contribution to the security of the American people themselves.

Whatever their respective motivations, once the president and the general secretary concluded that they wanted to proceed toward an INF agreement and were willing to provide the kind of discipline and leadership within their respective governments to obtain it, the various pieces of this complex document began to fall into place.

In January 1986, just three months after his meeting with Reagan in Geneva, Gorbachev publicly announced his willingness to accept a "zero" option for European-based US and Soviet INF missiles, which would be eliminated over a five- to eight-year period. Although press reporting on the October 1986 Reagan-Gorbachev meeting in Reykjavik focused mostly on the dramatic, last-minute collapse of a highly controversial breakthrough on offensive strategic arms, solid work was done on INF. Gorbachev agreed for the first time to reduce Soviet SS-20 deployments in Asia to an interim equal global limit of 100 per side outside of Europe. Interestingly, this triggered a strong negative reaction from Japan, China, and Australia, who rejected what they viewed as a differentiated US and Soviet approach between European and Asian security. They raised this concern at political levels with the Soviets, which led to Gorbachev's widely reported July 1987 statement to an Indonesian journalist that he would agree to the total, global elimination of all ground-launched INF missiles, including the SS-20 force stationed in the Asian territory of the Soviet Union.

In the spring of 1987, Gorbachev led another major departure from the Soviets' traditional opposition to reducing their shorter-range INF missiles—the SS-12s and SS-23s with ranges of up to 900 kilometers and 500 kilometers, respectively. He publicly offered a "second zero," namely, the elimination of all shorter-range missiles with ranges between 500 and 1,000 kilometers. Under this formula, the Soviets would eliminate the SS-12 and SS-23 missiles. The United States would destroy the Pershing

IA (PIA), which was no longer deployed in Europe as a US system, and cancel the Pershing IB, which was still to be developed.

Although this offer appeared to be strongly in the US favor, it succeeded in creating considerable political controversy among the European allies. They were worried that by lowering the threshold of the treaty, a ban on shorter-range missiles was a potentially dangerous step toward total denuclearization. Some were concerned that a ban could later inhibit the deployment of modernized short-range missiles with ranges under 500 kilometers, such as the follow-on version of the US Lance missile.

As events later unfolded in the spring of 1990, the United States subsequently scrapped plans to deploy new short-range nuclear missiles, notably the Follow-on-to-Lance (FTOL) system. The "Revolution of '89" in Eastern Europe raised serious doubts about the wisdom of deploying a system that was capable of reaching only countries that had effectively embraced democracy and disrupted the Warsaw Pact. One could speculate on whether the INF Treaty itself, even without that political upheaval, had so raised expectations about the demise of the Cold War that it would have proven difficult to deploy the FTOL missile. In any event, there is a notable irony here: in its determination to deploy the intermediate-range Pershing II and GLCM systems, the United States eventually deployed neither those systems nor short-range nuclear missile upgrades.

Gorbachev's "second zero" proposal also brought into focus another politically volatile issue—West Germany's PIA missile system. Modernization of this force had been a subject of vigorous debate in Bonn for years. The Soviets argued that because these missiles were armed with US warheads and fell within the 500-1,000 range limitation, they should also be eliminated. Washington replied that because US warheads for these missiles were provided under a long-established program of cooperation between the United States and the Federal Republic of Germany and because the launchers belonged to a third party, these systems should be excluded under the treaty. Quite apart from the various lines of argument, the Soviets had succeeded in portraying the West German PIA missile force as a potential obstacle to the treaty. Chancellor Helmut Kohl responded to this successful political squeeze play by announcing that Germany would dismantle its Pershing IA force, but outside the context of the treaty.

The two leaders, for their own internal political reasons, thus set the basic parameters of the INF Treaty: global double zero—that is, the worldwide elimination of all ground-launched missiles of both intermediate range (1,000-5,000 kilometers) and shorter-range (500-1,000 kilometers). Once these parameters had been established, a complex task of wrapping up a detailed treaty text remained. But the only question was when the INF Treaty would be ready for signature, not whether.

All this is not to gainsay the role of senior advisers and negotiators on both sides, not to mention the contributions of the teams of experts and backup groups in both delegations and in Washington and Moscow. On the US side, Secretary Shultz exercised leadership and persistence—a task made easier in the final stages of the negotiations by the resignations of Defense Secretary Caspar Weinberger and his deputy for policy affairs, Richard Perle, both noted for their skepticism toward US-Soviet arms control agreements. William Crowe, chairman of the Joint Chiefs of Staff, National Security Adviser General Colin Powell, and Ambassador Glitman played especially critical roles in the endgame. American officials are not privy to the internal roles played by various advisers on the Soviet side, but Foreign Minister Eduard Shevardnadze, Marshal Sergei Akhromeyev, Deputy Foreign Minister Viktor Karpov, and Colonel General Nikolai Cherov appeared to play key roles.

Finishing Up

The final few months of work on the treaty, which was signed December 8, 1987, were challenging and hectic, but took place among foreign ministers, ambassadors, and experts largely out of public view. The bulk of the work was devoted to ironing out details of complex counting rules and verification provisions. This work broke a great deal of new ground in the world of arms control negotiations, but was largely the domain of arms control and military specialists. President Reagan occasionally had to enter the fray to resolve interagency differences over remaining issues. (A notable example was his decision to overrule the Pentagon's desire to exclude conventionally-armed INF-range cruise missiles from the treaty by siding with the argument that such a provision would be unverifiable.) Presumably, Gorbachev may have entered the debate occasionally, as well, within the Kremlin on critical details related to verification. These details, however, were not dealt with as political issues.

The most important final political decision that both leaders took to secure the INF Treaty was relatively simple, but essential: setting the date for the summit meeting in Washington at which the treaty would be signed. During a trip to Washington by Foreign Minister Shevardnadze, at the end of September 1987, December 7 was set as the starting date for the summit. Without that deadline, the negotiations in Geneva would probably have continued for several more months. Only a month before the summit, one hundred "bracketed" passages remained in the treaty text, and a wealth of detailed treaty implementation procedures had to be set aside for resolution after treaty signature. Without the pressure of the summit deadline, the delegations in Geneva, and their backstopping committees in Washington and Moscow, would doubtless have moved forward at a more measured pace. This experience demonstrates once again that one of the most important powers that a chief executive has is the power to set deadlines.

Without underlying political imperatives on both sides and personal involvement at leadership levels, arms control negotiations become a cottage industry for specialists. The Mutual and Balanced Force Reductions (MBFR) in Vienna (1972-1989) were a classic case in point. There was nothing inherently wrong with the forum, the format, the substantive content, or the competence of the negotiators in Vienna. The problem was simply that there was no single point at which the leaders of the major participating countries all believed that an actual conventional force reductions agreement was in their own interest. If INF had not set the respective agendas and timetables of both Reagan and Gorbachev, the INF talks would have suffered the same fate as MBFR, a "process" of negotiations not intended to produce a concrete outcome.

The INF Treaty was achievable because of a rare confluence of events that brought the interests of the two nations and their leaders together at roughly the same time. The result was quite remarkable. The treaty itself, in bulk alone, surpasses any previous agreements of this kind. Its text, including protocols and appendices, far exceeds in length all of the arms control and disarmament agreements concluded since World War II combined. In substance, it is the first treaty actually to reduce nuclear arms and contains verification provisions so intrusive that they shatter a tradition, many centuries long, of the inviolable secrecy of military installations. The INF Treaty is a fitting benchmark for the dramatic turn of events that brought the Cold War to a close.

Indeed, one could finally speculate that the INF Treaty may have been a critical link to the subsequent political events that swept communism out of power in Eastern Europe. If the INF negotiations had failed, this would have perpetuated a climate of East-West tensions that would have required

Gorbachev, whether he wished it or not, to maintain a strong military presence. As it was, the demise of Cold War tensions between the military superpowers symbolized by the INF Treaty made it easier for him to justify his policy of liberalization in Eastern Europe, which opened the door to the political upheaval there. This example further illustrates the point elaborated in this chapter that arms control negotiations, while they may sometimes appear arcane to the layman and may find technocrats wandering around in the forest, are profoundly political in nature.

Notes

1. Cited in Arms Control and Disarmament Agency, *Understanding the INF Treaty* (Washington, DC: Government Printing Office, July 1989), p. 5.
2. *New York Times*, November 19, 1981, p. A-17.
3. *Washington Post*, November 22, 1985, p. A-9.
4. The Iran-contra affair refers to the efforts in 1985-86 of the Reagan administration to sell arms to Iran (allegedly in exchange for hostages) and to use the proceeds of the sales to finance anti-Sandinista guerrillas (the contras) in Nicaragua. Eventually, the president's national security adviser, Admiral John Poindexter, and one of his assistants, Colonel Oliver North, were convicted of lying to Congress.

5

US-Soviet Bilateral Relations Since Reykjavik

John M. Evans

THE UNITED STATES AND THE Soviet Union made considerable progress in a number of non-arms-control related areas in the period 1986-1990, or more precisely since the October 11-12, 1986, Reykjavik summit. This chapter surveys the accomplishments of that period, which culminated in the remarkable progress registered at the September 1989 Wyoming ministerial meeting and at the Malta (December 2-3, 1989) and Washington (May 30-June 3, 1990) summits.

Conscious of the need to pursue US interests vis-à-vis the Soviet Union in a comprehensive and balanced way, the Reagan administration chose to divide its agenda with Moscow into four parts: arms control, human rights, regional issues, and bilateral matters. The first three items were, and are, more or less self-explanatory, but the fourth, "bilateral matters," was actually an innocuous-sounding catch-all for some of the most difficult and intractable issues in US-Soviet relations—economic relations, reciprocity issues, certain security-related problems, but also such cooperative elements of the relationship as US-Soviet exchanges. This fourth agenda item yielded considerable dividends during the period after the Reykjavik summit, paving the way for continued progress in the Bush administration.

Secretary of State George P. Shultz used to say that US policy needed to be flexible enough to deal with the best and the worst of Soviet behavior.

This article covers aspects of recent US-Soviet negotiations other than those in the strategic and arms control fields. The views and opinions set forth are those of the author and do not necessarily reflect those of the Department of State or of the United States government. The author gratefully acknowledges the assistance of Stuart Swanson, a foreign service officer now assigned to the US Consulate General in Leningrad. Mr. Swanson worked in the Office of Soviet Union Affairs during the period in question and conducted the basic research for this chapter.

Nowhere was this principle put to a tougher test than in the area of bilateral relations. The October 1986 Reykjavik summit took place in the aftermath of the Daniloff affair,[1] which, along with Soviet resistance to a phased reduction of the size of the Soviet UN mission, precipitated a round of tit-for-tat expulsions of diplomats and the withdrawal of Soviet employees from the US embassy in Moscow and consulate general in Leningrad. But the Daniloff incident also posed a major test of the ability of Secretary Shultz and Soviet Foreign Minister Eduard Shevardnadze, working together, to resolve a thorny issue in the interests of both sides. As unpleasant as the matter was, settling it represented a victory for both foreign ministers.

Only a few weeks before the arrest of Nicholas Daniloff, the United States and the Soviet Union, recognizing that there was a host of unsolved administrative, consular, and other bilateral problems that could not regularly be addressed by ministers, had held the first meeting of the Bilateral Review Commission (BRC). The BRC was an attempt to get at some of the seemingly insoluble problems by providing a regular forum in which they could be addressed—and hopefully solved—at the deputy assistant secretary level. A second BRC was convened in March 1987 and a third in April 1988. Since then, BRC meetings have been held roughly every six months, often in conjunction with ministerial sessions. Although the record of achievement has been mixed, both sides would most likely testify to their usefulness.

Trade and Economic Relations

The Soviet Union would have preferred, and from time to time has suggested, that there be a separate agenda item on trade and economic cooperation. The United States has resisted that idea, arguing that the level of economic interaction did not support treating it separately. Despite the lack of a discrete economic item on the agenda, much was accomplished in this period, and the way was opened for even greater progress. Throughout the 1980s, the United States was on record as favoring an expansion of mutually beneficial nonstrategic trade with the Soviet Union, but the post-Afghanistan trade sanctions had clearly damaged the confidence of US business in the wisdom of pursuing trade in Eastern Europe and the Soviet Union. For its part, the Reagan administration made clear that the trade issue could not be separated from other issues in the overall relationship, namely, national security and human rights; as Secretary of State Shultz put it more than once, "linkage is a fact of life."

A small but significant step forward occurred in January 1987 when the Reagan administration, without fanfare, allowed export controls on oil and gas equipment and technology to lapse. These controls had actually been imposed in 1978 in response to the Soviet crackdown on human rights activists and were extended in response to the Soviet invasion of Afghanistan and the imposition of martial law in Poland. They were lifted in part because of an improving Soviet human rights record and in part because they had become ineffective. While these controls were in effect, the US share of the Soviet market in this sector slipped from more than 30 percent to less than 5 percent.

In April 1987, President Ronald Reagan approved a 4-million-ton sale of wheat to the Soviet Union to facilitate sales already agreed to under the Long Term Grain Agreement of 1983. This agreement requires the Soviets to buy a minimum of 9 million tons of grain from the United States per annum, including at least 4 million tons of corn and an equal amount of wheat. Negotiations on a new agreement broke down in 1988, leading to an extension of the existing agreement until the end of 1990. Soviet grain purchases from the United States in 1989 totaled a record 14 million tons of corn, 350,000 tons of sorghum, and 4.8 million tons of wheat.

In December 1987, at the Washington summit, the two sides announced plans to convene a meeting of the US-Soviet Joint Commercial Commission to develop ways of achieving an expansion of mutually beneficial trade. Commerce Secretary William Verity led the US delegation to that meeting in April 1988. The US government also gave a cautious endorsement to "commercially viable" joint ventures.

The real breakthrough in US-Soviet economic relations began in May 1989, when President George Bush announced, in a speech in Texas, that he was willing to work with the Congress to seek a waiver of the Jackson-Vanik amendment,[2] provided the Soviets passed and implemented an emigration law consistent with international standards. The human rights and freedom of emigration situation in the Soviet Union had, by this time, so greatly improved that this announcement met with only scattered opposition. Of course, signaling a willingness to seek a waiver of Jackson-Vanik did not make it happen overnight. For one thing, the amendment requires a commercial agreement; the 1972 trade agreement, which was negotiated but never entered into force, had to be renegotiated. At the

Joint Commercial Commission meeting in November 1989, the two sides agreed to set up a working group to identify the requirements for a new or updated agreement, which they negotiated in the first half of 1990.

In a related development, US and Soviet officials conducted technical discussions during 1989 aimed at resolving outstanding financial claims. At issue are some $187.7 million in US loans to the Aleksandr Kerensky government that the Bolsheviks repudiated, as well as several other pre-1933 financial claims. If a settlement is reached, possibly in 1990, it would lift the Soviet Union's status under the Johnson Act, which bars US citizens from engaging in certain financial transactions with a foreign government that is in default to the United States.

At the Wyoming ministerial meeting, the United States entered into much more thorough-going discussions with the Soviets than ever before about economic cooperation, and at the Malta summit several important steps were taken: President Bush and Chairman Mikhail Gorbachev agreed to negotiate a tax treaty to replace the rudimentary one signed in 1973; the president proposed starting talks as well on a bilateral investment treaty; and he offered to explore, once a Jackson-Vanik waiver was granted, options for removing the existing restrictions on US government loans to the Soviet Union—the Stevenson and Byrd amendments and certain provisions of the Export Import Bank Act.[3] In addition, at Malta, the Americans offered the Soviets technical advice on reforming their economy. This consisted of proposals to set up a continuing series of workshops and seminars, to provide technical advisory services, and to encourage the provision of management training in US universities.

The Wyoming ministerial meeting and the Malta summit set the stage for the remarkable progress on trade and economic matters that were codified in the signing of a bilateral trade agreement at the 1990 Washington summit. There Bush and Gorbachev initiated a pact that encouraged US businessmen to invest in and trade with the USSR. The way was cleared for the extension of US government credits and most favored nation status. President Bush decided to sign the agreement even though the Soviet parliament was still considering a draft emigration law that would have brought the USSR, in theory and in practice, into complete compliance with the Helsinki Final Act. In doing so, however, Bush opted not to send the agreement to the Senate for its advice and consent until the Soviet government formally adopted the new emigration legislation. The president acted this way, despite considerable pressure from conservative elements in the United States who sought to link this to the lifting of the Soviet trade embargo on Lithuania, to give Gorbachev a political boost at the time of growing domestic political instability in the Soviet Union and the erosion of his authority.

Bush also recognized the new reality of Soviet practice in 1989: more than 60,000 Jews had left the Soviet Union, supplemented by more than 20,000 "Volga Germans" and others; in the first half of 1990, Jewish emigration was running at an annual rate of more than 100,000. The sides also signed a new grain agreement that pledged the Soviets to purchase 9 million tons of grain annually for another five years. Finally, Moscow agreed to resume payment of the balance owed (about $187 million) in its World War II lend-lease loans.

Immediately following the Washington summit, the US government, in concert with its allies, moved to loosen the restrictions on some types of strategic material and manufactures to the Soviet Union and Eastern Europe.

Reciprocity Issues and the Commercial Presence

One noneconomic problem, among others, has proven to be a complicating factor in developing US-Soviet commercial relations. It is the question of how many businessmen of the other country each side would allow to live and work on its territory. Traditionally, the number of officials of Soviet state enterprises living in the United States has been higher than that of American businessmen living and working permanently in the Soviet Union. Washington has understandably been wary of permitting the entry of too many Soviet "businessmen," who have been presumed to constitute a security threat, into the United States. At the 1990 Washington summit, the sides agreed to seek to facilitate the conditions under which its businessmen worked in the Soviet Union and in the United States as part of an effort to expand trade and economic relations. The fact that more American businessmen than ever before are now resident, or seek to reside, in the Soviet Union will exert upward pressure on the numbers.

A related question is that of diplomatic representation. During the October 1986 expulsions of diplomatic personnel that followed the Daniloff episode, the United States imposed on the Soviet embassy in Washington and consulate general in San Francisco a ceiling of 251 employees, which corresponded to the number of US official personnel then in the Soviet Union. (UN personnel, for whom there is no analog in the Soviet Union, were put under a separate ceiling.) The concern had been that the overstaffed Soviet embassy in Washington was heavily involved in "activities incompatible with diplomatic status," as the euphemism for espionage has it. The Daniloff arrest provided the catalyst for establishing strictly reciprocal staffing levels in the two countries. Ironically, relations between Washington and Moscow have improved so dramatically since 1986 that the pressure to increase staffs on both sides has been tremendous. In no area has the pressure been greater than in the consular sections, which have had to deal with the exponential growth of travel by tourists, business and official travelers and, in Moscow, emigrants. In November 1988, the Soviets agreed to an overall phased increase of thirty-five positions, apportioned between the embassies and consulates, for a total of 286 on each side. Subsequently, in the spring of 1990, the sides agreed to a further reciprocal increase of fifty-five in the size of their representations.

Exchange of Consulates

In one area, the progress registered in the 1980s lagged far behind the realities. In 1974, President Richard Nixon and General Secretary Leonid Brezhnev had agreed to an exchange of consulates in Kiev and New York. Both sides needed the additional post, and, in 1976, advance teams were exchanged. In the wake of the Soviet invasion of Afghanistan, however, the United States suspended its plans to open the Kiev mission, withdrew its personnel, and asked the Soviets, who had purchased two brownstone houses on New York's upper East Side, to withdraw their personnel. At the Geneva summit in November 1985, the two sides agreed to renew the consulate exchange, but plans were again delayed by the Chernobyl nuclear accident.[4] The main obstacles, however, were in the security area. In the wake of the 1987 US marine spying scandal,[5] and amidst concerns about the bugging of the Moscow chancery,[6] the US House of Representatives passed an amendment forbidding the Soviets from occupying any new consulate in the United States until the US consulate in Kiev occupied "secure, permanent facilities." In the meantime, the Ukraine was not immune to the political winds sweeping the Soviet Union; the value to the United States of having a listening post in that large, important non-Russian republic, where nationalist sentiment was rising, increased many fold. In the meantime, the Germans, French, and Canadians announced plans to set up consulates of their own in Kiev. Eventually, after considerable effort by the State Department, authority was obtained in the Fiscal Year (FY) 1990/91 State Authorization Bill to proceed, on a reciprocal basis, with small posts in Kiev and New York. They were expected to open in late summer 1990.

As US-Soviet relations have broadened and deepened, and as power in the Soviet Union has become more decentralized, the need for additional consular posts in that enormous country has grown. Not only would the US government profit from having observers on the ground in, say, Tbilisi, Irkutsk, and Vladivostok, but the American traveling and business public would be better served if consular services were available in more locations. It would also help American travelers if Soviet visas could be obtained in US cities other than Washington and San Francisco. In response to new opportunities in Eastern Europe, the State Department decided in late 1989 to open consulates in Leipzig and Bratislava. The question of adding other small posts in the Soviet Union and Eastern Europe, in response to the new realities there, is under study.

US-Soviet Exchanges

At the Geneva summit in November 1985, the United States and the Soviet Union signed the US-USSR General Exchanges Agreement, thereby renewing an agreement on exchanges that had been allowed to lapse after the invasion of Afghanistan. The new agreement provided for official cultural and academic exchanges, including congressmen and students, exchanges of individuals in the arts, the media, sports, and the professions, and exchanges of exhibits and publications. Most important, the agreement opened the way for the private sector to become deeply involved in all manner of cooperative activities with Soviet counterpart organizations. The first post-Afghanistan official exhibit, "Information USA," opened in Moscow in June 1987 and was followed by "Design USA" in 1988. September 1989 saw the first Soviet undergraduates enrolled in American university degree programs. The 1990 Washington summit gave a further boost to these developments. President Bush and President Gorbachev agreed to the expansion of student exchange programs, and cultural exchanges and to the opening of cultural centers in their respective capitals.

With ever-increasing speed, US-Soviet exchanges after the Geneva summit broadened, deepened, and became more and more the province of the private sector. The State Department's Cultural Affairs Bureau had already been moved to the United States Information Agency (USIA) in the 1970s, and, after Geneva, the Office of the President's Exchange Initiative was set up in USIA to act as a clearinghouse for the many new kinds of exchanges that were being proposed from all sides. The State Department's Soviet Desk exercised policy guidance, but exchanges took on a rich life of their own.

Exchanges in the area of science and technology, which had been a major component of the détente-era exchanges in the 1970s, were put on a more realistic basis in the second half of the 1980s. In the aftermath of Afghanistan, Polish martial law, and the shootdown of Korean Airlines 007, the US government had reduced funding and other support for exchanges in this area, and four agreements (those on cooperation in space, energy, science and technology, and transportation) were allowed to lapse. In 1984, in a speech at the Smithsonian Institution, President Reagan called for reinvigorating four bilateral cooperative agreements—environmental protection, health, housing, and agriculture. In late 1985, the atomic energy agreement was extended through June 1988 (and later, through June 1990). In late 1986, the environmental protection agreement was extended through May 1992. In October 1986, despite a chilly political climate, the two sides negotiated a new bilateral civil space cooperation agreement that was signed the following April. At the Moscow summit in May 1988 a new transportation science and technology agreement was signed, and in January 1989, after arduous inter-agency discussions in Washington, an agreement on basic scientific research was signed to replace the earlier science and technology agreement.

The interagency discussions of possible reinvigorated exchanges with the Soviet Union in science and technology were marked by deep divisions between those who emphasized the benefits to the United States of more intensive engagement with the Soviet scientific establishment and those who saw dangers in such cooperation. Scientists, by and large, favored more interaction, and political developments supported this tendency. The world ocean agreement was extended at the Washington summit in December 1987, but had to be extended annually in 1988 and 1989, while hard negotiations continued within the US government. The resulting new agreement is scheduled to be signed in 1990, as is a new peaceful uses of atomic energy agreement that was completed in 1989. This agreement will include a protocol on nuclear reactor safety that was worked out by the Nuclear Regulatory Commission and Soviet officials after the Chernobyl disaster.

US-Soviet cooperation on environmental matters deserves special mention. At the 1987 Washington summit, the two sides put forward an initiative on global climate and environmental change. At the 1988 Moscow summit they called for greater use of the two countries' space programs to conduct global monitoring of the earth's environment and ecology and expanded bilateral space cooperation to this end. These directions were reemphasized at the September 1989 Wyoming ministerial meeting, where the two sides discussed bilateral environmental cooperation under the new "fifth" item added by the Bush administration to the US-Soviet agenda—"transnational issues."

Information Talks

A nagging problem in US-Soviet relations for years had been the proclivity of the Soviet media to engage in subtle forms of "disinformation" about the United States and its activities. Often this was done in so clever a manner—for example, by planting a story in a Third World paper of questionable repute and then picking it up—that the United States could do little more than protest through diplomatic channels. One of the most galling instances of disinformation was the persistent canard that the acquired immune deficiency syndrome (AIDS) virus had been created in US biological weapons laboratories at Fort Detrick, Maryland. Another was the allegation that the United States had collaborated with South Africa to produce an "ethnic weapon" that was selectively lethal to dark-skinned people. Jamming of Western broadcasts to the Soviet Union was another perennial problem. In an effort to get at these problems in a systematic way, the United States in 1987 proposed talks between media and cultural representatives under the aegis of the USIA and Novosti, the official Soviet news agency.[7]

The first two rounds of talks took place in April and September of 1988 between delegations led by USIA director Charles Wick and Novosti director Valentin Falin. Coming as they did at a time when *glasnost'* was in full sway in the Soviet Union, these talks were highly successful. They led to a cessation of Soviet jamming of Radio Free Europe/Radio Liberty, greater access for US officials to the Soviet media, a series of highly publicized interactive telebridges, and the establishment of a Voice of America Moscow bureau. Another continuing problem, that of free access by American journalists to trouble-spots in the Soviet Union, was successfully addressed in a further round of information talks conducted in the spring of 1990.

Human Rights

No discussion of the bilateral component of US-Soviet relations in the late 1980s would be complete without a mention of the dramatic background of progress in human rights against which advances in other areas were made. The earlier détente had proved unsustainable in no small part because of the human rights abuses of the late 1970s—the imprisonment of Anatoliy Shcharanskiy and Yuriy Orlov and dozens of others, the exile of Andrey Sakharov to Gor'kiy, and the denial of permission to emigrate to thousands of "refuseniks"—those denied permission to emigrate on various grounds, usually for security or family reasons. In December 1986, Sakharov was permitted to return from exile. Yuriy Orlov had been released earlier in the fall. The spring of 1987 saw the release of 140 political prisoners, the largest such release since the immediate post-Stalin period, and the tempo of progress quickened from then on, although it was not without its fits and starts.

The Reagan administration spoke out loudly and in no uncertain terms about human rights, both publicly and in private diplomatic channels, as well as at the Vienna Review Meeting of the Conference on Security and Cooperation in Europe (CSCE), which was in session from November 1986 until January 1989. One of the most difficult problems in the human rights area has been the alleged Soviet abuse of psychiatry for political purposes. In February and March 1989, the State Department, working closely with the National Institutes of Health and the CSCE commission, sent a delegation of American psychiatrists to the Soviet Union to assess the degree of change that had taken place in Soviet psychiatry. The conditions the US side demanded for the visit were unprecedented in Soviet experience, and several times the agreement to proceed almost fell through, but in the end it went forward, not without controversy, but it represented a milestone against which future progress will be marked.

Another area of US concern was unrestricted emigration. Washington maintained unceasing pressure on Moscow throughout the 1980s to allow refuseniks to leave as well as to change severely restrictive foreign travel regulations to permit any Soviet citizen to travel abroad. By 1987, Moscow began to respond constructively. In that year the number of Jews permitted to leave approached 25,000 and many longstanding refusenik cases were resolved positively. In 1989, more than 60,000 Jews emigrated and the pace of their departures in 1990 was running at an annual rate of more than 100,000. The previous high had been 52,000 in 1979. Furthermore, the previous trickle of Soviet "private" tourists began to swell. In 1988 the figure reached 20,000 to the United States alone and more than doubled in 1989. In 1990, some 80,000 Soviet visitors were expected to travel to the United States.

At the same time, in March 1989, the Soviet Union held elections to the newly created Congress of People's Deputies, opening a new chapter in the life of the Soviet Union. The following month saw troops of the Interior Ministry wielding shovels and employing toxic gas on demonstrators in Tbilisi, reminding the world that much remained to be accomplished in guaranteeing human rights and national self-determination in the world's last great land empire. The general direction of events, however, seemed clear and seemed to bear out the dictum of Lord Acton that "progress in the direction of organized and assured freedom is the characteristic fact of Modern History."

Notes

1. On August 20, 1986, American journalist Nicholas Daniloff was detained by the KGB on espionage charges. Daniloff's arrest came within days of the arrest on similar charges in New York of Gennadi Zakharov, an official of the Soviet Mission to the UN. After high-level diplomacy, both Daniloff and Zakharov were released and expelled to their homelands.
2. The Jackson-Vanik amendment, adopted in 1974, precluded the extension of most favored nation treatment and government credits to the Soviet Union in the absence of free emigration. The amendment was intended to prod Moscow to open its doors to Jewish emigration.
3. The Stevenson amendment to the Export Import Bank Act of 1974 set ceilings of $300 million on US government credits or credit guarantees in support of US exports to the Soviet Union. The Byrd amendment to Section 613 of the 1974 trade act denies the right to approve loans, guarantees, or insurance for exports to the Soviet Union in excess of $300 million without prior congressional approval. The Commodity Credit Corporation is excluded from the provisions of this amendment.
4. In April 1986, a fire in one of the four reactors at the Chernobyl nuclear power

plant (about 50 miles north of Kiev) led to the first major nonmilitary nuclear accident in history. Chernobyl caused the deaths of at least thirty-four people, led to the abandonment of hundreds of thousands of acres of rich agricultural land, and created a major international and domestic political problem for General Secretary Gorbachev.

5. In 1987, USMC Sergeant Clayton Lonetree was charged and convicted on espionage charges. Lonetree had served as a marine security guard at the embassy in Moscow in 1985-86. A Soviet employee of the embassy had seduced him, after which he had apparently begun to cooperate with the KGB. This conviction and an investigation into allegations of espionage by other marines assigned to that embassy prompted speculation that Lonetree and other marines had given the KGB access not only to US secrets but also to sensitive elements of the embassy. The latter allegations were never confirmed.

6. In 1986, US technical security officers discovered that the new US embassy in Moscow, then in the final stage of construction, had been subjected to a sophisticated technical attack aimed at undermining its security. The discovery touched off a major scandal in Washington and led to a halt in the embassy's construction. The US government continues to deny the Soviets the right to occupy and use their new embassy in Washington.

7. Novosti is the official news agency. It serves as the "umbrella" organization under which TASS, *Moscow News*, Moscow Radio, Moscow TV, etc., function.

6

Ending the Iran-Iraq War

Sohrab C. Sobhani

ON AUGUST 15, 1990, the press reported that in a letter to President Ali Akbar Hashemi Rafsanjani of Iran, Saddam Hussein, the president of Iraq, accepted Iran's conditions for a peace treaty, abandoning Iraq's claim over the disputed Shatt al-Arab waterway that links Iraq to the Gulf. The Iraqi offer reportedly agreed also to return bits of Iranian territory still occupied by Iraq and to hand back Iranian prisoners of war. The move appeared to represent the full Iraqi acceptance of United Nations Security Council Resolution 598, which established the cease-fire between the two countries that followed eight years of bitter warfare.

The Iraqi move, especially relating to the Shatt al-Arab, represented a dramatic concession of the central issue of the war and was clearly made as a result of the international pressure on Baghdad following the invasion of Kuwait and with the hope of securing Iranian cooperation in circumventing economic sanctions.

The following essay, prepared before the start of the Gulf crisis in August 1990, provides an account of the negotiations that led to Resolution 598 and of the issues that remained following the cease-fire. As *The Diplomatic Record* went to press it was unclear how much of the conditions of Saddam Hussein's offer were being fulfilled. The essay, however, gives the background that underlines both the extraordinary nature of President Hussein's latest move and of the longstanding enmity between the two countries, which current maneuvers may not totally erase.

On August 20, 1988, after almost eight years of fighting, Iran and Iraq agreed to a cease-fire under UN Security Council Resolution 598 (see pp. 111-112). The Security Council was convinced that a comprehensive, just, honorable, and durable settlement should be achieved between Iran and Iraq and hoped that the two nations would resolve their dispute immediately. Both parties, since that time, have repeatedly expressed their commitment to achieving the full implementation of Resolution 598, but, largely because of mutual mistrust, the divergence in their interpretations of how this is to be accomplished has prevented forward movement.

The conflict between the two parties has been characteristic of a protracted regional dispute whose dimensions reflect tensions—historical, geopolitical, ideological, and legal—that have, over the years, resisted military, negotiated, and imposed solutions. Although temporarily subdued from time to time, tensions resurfaced with shifts in the balance of power between the two states. Thus, Iran's 1969 abrogation of the 1937 Frontier Treaty and negotiation of the 1975 Algiers accords reflected a power equation favorable to Tehran. On the other hand, Iraq's abrogation of the 1975 accords reflected the dynamic changes in the power equation resulting from the shah's departure and Iran's destabilization. One must therefore begin the study of the background of Resolution 598 against this geopolitical backdrop.

Conceptual Framework: Sources of Iranian and Iraqi Conduct

Iran and Iraq are components of an inherently anarchic interstate system. This system is unruly because it lacks an overarching authority that has a monopoly of legitimate force to judge the grievances of states and compel them to behave peacefully. Because states like Iran and Iraq exist in such a chaotic and hostile geopolitical environment, their leaders feel insecure and "worry about their survival, and the worry conditions their behavior."[1] As one scholar put it:

> In an anarchic, self-help system, the very search for security turns into the root cause of insecurity as each nation's quest poses a threat to the other. Because there is no ultimate guardian, nations must assume the worst. Because they act on their worst assumptions, they excite the worst suspicions of their neighbors and rivals whose countervailing responses merely seem to buttress the former's initial anxiety.[2]

This is precisely the case with Iranian-Iraqi relations. By the nature of their deep-seated tensions over the last few decades, Iran and Iraq have been locked into a precarious security dilemma: An action-reaction spiral has occurred—and continues to occur—between the two states such that each is forced to engage in security-seeking measures, whether through war or at the negotiating table.

The Iraqi worldview is best illustrated by President Saddam Hussein in his speech following the outbreak of hostilities between Iran and Iraq in September 1980:

> Our area has been living for several years under conditions of threat, aggression, instability and under the fear of crises and explosive situations. The previous Iranian regime had assumed a serious aggressive role in the region. Induced by world imperialism and zionism, it had carried out the role of the so-called Gulf Policeman. When the new regime assumed office, we hoped that it would depart from these aggressive policies and vicious attitudes. However, shortly afterwards, the regime began to behave exactly as the previous one. The battle that we have waged against the Iranian regime [is] a battle in defense of the honor, sovereignty, constant historical rights, and legitimate vital interests of our country.[3]

This Iraqi perception of Iran's bellicosity has extended from the battlefront to the talks aimed at implementing Resolution 598. At the opening round of talks in November 1988, for example, Iraqi Foreign Minister Tariq Aziz described his view of Iran's negotiating position on outstanding territorial issues as follows:

> The Iranian mind and thinking is very sick, and the Iranian leadership is suffering from schizophrenia. The one familiar with history finds that Iran has been for longer periods of time a part of Iraq and not the contrary as claimed by the Iranian Foreign Minister Velayati who said that Iraq is a new country whose lifetime spans no more than 40 years and that nothing called Iraq before existed. Has he forgotten that Iran for long periods of time was part of the Kingdom of Assyria and Babylonia. All at once, he reveals the truth pertaining to his chauvinism and his Persian racism.[4]

As with Iraq, Iran's conduct both during the war and the cease-fire talks currently under way was a function of what it perceived to be a patently anarchic regional and international system. Despite the change of regime in Tehran, the challenge of Iraqi hegemony—particularly in the Persian Gulf—continued unabated and manifested itself in the crudest form during eight years of war. From Iran's vantage point, this challenge has not dissipated and has impinged on talks aimed at implementing Resolution 598. In addition, Iran's current security dilemma stems from and is reflective of a major feature of the Shiite world view. Because of its anarchic nature, the international milieu is seen as threatening, a perception in which the threat derives from hostile attitudes toward the Shiite state, so that the state is viewed as an effect and various external factors as cause. In other words, in the unruly international system, the Shiite state is perceived as oppressed while the non-Shiite states are the oppressors. The Islamic Republic of Iran, therefore, is not likely to hold itself accountable when things go wrong and will generally react by turning anger and hostility outward toward others—perceived Sunni oppressors, an arbitrary and unjust government, imperialists, or minority groups such as Jews and Bahais. This world view has been expounded by Iran's Friday prayer leaders, who as spokesmen for the regime, have described the identity of the external enemies. Therefore, since 1980, in addition to "American imperialism, international Zionism, and the Wahhabis of Saudi Arabia," the Baathist government of Iraq has been viewed as a major external threat to the survival of the Islamic Republic.

This position was recently expounded upon by Iran's Deputy Foreign Minister Ali Mohammad Besharati:

> If we were to study the general course of the Islamic revolution, we would realize that it automatically raises many hostilities. In verse 120 of the holy chapter of *baqarah* [Koranic chapter] God tells the apostle [Prophet Muhammad]: The Jews and the Christians will never be happy with you unless you submit to their demands and follow their way of life. But you tell them that the correct way of life is what God has shown you. Meanwhile, O you prophet, if you were to follow their way of life, if you were to submit to their demands and if you were to take any notice of their proposals after so much succor and so many victories that Almighty God has granted you, you must not expect any favor from [*sic*] us from God again. It seems as if Almighty God has made this divine revelation to the Muslim people of Iran through his angel reading the same verse to us. We view the talks, the Resolution 598, and all the problems of the post-cease-fire period as the other side of the war coin. This is, the conspiracies of global arrogance has [*sic*] two sides: One side of it is the war, the other side is talks. We do not believe that these two are separate from each other.[5]

The views expressed by both the Iranian and Iraqi delegations reflects a zero-sum view of relations between the two nations and their negotiations to end the conflict. This view has major implications for the UN secretary-general's mediation efforts and the challenge he faces: an attempt by both parties to combat conditions of perceived victimization stemming from a protracted conflict, an absence of security and valued neighborly relationships, and the uniqueness of their security predicament. The reality facing UN mediators is that longstanding ideological, geopolitical, and historical cleavages will not be traded, exchanged, or bargained over. They are not subject to negotiation.[6] Any agreement arrived at as a result of UN efforts, therefore, that may give certain advantages to one party but not touch upon the underlying issues in the conflict, will not last.

The sense of insecurity outlined above manifests itself in the negotiating styles of both Iran and Iraq as well. Those styles are shaped by each nation's culture, history, political system, and place in the world and motivated by pride in their past. Their leaders are highly suspicious of negotiations; historically their independence has been threatened or violated by the collusion and intervention of external powers. Furthermore, Iran and Iraq see the negotiations as part of the continued struggle for increased power and influence by the other. Should the objectives of one party be realized, as a result of the implementation of the resolution, the losing party will find it difficult to save face and may attempt to sabotage the agreement. Face-saving is more important than are the details of the reconciliation. The point is to let the intermediary explore positions carefully before either party is required to make any clear commitment. This is precisely what the Swedish team headed by Ambassador Jan Eliasson has attempted to accomplish.

UN Mediation: The Swedish Connection

On September 1, 1988, Jan Eliasson was appointed "Personal Representative of the Secretary-General on Matters Pertaining to the Implementation of Security Council Resolution 598." In this function, Eliasson represents the United Nations and the secretary-general. Prior to the appointment, the secretary-general obtained the Swedish government's agreement to this arrangement. The fact that the UN secretary-general turned to Sweden for the resolution of the conflict may be indicative of Sweden's strong support of the UN as an organization and the fact that Sweden is not thought to have any direct interests of its own in the Iran-Iraq conflict. Furthermore, the Swedish delegation, which reports directly to the secretary-general, has been capable of gaining the confidence of the parties concerned and has not been suspected of harboring ulterior motives or representing the interests of the great powers. Sweden's policy of neutrality has thus provided it with special opportunities to contribute to peaceful cooperation and the resolution of conflicts such as the one between Iran and Iraq. Throughout the negotiations, Eliasson has emphasized that the mediator's suggestions are as a rule only advisory and nonbinding on the disputing parties.

The conditions facing Eliasson are different from those facing his predecessors. As has been stated, Sweden's only objective is to achieve a peaceful resolution of the dispute. Of this, there is no doubt among the parties. Thus, despite the all-pervading interest in putting an end to the war and suffering, a certain amount of caution has nevertheless occasionally been necessary in matters directly related to the conflict. For example, when the war between Iran and Iraq, for the first and hitherto only time, became a subject of a General Assembly resolution in the autumn of 1982, Sweden, to maintain its impartiality, decided not to take a position. Instead, it chose the unusual route of not participating in the vote.

Although a cease-fire is now in effect, and both parties have committed themselves to the full implementation of Resolution 598 and to the talks under UN auspices, Eliasson recognizes that much work needs to be done.[7] First, the resolution contains several provisions that have to be implemented. Second, the Security Council must throw its political weight behind the UN mediator in order to enhance the latter's hand and generate respect for the office of the secretary-general and the Security Council. This weight was forthcoming immediately after Iran accepted Resolution 598, which subsequently led to the creation of the United Nations Iran-Iraq Military Observer Group (UNIIMOG).

UNIIMOG: Cooperation Under Anarchy

The building of bridges from conflict to conciliation is only possible when time is allowed for changes in perceptions, mentality, tactics, definitions, and acceptability levels. The observer group's mandate must be viewed in this context: a temporary measure in conjunction with the cease-fire that provides some breathing space so that the parties may enter into and continue negotiations.

On August 9, 1988, the Security Council adopted Resolution 619 unanimously, establishing UNIIMOG for an initial period of six months. Since then the mandate has been renewed several times and was last extended on March 31, 1990. The task of its 350 unarmed troops is to supervise the cease-fire and withdrawal of troops along the 740-mile border to internationally recognized boundaries. Since its inception, UNIIMOG has developed into a vital complement to mediation efforts while serving as a mediating institution at the local level. The observer group's functions, however, are limited in the sense that they may contribute to peacekeeping, but will not by themselves lead to peacemaking. In general, operations are conditional on decisions by the UN Security Council and require the agreement and permission of the great powers. They also presume the support or acceptance of the parties to the conflict as well as a reasonably good climate of cooperation in order to resolve problems that may occur. Thus, while it serves as a down payment on confidence, UNIIMOG is a temporary, vulnerable, and provisional concession, even though it has effectively removed both the danger and possibility of unilateral acts by either party.

Despite its limited mandate, the observer group has provided stability to the negotiation process, a fact not forgotten by UN Secretary-General Javier Perez de Cuellar in his September 22, 1989, report to the Security Council:

> For its part, UNIIMOG has played an indispensable role in ensuring the maintenance of the cease-fire and I am convinced that its continued presence is an essential condition for further progress towards the full implementation of Resolution 598 (1987). Both parties have assured me of their support for UNIIMOG and of their agreement that its mandate should be extended.[8]

The Pre-Negotiation Phase: Background

Delineating the discrete military and political events that drove the Iran-Iraq war to a stalemate is a relatively simple process. Shortly after the outbreak of the war in September 1980, the UN secretary-general offered his good offices to both sides to help settle the conflict. He directed the attention of the Security Council to the war, invoking Article 99 of the UN Charter.[9] On September 28, 1980, the Security Council adopted Resolution 479, calling for a settlement of the dispute and supporting the secretary-general's offer to mediate. In November 1980, Swedish Prime Minister Olav Palme was named special representative and visited the area for the first time in that capacity. (It should be noted that Jan Eliasson accompanied the late prime minister on missions to Iran and Iraq from 1980 to 1986.) During 1981 and 1982, talks continued and some prisoners of war were exchanged. The Security Council on July 12, 1982, adopted Resolution

514 calling for a cease-fire, withdrawal of troops to international boundaries, and dispatch of UN observers to the area. On October 4, it adopted Resolution 522, reaffirming provisions of Resolution 514. Between 1982 and 1987, the General Assembly also adopted resolutions supporting the peace efforts and calling for a cease-fire.

In 1983, the UN sent the first of a number of special missions to the area to inspect alleged military attacks against civilian areas. Later, other missions investigated alleged use of chemical weapons and the conditions of prisoners of war. On October 31, the Security Council adopted Resolution 540 calling for an end to military operations against civilian targets and affirming the right of free navigation in the Gulf. On July 1, 1984, the Security Council adopted Resolution 552 asking for respect for the rights of free navigation and an end to attacks on commercial ships. In the same month, a truce was begun in the so-called war of the cities that lasted nine months. In March 1985, the secretary-general presented representatives of Iran and Iraq with an eight-point peace plan; the following month he personally visited Tehran and Baghdad to continue discussions. On February 24, 1986, the Security Council adopted Resolution 582, deploring the initial acts that caused the war and reaffirming its call for a cease-fire and troop withdrawal to international borders. In Resolution 588, adopted on October 8, the Council asked for implementation of Resolution 582. Following intensified diplomatic activity, including that by the five permanent members of the Security Council, the Council adopted Resolution 598 on July 20, 1987, which became the framework for reaching the cease-fire agreement in 1988.[10]

Broader geopolitical, economic, and social forces shaped the belligerents' eventual acceptance of the cease-fire resolution and the negotiating table.[11] The first is that the United States and the Soviet Union, confronted by a regional war not of their making—but one that posed a strong threat to their respective national interests and the balance of power in the Persian Gulf—chose primarily diplomatic rather than military means to pursue an end to the war. The common denominator of US and Soviet foreign policy regarding the Iran-Iraq war was to pursue a policy of strategic denial aimed at preventing the emergence of either Iranian or Iraqi hegemony in the region and its implications for the balance of power in the Middle East. Both superpowers agreed on the need to contain the violence of the Persian Gulf war and bring it to a diplomatic, yet inconclusive end for two mutually reinforcing reasons. First, both Moscow and Washington desired an end to the war that would maintain the Persian Gulf's status quo antebellum while avoiding a direct superpower military conflict: The victorious power should not be in a position to dominate and destabilize the region. The second impetus for US-Soviet cooperation was that the Iran-Iraq war provided—with the assistance of third-party arms producers and distributors—an arena for unchecked proliferation of weaponry. The destabilizing potential of these weapons, as evidenced in the war of the cities, convinced the superpowers that one way to temper this proliferation was to exert pressure on the belligerents to accept 598. These two basic reasons are spelled out, both explicitly and implicitly, in the text of Resolution 598.[12]

Until the last year of the war, Iran held the advantage. When the combination of internal and international pressures—Iraqi military victories, internal Iranian discord and flagging revolutionary zeal, and increased international military activity in the Persian Gulf—began to threaten the regime itself, however, Tehran looked to Resolution 598 as a face-saving means of ceasing hostilities with Iraq.

According to some military analysts, by April 1988 it had become clear that Baghdad had achieved the final military advantage in the war. A series of Iraqi offensives regained strategic Iraqi territory, which Iran had taken two years to conquer, including the Fao Peninsula, the Majnoon Islands, and the Halabjeh border area. In the Persian Gulf itself, the escalating tanker war had drawn the US Navy into the conflict, culminating on April 17, 1988—the same day that Iraq regained control over Fao—in the destruction of two oil platforms and six Iranian naval vessels. This combination of land and naval defeats, in addition to the tragic downing of Iran Air 655 on July 3, 1988, which convinced Iran of American determination to force an end to the war, marked the psychological turning point in the conflict. The regime realized that for the first time in the eight-year war, the success of the war and the survival of the Islamic Republic itself had become inextricably intertwined.[13]

In short, the following factors and events compelled the Tehran regime to fear for its own future: Iranian military ineffectiveness and inefficiency; an economy plagued by material deficiencies and a lack of trained personnel; the continued depression of the oil industry; an American and international determination to force an Iranian capitulation; and domestic war weariness, coinciding with an internal and grave concern for Ayatollah Khomeini's death. Diplomatically, Iran had sought support for its position that before a cease-fire could take effect, Iraq should be named the aggressor in the war. This position was clearly spelled out by Iran's foreign minister, Ali Akbar Velayati:

> Before we officially agreed to [UN Resolution 598] the Majlis Speaker [Mr. Rafsanjani]... called for changing the sequence of the first and sixth articles; that is, he asked that the sixth article take the place of the first article. When the UN secretary-general was exchanging views with us regarding his plan to implement Resolution No. 598, he told us that he would form a committee to identify the responsibility for the war (article 6) at the same time the cease-fire announcement was made. This means the sequence of the articles will be different from what it was before. When that arrangement came closer to our point of view, we announced our acceptance of the resolution.[14]

Tehran also actively campaigned for a strong condemnation of Iraqi use of chemical weapons in the war. When neither of these demands was satisfied, particularly after Iraq's acceptance of the cease-fire resolution in July 1987, Iran fully understood the extent of its isolation. Faced with these factors and steady losses on the battlefield, the Iranian government accepted the inevitability of defeat and searched for a means to end the war with a minimum of damage to its credibility. That opportunity presented itself with the shooting down of Iran Air 655. The sheer magnitude of the disaster and the apparent willingness of the United States to continue vigorous military actions gave the Iranian government the domestic and international justification it needed to accept UN Resolution 598 and agree to a cease-fire.[15]

This decision is reflected in Iran's official response to Secretary-General Perez de Cuellar. On July 17, Iranian President Ali Khamenei wrote to the secretary-general that his nation would accept Resolution 598 "because of the importance it attaches to saving lives of human beings and the establishment of justice and regional and international peace and security."[16] The "fire of war has gained unprecedented dimensions," he stated, bringing other countries into the war and even engulfing innocent civilians, referring to the deaths of 290 Iranians over the Persian Gulf after the downing of Iran Air 655.[17]

On July 19, in a statement made available to the United Nations, Iraq's Deputy Prime Minister Tariq Aziz said that while his country was "wary" of Iran's intentions, nevertheless it approached the new developments "with open minds."[18] Iraq would "not have any truck with any partial measures that do not lead surely and within a clear, sound and agreed plan, to a comprehensive and lasting peace," he said.[19] Approaching Resolution 598 "in good will and in accordance with the sequence of its operative paragraphs" would be "the serious way" to achieve ultimately a lasting peace accord.[20]

Why did Iran wait a year to accept Resolution 598? Although the conventional reasons for this decision are spelled out above, a more fundamental and justifiable explanation—in view of Iran's security predicament elaborated earlier—is Tehran's mistrust of the United Nations in general and the Security Council in particular. The Iranian perception of a conspiratorial Security Council—three of whose members do not have normal relations with Iran—is reflected in the August 11, 1987, letter to Perez de Cuellar from Iran's permanent representative in response to the adoption of UN Resolution 598:

> The Security Council is obliged to explain why the Iran-Iraq war, exactly at the time when it is approaching its final stages, has turned into a breach of peace, thus necessitating recourse to Article 39 of the Charter. Ironically enough, the initiation of the war by Iraq on 22 September 1980 and occupation of a vast part of the territory of the Islamic Republic of Iran was a breach of world peace. The Security Council, however, chose to remain silent then. Little wonder, then, that the United States, in an outright show of support for Iraq, even forced the Security Council to oppose the amendment of some permanent and non-permanent members of the Council as to considering the war from the very outset as a breach of peace.[21]

It is interesting to note, however, that the letter goes on to "renew [the Islamic Republic's] confidence in the Secretary-General and is prepared to continue cooperation with him within the framework of his independent efforts and initiatives."[22] With Iran's "cooperation" secured after Ali Khamenei's letter to the UN secretary-general, the stage was set to begin negotiations on implementing Resolution 598.

Although both parties agreed on a definition of the problem, their perceptions of the shape of a possible solution was divergent. Some ten days before the opening of direct talks, scheduled for August 25 in Geneva, the secretary-general provided the parties with specific ideas from the elaborated implementation plan relating to arrangements for the cease-fire. Perez de Cuellar's proposal called for a timetable to be attached to the specific paragraphs of the resolution, with "D-Day" (the starting time for the cease-fire) set at 0300 hours Greenwich mean time, August 20.[23]

Thus, with reference to paragraph 1 of the resolution, the withdrawal of "all forces to the internationally recognized boundaries without delay" was set for D-Day plus three—August 23.[24] Paragraph 2 calls for "the Secretary-

General to dispatch a team of United Nations Observers to verify, confirm, and supervise the cease-fire and withdrawal . . . and to submit a report thereon to the Security Council."[25] This was to occur on D-Day plus 13. With reference to the release and repatriation without delay of POWs addressed in paragraph 3, repatriation was set to commence on D-Day plus 21 and to be completed by D-Day plus 81 according to the Third Geneva Convention of August 12, 1949. No D-Day was attached to paragraph 4, which calls upon both Iran and Iraq to "achieve a comprehensive, just and honorable settlement, acceptable to both sides, of all outstanding issues," or paragraph 5, stipulating that "all other States exercise the utmost restraint and to refrain from any act which may lead to further escalation and widening of the conflict, and thus to facilitate the implementation of the present resolution."[26] The decision not to set a date for paragraphs 4 and 5 was made by the secretary-general. With reference to paragraph 6, requesting "the Secretary-General to explore, in consultation with Iran and Iraq, the question of entrusting an impartial body with inquiring into responsibility for the conflict," the designated team was to commence its work on D-Day plus 21 and complete its report by D-Day plus 90.[27] And finally, the report by a team of experts who would study the question of reconstruction, stipulated in paragraph 7, was to be completed and the team report back to the Security Council by D-Day plus 90.

The Iranian delegation responded favorably to the proposal because it set specific timetables on issues of immediate importance to Iran such as those stipulated in paragraph 1 (calling for an immediate cease-fire and withdrawal of all forces to internationally recognized boundaries), paragraph 2 (verification, confirmation, and supervision of the cease-fire and withdrawal), and paragraph 6 (entrusting an impartial body with inquiring into responsibility for the conflict). On the other hand, the fact that no timetable was set for paragraphs 4 and 5 seems to have been the reason behind Iraq's rejection of the proposal. Iraq's position was that the resolution must be viewed in the context of an overall peace plan and not a truce. This point was spelled out by Saddam Hussein on August 6, 1988:

> You recall how Khomeyni said in his speech that he accepted the Security Council Resolution 598 as if he were taking poison. . . . All this made us ask for direct negotiations and reject a truce. . . . This is an initial test of intentions to see whether the Iranian rulers' approval of the Security Council Resolution is meant to establish a complete, comprehensive, and lasting peace devoid of personal aims and ambitions against Iraq and the Arab nation, or if it is meant—as they announced—to alleviate military, national, and international pressure on them.[28]

Although this pre-negotiation phase allowed both Iran and Iraq to assess and come to terms with the costs and benefits of concessions and agreements before making any firm commitments, their perceptions of what UN Resolution 598 entailed differed. As a result, Iraq and Iran entered the first round of negotiations with a distorted perception of Resolution 598—a means to an end or an end in itself?

The Negotiation Phase: To Requite or Not?

The first round of talks in Geneva (August 25-28) ended with Perez de Cuellar reporting "unexpected difficulties" over the withdrawal of forces to the internationally recognized boundaries.[29] This unexpected difficulty was expounded upon by Khamenei, arguing that "the first issue which should have been raised and implemented was the withdrawal of forces."[30] He then went on to say: "Another problem is the fact that in connection with the border dispute and withdrawal to internationally recognized boundaries, the criterion and focus is the Algiers Agreement."[31] Iran basically wanted to finalize the timetable presented by the secretary-general for implementing paragraphs 1 and 2 of Resolution 598, claiming that in the process Iraq was raising new "pre-conditions," including the clearing of the Shatt-al-Arab waterway.[32] The Iraqi response, presented by Sa'dun Hammadi, minister of state for foreign affairs, came within a day:

> In reply to the ... statements, by ... the president of the [Islamic] Republic [of Iran], ... we wish to make the following clear:
>
> 2. The repeated statements on the 1975 agreement also prove the lack of seriousness of the Iranian regime. This regime is adhering to an agreement that the Iranian side did not respect in its most important clauses—namely, the noninterference in internal affairs ... and threatening the security and safety of Iraq. This totally contradicts the spirit and letter of that agreement. This has obliged Iraq to abrogate that agreement after Iranian conduct rendered it useless.
>
> 3. Shatt al-Arab is a sovereign Iraqi river, and it has always been a sovereign Iraqi river throughout history. It is Iraq's only outlet to the Gulf and the artery connecting it to the outside world. Any attempt to undermine Iraq's full sovereignty over this vital waterway will be totally rejected by us.[33]

The Iraqi precondition concerning the dredging of the Shatt al-Arab under UN auspices and not according to the 1975 Algiers accord was an attempt to render the accord as inoperative within the context of paragraph 1 of Resolution 598, which calls for a withdrawal to internationally recognized boundaries. According to the accord, the internationally recognized boundary between the two states is "the median line of the main navigable channel at the lowest navigable level, starting from the point at which the land frontier between Iran and Iraq enters the Shatt al-Arab and continues to the sea,"[34] thus restricting Iraq's claims to complete sovereignty over its only outlet to the sea.

UN mediation efforts continued through September; at one point during the sessions the Iranian delegation submitted a proposal to Ambassador Eliasson for consideration. Details of this alleged Iranian attempt to break the deadlock were revealed by the Kuwaiti newspaper *al-Qabas*:

> Well-informed Western diplomatic sources have revealed to Al-Qabas that the Iranian delegation to the talks has submitted to Jan Eliasson the following new proposals which aim, according to the Iranian viewpoint, to get the talks moving:
>
> 1. Iran is ready to agree to guarantee full freedom of shipping for Iraqi ships in the Shatt al-Arab in return for Iraq's withdrawal of all its troops from Iranian territories within a short period of time.
>
> 2. Iran is ready to accept the dispatch of a team of UN experts and engineers to the Shatt al-Arab to prepare a study on dredging this waterway. However, Iran rejects Iraqi demands that the United Nations and the international community guarantee the clearing of the Shatt al-Arab. In this respect, the Iranians said that their acceptance of the Iraqi demands means abandoning the 1975 Algiers Agreement, which states in one of the protocols attached to it, that Iran and Iraq will carry out a common survey of the Shatt al-Arab once every 10 years.[35]

Iraq rejected these Iranian proposals for the following reasons:

> 1. Iraq refuses to barter the freedom of shipping for the withdrawal of troops to the international borders. It also refuses to link the two issues. Iraq believes that Resolution No. 598 must be implemented step by step and clause by clause. Therefore a full understanding of the cease-fire on land, at sea and in the air, must be achieved at the beginning. This must include the freedom of shipping and international commitment to clear the Shatt al-Arab. After agreement is reached on this subject, the withdrawal of troops to the international borders can be discussed.
>
> 2. The Iraqi side believes that sending a team of international experts and engineers to study the dredging of the Shatt al-Arab . . . must be accompanied by an international commitment to clear the waterway so that it becomes fit for shipping.[36]

From Iraq's perspective, the point on which the Iranian position had not changed was the clearing of the Shatt al-Arab. Iraq continued to demand that the UN secretary-general assume the task of clearing the Shatt al-Arab without affecting its legal status, which Iraq claimed it would discuss at a later stage. Iran rejected this and set the condition that the clearing of the Shatt al-Arab be carried out under the 1975 Algiers agreement. Iran viewed Iraq's position as an attempt to lend international legitimacy to its unilateral abrogation of the accord. For Iraq, this meant that Iran was setting preconditions for the Shatt al-Arab clearing operation, thus exploiting Iraq's need for the clearing of the Shatt al-Arab in order to pressure Baghdad into accepting the 1975 Algiers accord. Iran and Iraq were so firmly entrenched in their respective positions that face-saving on this particular issue became more important than the details of reconciling the divergent views.

It is interesting to note that throughout this round and the ones that followed, both parties consolidated their own internal support for a nonaccommodative policy as well, preparing the home front for a win in the negotiation process as opposed to a conciliatory mentality. The following commentary by the Iranian media at the conclusion of talks in November 1988 provides insights in this regard:

> The outcome of this round of talks and the Iraqi foreign minister's swift declaration of his country's intention not to raise the issue of the Arvand River outside the framework of the resolution is, in fact, a major victory for the Islamic Republic of Iran's diplomacy within the confines of the peace talks between the two countries. A cursory glance at the talks from the 1st day to the present reveals that, despite all of the Iraqi regime's obstructionism and pronouncements of unprincipled preconditions, which served only to waste time, bring the talks to an impasse, and delay the precise implementation of Resolution No. 598, the Islamic Republic of Iran did not accept any kind of precondition.[37]

While the drama of "who is winning in the talks" was being played out within Iran and Iraq, two other rounds of joint meetings at the ministerial levels took place. One was held in New York on October 1, 1988, and another at Geneva during the period between October 31 and November 11. Together, these rounds of talks included a total of eleven plenary meetings between the foreign ministers of Iran and Iraq. In an effort to break the seemingly unresolvable deadlock, the UN secretary-general presented a novel approach. He suggested that both sides agree to a set of assurances, which would be in conformity with relevant principles of international law. Agreement on a set of legal principles with direct bearing on 598 would, it was hoped, create a confluence of positions on general rules and serve as a confidence-building mechanism. This creative approach, which had been hammered out in spring 1988 by the UN, Iranian, and Iraqi technical teams, was introduced during Perez de Cuellar's presentation at a joint meeting on October 1, covering the following substantive points drawn from the elaborated implementation plan:[38]

- Consolidating arrangements governing the cease-fire, including freedom of navigation through the Strait of Hormuz;

- Withdrawing forces to the internationally recognized boundaries within a time frame of some two weeks;

- Undertaking a procedure for the release and repatriation of prisoners of war to be concluded within a specific time frame;

- Proceeding immediately with the unimpeded clearing of the Shatt al-Arab.

With regard to this initiative, the parties appeared to concur in principle on some of these suggestions as it related to the following considerations:

- Freedom of navigation on the high seas and in the Strait of Hormuz for the ships of both sides;

- Expeditious withdrawal of forces to internationally recognized boundaries;

- The Third Geneva Convention as it pertains to the issue of prisoners of war;

- The usefulness to both sides of restoring the Shatt al-Arab to navigation.

Unfortunately, as the secretary-general indicated in his February 2, 1989, report to the Security Council, the common ground between the parties on the issues listed above "should not be construed as having gone substantially beyond a convergence of views in principle."[39] The parties continued to hold divergent views on what constitutes a cease-fire. They held different views also on when the withdrawal of forces to internationally recognized boundaries would begin. On the question of the restoration of the Shatt al-Arab to navigation, the parties maintained different positions as to the context and manner in which the matter would be addressed. Although these divergences emerged in the context of a more fundamental disagreement on the wider issue of the framework for the conduct of the direct talks, they also stemmed from their view of negotiations as an exercise of mutual power, thus recognizing the risky undertaking. Even the talks on the repatriation of POWs could not escape this zero-sum mentality.

On October 4, 1988, the International Committee of the Red Cross (ICRC) sent a memorandum to the foreign ministers of both Iran and Iraq appealing to the two countries' governments "to make the necessary arrangements to implement Article 118 of the 1949 Third Geneva Convention on the release of POW's and their repatriation."[40] In agreeing to the ICRC's request, Iraq stressed that its acceptance of the measure was not linked to the other topics included in UN Resolution 598 and that its decision would not affect the implementation of the resolution according to the sequence of its provisions. The Iranian response, however, was different. Velayati stated that Iran would approve of the exchange of prisoners of war only within the framework of Resolution 598 and on the basis of its third article. He emphasized that Iran "will never agree to the exchange of POWs out of the Resolution 598 or the UN chief's implementation plan," and considered Iraq's acceptance as "a purely propaganda move, [therefore] in an attempt to escape public pressure, [Iraq] has proposed the exchange of POWs before the execution of other articles of the Resolution 598."[41] Not surprisingly, at the conclusion of the third round of direct negotiations in November, Ambassador Eliasson confessed that "we are unable to make progress on the essential issues."[42] He did, however, emphasize that "the resolution is an indivisible whole as confirmed by the UN Security Council"—a clear reference to Iran's stated position.[43] On the other hand, he indicated "an urgent need to make progress on the essential issues," referring to the specific paragraphs of Resolution 598, such as the exchange of POWs.[44]

The issue of the exchange of POWs was revived in 1989. Prior to the fifth round of direct talks scheduled for April, on March 5, 1989, Saddam Hussein said Iraq was prepared for an immediate exchange of all war prisoners, "without regard for the final results of the negotiations and the different stages on the way to global and lasting peace" in accordance with Resolution 598."[45] From Iraq's vantage point, a reciprocal move by Iran would alleviate Baghdad's deep-seated mistrust of Tehran's intentions and demonstrate Iran's "good-will." In other words, Baghdad viewed the "price-tag" for its magnanimity as being minimal: requital by Iran in kind. Tehran's perception of Baghdad's "magnanimity," however, was different and remained unchanged. In a March 17 letter to the secretary-general, Velayati said the Iraqi proposal for the exchange of prisoners, disregarding the final outcome of negotiations, was aimed at changing the order of priorities in Resolution 598 "based on international law" and at "impairing the whole resolution."[46] By its proposal, Iraq was "trying to deviate the negotiations from their determined framework."[47] He affirmed that Iran was ready for the exchange of all prisoners within the framework of Resolution 598 following the withdrawal of all forces to internationally recognized borders. Clearly, for Iran, the withdrawal was and continues to be the resolution's most important element.

At the fifth round of joint plenary meetings, April 20-23, Perez de Cuellar met with the foreign minister of Iran and the deputy prime minister of Iraq. No progress was made, however, as a result of the secretary-general's mediation efforts. Velayati claimed that Baghdad's refusal to withdraw from Iran seriously threatened regional peace and urged Perez de Cuellar to announce a date for the withdrawal of Iraqi troops from 2,000 square kilometers of Iranian territory and a procedure for its verification. "This continued occupation," he stated, "reflects Baghdad's expansionist aspirations."[48] By the end of this round, and as a result of frustrations over the deadlock, Iran and Iraq began questioning the authority of the each other's negotiating team—yet another ploy not to requite. The Iraqi delegation pointed to reports in the Western press concerning Velayati's mandate to negotiate on behalf of Iran. The Iranian foreign minister, in turn, firmly denied the rumors that his position had been weakened following the resignation of top officials at his ministry, including members of Iran's negotiating team. He was apparently referring to the resignations of deputy foreign minister for European and American Affairs, Mohammad Javad Larijani, and UN envoy Mohammad Ja'far Mahallati. For his part, Velayati stated that the difficulty at the fifth round of talks was a result of "clashes and differences of opinions among the Iraqi authorities. This has intensified the state of the Iraqi delegation's lack of authority in the tripartite Geneva talks."[49] These distorted perceptions of the other team's mandate added to the difficulties already facing the secretary-general and his personal representative.

In May and June 1989, extensive consultations continued with officials of Iran and Iraq with a view to exploring the prospects for a more fruitful joint ministerial meeting than those previously held. Unfortunately, this round of talks did not produce any breakthroughs.

On July 4, 1989, Perez de Cuellar met in Geneva with Ali Akbar Velayati and on July 6 in Rome with Tariq Aziz. At both meetings he stressed the UN concern that almost a year after the cease-fire had taken effect only parts of paragraphs 1 and 2 of the resolution had been implemented. Both parties pointed the finger at the lack of political will in Tehran and Baghdad to implement Resolution 598. The Iraqis pointed to changes in Iranian politics following the death of Ayatollah Khomeini and the division between hardliners and moderates as reasons for the lack of consensus within the Islamic Republic concerning Resolution 598. The Iranian perception of Iraqi intransigence was recently spelled out by the deputy foreign minister:

> Iraq does not wish to solve its dispute with us. Why? Because the eight-year war left Saddam Hussein with 2 million wounded, 600,000 dead, financial losses of 150 billion [dollars], and 10 ruined cities. If Saddam were to return this occupied territory in exchange for his POWs, the people of Iraq would ask Saddam: What was the outcome of the eight-year war and so many losses? What did you achieve? To avoid such a problem, Saddam does not wish to solve the crisis.[50]

In preparation for his proposed meetings with leaders of the delegations of Iran and Iraq to the Non-Aligned Summit meeting in Belgrade, Ambassador Eliasson met in Geneva from August 20-23, 1989, with representatives of both governments. On September 4, Perez de Cuellar met in Belgrade with Velayati and on September 5 with Tariq Aziz. Both sides agreed that another round of talks as previously held in Geneva and New York would not be fruitful at that stage. It appears that by this time a general feeling of frustration had prevailed over all the parties involved. The Iranians felt that the UN secretary-general's vagueness on the contentious issues had weakened the negotiating process. Although they recognized that it served to diffuse tension by allowing each party to interpret the secretary-general's statements differently, vagueness often led to ambivalence. Thus, the lack of enforcement mechanisms, coupled with ambivalence, weakened the UN role. The Iraqis felt that the mediator's creativity was, time and again, tempered by a need to maintain strict impartiality. In other words, in the interest of maintaining impartiality, when a creative idea was not acceptable to one or the other of the parties, the initiative would be dropped. For their part, the mediators realized the importance of the role of the Security Council and recognized the latter's unwillingness to throw its political weight into the mediation efforts, thus weakening the mediator's position vis-à-vis the two belligerents.

Despite their frustrations, both parties gave favorable consideration to Perez de Cuellar's suggestion that, at a mutually convenient time in the fall, Ambassador Eliasson arrange an open-ended visit to the area in an effort to further the implementation of the resolution. Eliasson's "shuttle diplomacy" ended in December 1989 with Iran agreeing to an exchange of POWs in return for Iraq's withdrawal to internationally recognized borders. This arrangement, Tehran stressed, would accelerate the implementation of the other articles of the UN resolution. On the other hand, Baghdad maintained that it had not received from Ambassador Eliasson any substantive clarification indicating a serious change in the Iranian position on Iraq's sovereignty over the Shatt al-Arab, Tehran's attitude toward the POWs, or its view on the implementation of the resolution as a peace plan. From Iraq's vantage point, the Iranian government remained vague, selective, and noncommittal in its position on the foregoing issues.

The seemingly unresolvable positions held by both parties were made more difficult as a result of distorted perceptions by both Iran and Iraq of statements emanating from Tehran and Baghdad. The following comments by Iraq's ambassador to the UN illustrate this point:

> [Velayati's January 17 statements] at Tehran University to a number of traitors described . . . as "the Iraqi opposition," . . . reflect the real intention of the Iranian government, which has not relinquished its policy based on interfering in the internal affairs of world states. [The] . . . statements run contrary to those made behind closed doors by Iranian officials during their deliberation with the UN Secretary General, his personal representative, and the UN Security Council members . . . Velayati's statements are indicative of the selective approach and deceptive, procrastinating, and prevaricating policy pursued by the Iranian government regarding the peace process.[51]

Although selective and distorted perceptions dominated the negotiations through January, neither party was deterred from attempting to gain concessions by redefining the issues. In an effort to gain support for its position on linking the exchange of POWs to the withdrawal of Iraqi forces, the chief of Iran's UN mission pointed out that the homelessness of 87,751 Iranians as a result of Iraq's continued occupation of Iranian border areas was by no means a less humanitarian issue than the exchange of POWs.[52] Unfortunately, for Iranian refugees, as well as Iraqi and Iranian POWs, 60,000 of whom remain unregistered (30,000 POWs in Iran and another 30,000 in Iraq), the anguish and sorrow continued through March 1990.

Conclusion

In March, the UN secretary-general handed to the representatives of both Iran and Iraq at the United Nations his proposal for resumption of peace talks to implement Security Council Resolution 598. These were the issues that remained at the beginning of the summer of 1990:[53]

- Iraq insisted that Resolution 598 be fully implemented as a peace plan and not a temporary settlement. Baghdad's main concern has been the implementation of the other provisions of the resolution once the withdrawal to the internationally recognized boundaries has been carried out. Furthermore, it maintained that the direct talks it had envisaged to reach a common understanding of the provisions of the resolution as a whole have yet to take place.

- Iran, on the other hand, has maintained that Iraq wanted to turn Resolution 598 into an open forum and arrive at a settlement outside the framework of 598 because the resolution did not recognize Iraq's claim to sovereignty over the Shatt al-Arab. Thus, Tehran maintained that the withdrawal to the internationally recognized boundaries was a mandatory provision of the resolution that should be carried out without delay or preconditions. It asserted that the withdrawal should be implemented as a first step, together with the cease-fire, in accordance with paragraph 1 of the resolution.

- Both Iran and Iraq took different views of how and when to implement paragraph 3 concerning release and repatriation of prisoners of war. Iraq stated that on a basis of reciprocity and in the context of the Third Geneva Convention it was prepared to release and repatriate all prisoners of war immediately. Iran made clear its readiness to repatriate the prisoners of war in the context of the implementation of the resolution, and thus not before the withdrawal was carried out. It should be noted that throughout Secretary-General Perez de Cuellar's discussions and those of Ambassador Eliasson they continued to urge the parties, regardless of reciprocity, to allow the ICRC to proceed with visits to, as well as registration and notification of, all prisoners of war being held in their countries.

- As for the withdrawal of foreign troops, Baghdad repeatedly stated that it held no claim to Iranian territory. The concern was expressed by Iraq that if withdrawal were to take place in isolation, it would perpetuate the situation of no war, no peace, and instability in the region. Tehran expressed the concern that Iraq was procrastinating on the withdrawal by questioning Iran's intentions as to their future relations.

In addition to these basic differences, the atmosphere that surrounded efforts to implement the resolution were not conducive to early success. The talks were characterized by mistrust, selective and distorted perceptions, negative attitudes and images, poor communications, and a competitive win-lose orientation that attempted to force or extract capitulation for the adversary. Both parties viewed the efforts as acts of nonviolence intended to compel the other to fulfill its will—the reverse of Karl von Clausewitz's dictum of "war as a continuation of politics by other means." For both Iran and Iraq, the negotiations were not merely a diplomatic endeavor; they were a political struggle for survival, a continuation of their war by other means.

Appendix 6.1 UN Resolution 598

RESOLUTION 598 (1987)

Adopted by the Security Council at its 2750th meeting,
on 20 July 1987

The Security Council,

Reaffirming its resolution 582 (1986),

Deeply concerned that, despite its calls for a cease-fire, the conflict between Iran and Iraq continues unabated, with further heavy loss of human life and material destruction,

Deploring the initiation and continuation of the conflict,

Deploring also the bombing of purely civilian population centres, attacks on neutral shipping or civilian aircraft, the violation of international humanitarian law and other laws of armed conflict, and, in particular, the use of chemical weapons contrary to obligations under the 1925 Geneva Protocol,

Deeply concerned that further escalation and widening of the conflict may take place,

Determined to bring to an end all military actions between Iran and Iraq,

Convinced that a comprehensive, just, honourable and durable settlement should be achieved between Iran and Iraq,

Recalling the provisions of the Charter of the United Nations, and in particular the obligation of all Member States to settle their international disputes by peaceful means in such a manner that international peace and security and justice are not endangered,

Determining that there exists a breach of the peace as regards the conflict between Iran and Iraq,

Acting under Articles 39 and 40 of the Charter of the United Nations,

1. *Demands* that, as a first step towards a negotiated settlement, Iran and Iraq observe an immediate cease-fire, discontinue all military actions on land, at sea and in the air, and withdraw all forces to the internationally recognized boundaries without delay;

2. *Requests* the Secretary-General to dispatch a team of United Nations Observers to verify, confirm and supervise the cease-fire and withdrawal and further requests the

Secretary-General to make the necessary arrangements in consultation with the Parties and to submit a report thereon to the Security Council;

3. *Urges* that prisoners-of-war be released and repatriated without delay after the cessation of active hostilities in accordance with the Third Geneva Convention of 12 August 1949;

4. *Calls upon* Iran and Iraq to co-operate with the Secretary-General in implementing this resolution and in mediation efforts to achieve a comprehensive, just and honourable settlement, acceptable to both sides, of all outstanding issues, in accordance with the principles contained in the Charter of the United Nations;

5. *Calls upon* all other States to exercise the utmost restraint and to refrain from any act which may lead to further escalation and widening of the conflict, and thus to facilitate the implementation of the present resolution;

6. *Requests* the Secretary-General to explore, in consultation with Iran and Iraq, the question of entrusting an impartial body with inquiring into responsibility for the conflict and to report to the Security Council as soon as possible;

7. *Recognizes* the magnitude of the damage inflicted during the conflict and the need for reconstruction efforts, with appropriate international assistance, once the conflict is ended and, in this regard, requests the Secretary-General to assign a team of experts to study the question of reconstruction and to report to the Security Council;

8. *Further requests* the Secretary-General to examine, in consultation with Iran and Iraq and with other States of the region, measures to enhance the security and stability of the region;

9. *Requests* the Secretary-General to keep the Security Council informed on the implementation of this resolution;

10. *Decides* to meet again as necessary to consider further steps to ensure compliance with this resolution.

United Nations Security Council, S/RES/598 (1987), 20 July 1987.

Notes

1. Kenneth Waltz, *Theory of International Politics* (New York: Random House, 1979), p. 105.
2. Cited in Avner Yaniv, *Dilemmas of Security* (Oxford: Oxford University Press, 1987), p. 7.
3. The entire text of President Saddam Hussein's speech appears in *Iraqi-Iranian Conflict: Documentary Dossier*, prepared by the Iraqi Ministry of Foreign Affairs (Baghdad: January 1981).
4. Foreign Broadcast Information Service (FBIS/NES), November 2, 1988, p. 28.
5. Comments by Besharati in FBIS/NES, March 14, 1990, p. 33.
6. Edward E. Azar, "Protracted International Conflicts: Ten Propositions," in *International Conflict Resolution*, eds. Edward E. Azar and John W. Burton (Boulder, CO: Lynne Rienner Publishers, 1986), p. 30.
7. Jan Eliasson, *Sweden and International Mediation* (Stockholm: Ministry of Foreign Affairs, 1989), pp. 11-14.
8. Report of the secretary-general on the United Nations Iran-Iraq Military Observer Group, S/20862, New York: United Nations, September 22, 1989, p. 11.
9. Article 99 of the UN charter falls under the section concerning the office of the Secretariat.
10. *UN Chronicle* (New York: United Nations, December 1988), pp. 24-25.
11. Richard Morgan Wilbur, "The Iran-Iraq War: An Analysis of the Cease-fire," *The Fletcher Forum of World Affairs* (Winter 1990), Vol. 14, No. 1: 112-115.
12. See Appendix 6.1.
13. Wilbur, "The Iran-Iraq War," pp. 112-115.
14. FBIS/NES, September 7, 1988, p. 48.
15. Wilbur, "The Iran-Iraq War," pp. 119-125.
16. *UN Chronicle*, December 1988, p. 22.
17. *Ibid.*
18. *Ibid.*
19. *Ibid.*
20. *Ibid*, p. 23.
21. For the text of Ambassador Said Rajaie Khorasani's response see UN document S/19031, August 11, 1987, p. 2.
22. *Ibid*, p. 4.
23. Conversation with Dr. Javad Zarif, deputy chief of the Iranian Mission to the UN, February 1990.
24. See text of UN Resolution 598 (1987).
25. *Ibid.*
26. *Ibid.*
27. *Ibid.*
28. FBIS/NES, August 8, 1988, p. 21.
29. See *UN Chronicle*, December 1988, p. 23.
30. Comments by Ali Khamenei in FBIS/NES, August 29, 1988, p. 61.
31. *Ibid*, p. 61.

32. See comments by Ali Akbar Velayati in FBIS/NES, August 29, 1988, p. 53.
33. FBIS/NES, August 30, 1988, p. 23-24.
34. Article 2 of the "Protocol Concerning the Delimitation of the River Frontier Between Iran and Iraq," signed on June 13, 1975, between Iran and Iraq. For the complete text of the Algiers agreement see Tareq Y. Ismael, *Iran and Iraq: Roots of the Conflict*, (Syracuse: Syracuse University Press, 1982), pp. 58-68.
35. Commentary by *al-Qabas* in FBIS/NES, September 13, 1988, p. 56-57.
36. *Ibid.*
37. FBIS/NES, November 7, 1988, p. 60.
38. See report by the secretary-general in UN document S/20442, February 2, 1989.
39. For the text of the report by the secretary-general see UN document S/20442, February 2, 1989.
40. FBIS/NES, October 21, 1988, p. 17.
41. *Ibid*, p. 42.
42. Comments by Jan Eliasson in FBIS/NES, November 14, 1988, p. 27.
43. *Ibid.*
44. *Ibid.*
45. FBIS/NES, March 6, 1989, p. 28.
46. *UN Chronicle*, June 1989, p. 25.
47. *Ibid.*
48. FBIS/NES, April 20, 1989, p. 43.
49. Comments by Velayati in FBIS/NES, April 24, 1989, p. 68.
50. FBIS/NES, March 14, 1990, p. 33.
51. Comments by Ambassador Abd-al-Amir al-Anbari in FBIS/NES, January 25, 1990, p. 20.
52. See comments by Kamal Kharrazi in FBIS/NES, January 31, 1990, p. 60.
53. For the text of the report by the UN secretary-general, see UN document S/20862, September 22, 1989, p. 70.

7

The Negotiations on a Chemical Weapons Ban in 1989

Barend ter Haar

IN 1989 THE NEGOTIATIONS on a worldwide ban on chemical weapons (CW) accelerated further, but, although important progress was made, no final breakthrough took place. At the beginning of 1990 the negotiators were still wrestling with the elaboration of an effective verification regime, and the review of the US position regarding a comprehensive ban on chemical weapons was still going on.

Negotiations on a worldwide ban on chemical and biological weapons started in 1968. In 1972 a separate ban on the development, production, and storage of biological weapons was signed. These weapons were not considered to present a serious military risk, and therefore the Western countries were willing to accept the absence of a credible regime for verification. Chemical weapons, however, were considered to be too great a military threat to base a treaty solely on trust that other parties would honor their obligations.

The Soviet Union was adamantly against allowing foreign inspectors on its territory. So, despite draft-conventions presented by Japan (1974) and the United Kingdom (1976) and despite years of bilateral negotiations between the United States and the USSR, the negotiations made little headway. The turning point came in the 1980s when the Soviet Union step-by-step completely reversed its position into that of the champion of intrusive verification.

With the introduction of the *basic provisions* of the Soviet Union in 1982, the *detailed views* of the United States in 1983, and the draft convention introduced by Vice President George Bush in April 1984, the pace of the negotiations in the Conference on Disarmament (CD) quickened. In the following years, the use of chemical weapons in the war between Iraq and

Iran and the indications that several countries were trying to acquire chemical weapons led to more political attention and to a further intensification of the negotiations.

The Paris Conference

Not since World War I had lethal chemical weapons been used on such a large scale as in the summer of 1988. Among the victims were not only many Iranian soldiers, but many civilians as well. As long as the war between Iraq and Iran continued, the international community had not reacted strongly against the clear evidence of the use of chemical weapons by Iraq; it was felt that any sanction against Iraq would be seen as siding with Iran. When the cease-fire was finally declared, the way was free for an effort to strengthen the shattered image of the Geneva Protocol—both Iraq and Iran were party to that protocol. In September 1988, President Ronald Reagan proposed to hold a high-level conference to strengthen the Geneva Protocol and to stem the proliferation of chemical weapons.[1] President François Mitterand responded to Reagan's proposal by offering accommodation for the conference in Paris. The proposal to reaffirm the ban on the use of chemical weapons met with—at least officially—general approval. The American suggestion to couple such a reaffirmation of the Geneva Protocol with a kind of nonproliferation commitment was, however, met with much less enthusiasm. Many third world countries opposed any nonproliferation policy as discriminatory; in addition, it was feared that if progress were made in the direction of such a commitment, Washington might lose its interest in a worldwide ban of chemical weapons.

The conference was held from January 7-11, 1989, and was attended by about 149 countries, including the countries that are often mentioned in connection with chemical weapons like Iran, Iraq, Israel, Libya, and Syria. Around eighty of the delegations were headed by foreign ministers. Although the reason for the conference clearly was the Iraqi use of chemical weapons, the conference was not meant to deal with this or any other specific problem, because that would have prevented the conference from adopting the final declaration with consensus. The use of chemical weapons by Iraq was not, therefore, specifically addressed in the final declaration.

The United States, in particular, pressed for a condemnation of the continuing proliferation of chemical weapons. Several delegations argued, however, that because the United States was itself producing chemical

The Negotiations on a Chemical Weapons Ban in 1989   117

weapons, it was not in a position to condemn others for pursuing the same goal. The resulting compromise was that the conference linked the risk of the use of chemical weapons both to remaining stocks and to the spread of these weapons. Neither retaining nor acquiring chemical weapons were explicitly condemned, but the necessity was expressed "to exercise restraint and to act responsibly in accordance with the purpose of the present declaration."[2] For most delegations the crux of the matter was that only a worldwide ban would be able to solve the problem of proliferation.

The conference was a success in several respects. Fourteen countries decided to become party to the Geneva Protocol, making membership virtually global. It was also useful that the participants called on the CD "to redouble its efforts" to resolve the remaining issues, because lack of manpower and of resources for verification research seriously hampered progress. Although few governments took their commitment to "redouble efforts" literally, the fact that the declaration was agreed at such a high level certainly stimulated some governments to make available more manpower to carry on the negotiations and possibly more money for development of verification techniques.

The most important result, however, might be that all participating countries, including those believed to be interested in acquiring a chemical weapons capability, not only condemned the use of chemical weapons, but also stressed the necessity of an early conclusion of a global and effectively verifiable ban. Because the accession of all relevant states will, in the end, decide the success of the convention, this consensus was a hopeful sign. That the conference stated that "any state wishing to contribute to these negotiations should be able to do so,"[3] was another positive development and opened the way for admission of Iraq as an observer to the negotiations[4] and also Israel[5] in February 1990.

The Canberra Conference

The use of chemical weapons by Iraq would not have been possible had Iraq been unable to buy the necessary equipment, technology, and chemicals from the chemical industries in other, mainly Western countries. Other countries such as Iran, Libya, and Syria seemed to be trying to follow the Iraqi example. In reaction, most industrial nations took measures to prevent any further involvement of their industries, trading houses, and engineering firms. Probably in response to the widely publicized role that a few German firms played in Libyan efforts to acquire a chemical weapons production plant, the US government felt that a strong commitment should be sought from the chemical industries around the world to prevent further proliferation of these weapons. Other governments reacted to this idea as they did in the case of the Paris conference: The only effective and acceptable way for all countries to prevent proliferation is through a complete ban of chemical weapons. Several nonaligned countries made clear that they would not attend a conference that had as its main purpose the denial to them of what the two superpowers kept for themselves. The Australian government, which hosted the conference, therefore stated clearly that the purpose of the conference was to contribute to a successful conclusion and implementation of a worldwide ban.

Representatives of governments and the chemical industry met in Canberra for the Government-Industry Conference against Chemical Weapons on September 18-22, 1989. The conference did discuss practical ways to bring the goal of a worldwide ban closer.[6] The Australian government declared it would set up a national Chemical Weapons Convention Secretariat as the nucleus of a future national authority.

The main accomplishment of the conference, however, was probably the unreserved commitment of representatives of more than 90 percent of the world's chemical industries to a worldwide ban of chemical weapons, including the necessary verification. As the negotiations on a chemical weapons ban proceeded, it had become increasingly obvious that a regime to monitor the civil chemical industry would eventually become the cornerstone of the convention. Developing such a regime would not be possible without the close cooperation of the chemical industry. A few governments among them—those of the Netherlands and the United States—therefore started an informal dialogue with their industry early on in the negotiations. In most countries, however, such a dialogue had not yet begun when, in 1987, the ad hoc Committee on Chemical Weapons held its first informal consultations with representatives of the chemical industry. Contacts with the chemical industry often went through two stages. The initial reaction to the prospect of a new set of inspections and obligations was always reserved. Industry, however, usually quickly understood that the burden of inspections would be small compared with existing inspections for labor safety and environmental protection and, therefore, would be turned into an ally of government in efforts to ban chemical weapons.[7] This alliance was strongly confirmed at the Canberra conference.

Multilateral, National, and Bilateral Negotiations

Since the start of the negotiations in 1968, the main negotiating forum has been the CD[8] in Geneva and its predecessors.[9] Formally, the plenary is the main body of the CD, but this is, in fact, solely a forum for reading out prepared statements and a meeting place to talk with colleagues in the corridors. The ad hoc Committee on Chemical Weapons of the CD is responsible for the negotiations on a Chemical Weapons Convention. The actual negotiations, however, take place in formal and informal meetings of the working groups of this Committee and in special contact groups. The CD convenes for two sessions of three months each, a spring session in the months February, March, and April and a summer session in June, July, and August.[10] The ad hoc Committee on Chemical Weapons also convenes, formally or informally, in the period between the summer session and the spring session, usually during three weeks starting at the end of November, and during a three-week period in January, immediately preceding the spring session of the CD.

The projected convention will probably, at least in principle, open the most secret military and commercial locations and facilities. That is why the most heated negotiations on a chemical weapons ban often do not take place in Geneva, but in national capitals, usually between the Ministry of Foreign Affairs on the one hand and the Ministry of Economic Affairs or the Ministry of Defense on the other. These internal negotiations are easily overlooked, because they usually take place in secret. When a delegation stubbornly adheres to a position that lacks logic—and certainly when the delegation has visible difficulty in explaining its position—the reason is often that negotiations at home have led to an unfortunate compromise.

The two superpowers possess the major part of all chemical weapon stocks.[11] It is therefore obvious that bilateral negotiations between them can play an important part in the multilateral negotiations on a worldwide ban. The relationship between the bilateral and the multilateral negotiations is, however, not without some inherent tension. As long as the bilaterals concentrate on detailed arrangements for the declaration and destruction of the chemical weapons of both countries, the results are generally welcomed— although the United States and the Soviet Union have an understandable inclination to save their most effective chemical weapons as long as possible, while countries without chemical weapons would rather see the most dangerous weapons destroyed first. Bilateral negotiations on subjects that might directly affect the industry and the armed forces of every party would, however, be viewed with suspicion. The bilaterals therefore mainly concentrate on the problems of declaring and destroying stocks and chemical weapon production plants and on bilateral measures to strengthen confidence between the two countries before the convention enters into force. An additional problem of the bilaterals is that they draw scarce manpower away from the multilateral negotiations. According to other delegations, this has led to an appreciable slowing down of the pace of the multilateral negotiations.

The Agreed Concept of the Convention

Any discussion of the issues still outstanding should start with a recognition of the agreement that exists on the following basic elements of the convention:

1. A comprehensive ban on chemical weapons;
2. An obligation to destroy CW stocks and production plants;
3. Routine verification to give parties confidence in compliance;
4. A verification regime to resolve doubts about compliance; and
5. An international organization to implement the convention.

The central provision of the CW convention is the prohibition of developing, producing, retaining, transferring, and using chemical weapons. Every chemical compound that is intended either to be used as a warfare agent or as a precursor for the production of these agents is to be considered a chemical weapon. This *general purpose* criterion means that it is essentially only the intention that counts.[12] Protection against chemical weapons is permitted, and chemicals that are produced or used for testing of protection equipment are not considered to be chemical weapons.[13]

The logical consequence of the ban on producing, retaining, and transferring chemical weapons is the obligation to destroy chemical weapon stocks and chemical weapon production plants. To assure all parties that such destruction indeed takes place, after the convention enters into force all plants and stockpiles will have to be declared, sealed, and put under a system of international on-site inspection. This verification regime will stay in force until all stocks and production plants are destroyed.

Many civil chemical plants have, to a lesser or greater degree, the capability to produce chemical weapons. The obligation to destroy plants that have been making certain chemicals for chemical weapon purposes only makes sense if parties feel confident that these civil plants are not used for the same purpose. To give parties such confidence, an elaborate verification regime is foreseen.

Routine inspections will give confidence, but no certainty that the convention is complied with. The only way to solve possible doubts about violations at locations that are not under routine inspection is to give all parties the right to request inspection of any location or facility on the territory of an other state party. This is the concept underlying the regime for challenge inspections. As explained later, it is not yet clear whether all states—including the United States, which proposed the concept—are willing to accept the openness necessary for an effective functioning of this system.

The inspections will have to be carried out by the inspectors of the Technical Secretariat. The secretariat will be part of an international organization that will be set up to implement the CW convention. The highest organ in this organization will be the Conference of States Parties, but an executive council will supervise the implementation of the convention on a more frequent basis. Whereas all states parties will take part in the Conference of States Parties, membership of the executive council will be limited to about twenty-five countries.

The Remaining Issues

The paradox of progress in complicated negotiations is that initially the number of outstanding issues does not become smaller but only seems to grow. Large stumbling blocks in the negotiations sometimes simply cannot be removed but have to be shattered, resulting in innumerable smaller problems that have to be removed one by one. The discussion here of the remaining issues has to be limited, therefore, to those that are most salient.

Little progress was made in 1989 on the composition of the executive council. The discussion on composition is familiar because of experience in other United Nations forums: Should the seats be distributed evenly among all regional groups, or should certain groups—countries with a large chemical industry, or military powerful countries—be more strongly represented? It is clear that some kind of compromise must be struck. As long as negotiations seem to drag, however, little stimulus exists for any delegation to give in.

Much more difficult will be to find an adequate answer for the request of several nonaligned states that effective measures be taken in case a party to the convention is attacked or threatened by chemical weapons. The lukewarm reactions of the world community to Iraq's repeated violations of the Geneva Protocol testify to the difficult character of this issue. Two types of measures could be considered: direct assistance to the attacked party and sanctions against the attacker. The dilemma is that a strict obligation to give assistance—to Iran against the Iraqi use of chemical weapons, for example— might involve parties deeper in a conflict than they would like, whereas making assistance voluntary might leave an attacked party in the cold when other parties drag their feet. For the same reasons, it is difficult to agree on a meaningful system of sanctions—such as an arms embargo.

Two other issues should be mentioned, even though the negotiations in Geneva have so far been successful in avoiding them: the relationship between chemical and nuclear weapons and the costs of a ban on chemical weapons. The first issue surfaced at the Paris conference where some Arab delegations claimed that the danger posed by the risk of the use of chemical weapons cannot be isolated from the risk of the use of nuclear weapons. The reasoning behind this argument seemed to be that some countries might want to keep a chemical option against a possible Israeli nuclear weapon. Accepting a link between chemical and nuclear disarmament would kill the prospects for a CW convention.

The Geneva Protocol did not cost much more than the paper it was written upon and the meals and lodgings of the diplomats who negotiated the text. But the day of such cheap agreements is definitely gone, now that verification is considered to be essential. Both the preparation for the entry into force and the implementation of the verification regime will cost substantial sums of money. So far this question has been mainly passed over.

Security Stocks and the Destruction of Stocks and Plants

The rolling text[14] stipulates that shortly after the entry into force of the convention all stocks and plants of chemical weapons will have to be declared and sealed, in anticipation of their destruction during the first ten years. In July 1987, however, France suggested that parties should have the right to produce and possess a so-called security stock of chemical weapons until eight years after the entry into force. According to France, this was necessary to ensure that during these years parties with large stocks would not have undue advantage over parties with only limited or no stocks. Apart from the US delegation, which did not take a position, all delegations opposed the

French proposal, as it went against both letter and spirit of the envisaged convention. The problem seemed to be solved when President Mitterand, in his speech before the General Assembly of the United Nations in September 1988, withdrew the French proposal.

The spirit of security stocks did not return into the bottle so easily, however. In September 1989, President Bush, in an address to the General Assembly of the United Nations, announced that the United States was ready to destroy 98 percent of its chemical weapons stockpile in the first eight years of the convention. Destruction of the remaining 2 percent was, however, made dependent on the accession of all nations that are capable of building chemical weapons.[15] Furthermore, it became clear that the United States would like to keep open the option of continuing to produce chemical weapons after the entry into force of the convention. Possibly as a reaction to worldwide disapproval, the United States expressed at the Malta summit in December 1989 its willingness to drop this position.[16]

At the beginning of 1990 the United States had not yet given up its desire to keep a security stockpile as long as not all CW-capable countries had become party to the convention. According to many delegations, acceptance of this principle would fundamentally change the character of the convention. The agreement on such a principle would encourage countries to build a stockpile of chemical weapons before the entry into force in order to be prepared in the event that one or more countries would decide that, in their view, not all CW-capable nations had become party.

Verification of Nonproduction

By far the most time-consuming part of the negotiations is the development of a regime that should give parties confidence that the permitted civil capabilities of other parties are not used for the production of chemical weapons. The most obvious example of such a capability is, of course, the production of super-toxic lethal chemicals for the development and testing of protective measures against chemical weapons. Such production will therefore be strictly limited[17] and intrusively verified. A much larger capability is hidden in the civil production and use of chemicals that can be used for the production of warfare agents or even directly as such.[18] Efforts to develop a regime for verification of nonproduction have so far been mainly directed at these chemicals.

The backbone of this regime is a classification of the most relevant chemical compounds into three lists that will be subjected to three different regimes. (See Table 7.1.) In 1989 the lists of chemicals were brought together with definitions and guidelines for placing a chemical compound on a list in a new *Annex on Chemicals*.

List 1 contains:

- Super-toxic lethal compounds that have been used as chemical weapons, such as the nerve agents and mustard gases;

- BZ, an incapacitant that had been weaponized by the United States;

- A few key precursors[19] that can be used in binary weapons.[20]

List 2 now contains:

- Specific key precursors of the chemicals on list 1;

- Lethal chemicals that possibly could be used as warfare agents but were never weaponized. (The origin of this category was a separate list 4 for super toxic lethal chemicals that were not included in list 1.)

List 3 contains:

- Precursors of the chemicals on lists 1 and 2;

- A number of toxic chemicals that can be used as warfare agents.

The paper of the rolling text never blushed, but some negotiators probably did when it became manifest how loosely the word verification had been used and how little the diplomats and chemical weapon experts in fact knew about the chemical industry. Most of them had probably never seen a chemical factory from the inside. The proposed inspection procedures were tried out for the first time in 1986 in a plant in the Netherlands. This trial inspection indicated that verification of nonproduction would be possible, but also complicated. In 1988 the Soviet Union suggested that all countries that felt able to do so should hold a national trial inspection. On the basis of the results of these national trials, international trial inspections should be

Table 7.1 Regimes for Use of Chemicals

	Declaration	Routine Verification	Production Limits
List 1	yes	yes	1 metric ton
List 2	yes	yes	none
List 3	yes	no	none

held. About twenty countries conducted national trial inspections. If they did not always contribute much to refining the convention, they certainly helped to make national governments better aware of the problems involved. The inspections also stimulated contacts between government and industry.

In the original concept of Article VI—still in the rolling text at the beginning of 1990—verification of nonproduction was limited to facilities[21] that produce or use chemicals on list 2 in quantities above certain thresholds. In practice this would mean that about 90 percent of the routine verification effort would be directed at the sophisticated civil chemical industry of the West. More disquieting was that most plants that had the capability to produce warfare agents would not fall under the scope of these routine inspections. One obvious category of such plants includes those that produce or use the chemicals on list 3. Australia therefore suggested that these plants be brought under a mild inspection regime called spot checks.

This proposal would, however, still leave many relevant plants outside the scope of routine inspections. Some of the pharmaceutical or pesticide plants that were suspected of producing chemical warfare agents fell in that category. The problem was that most if not all chemical plants could, after minor or major adjustments, have some capability of producing chemical weapons. Because of the large variety of chemical plants and the diversity of chemical warfare agents, no clear and objective criterion could be devised to distinguish plants that are "really capable" from plants that are not.

The Federal Republic of Germany drew the only possible conclusion and in January 1988[22] boldly proposed to bring the whole chemical industry under a regime of routine ad hoc checks. The purpose of these checks would be to verify on a routine basis whether, at the time of the check, any chemicals on one of the lists were produced without being reported. The basis of these checks would be a register of all chemical plants. As so often was the case during these negotiations, the solution to the original problem raised a number of new problems. Chemical processing also takes place in industries that are usually not considered to be part of the chemical industry such as the electrotechnical industry, the nuclear industry, and the food industry. Should every such plant with a chemical processing capability fall under the regime of ad hoc checks? Would it be feasible to inspect such a large number of facilities on a random basis? Should some facilities have a larger chance of being inspected than others, and how would that be decided? What would happen if an inspection team found that undeclared production took place of a compound on list 2 or 3? To ascertain that the amount produced was below the threshold for declaration, a quantitative analysis would be required, but such an analysis would be much more intrusive than the ad hoc checks were supposed to be.

In March 1988, the Czechoslovakian chairman of working group A made an even more radical proposal.[23] The Technical Secretariat itself would have the right to request an ad hoc inspection. Such inspections were not to be limited to registered chemical plants, but could be requested anywhere, including places that might be suspected as chemical weapon storage facilities. This type of inspection came close to the concept of challenge inspections. The difference was that an ad hoc inspection was supposed to be a routine matter, whereas a challenge inspection would only take place in case of serious doubts about compliance. Another important difference was that challenge inspections could only be requested by states' parties[24] while ad hoc inspections could be requested by the Technical Secretariat. Several delegations believed that this would give too much power to the secretariat.

At the beginning of 1989 the United Kingdom therefore proposed to limit the right to request ad hoc inspections to the states parties. The number of inspections a party would be allowed to request in a year would be limited by quota. A limit would also be placed on the number of ad hoc inspections a party would have to allow. During 1989 intensive negotiations took place behind the scenes on a possible synthesis of the different ideas. Such a synthesis would possibly include the right of parties to request an ad hoc inspection, but be limited to registered chemical production facilities.

In the discussions with the chemical industry it became evident that the chemical industry would be little concerned by the prospect of inspections, as long as they felt assured that their commercial and technical secrets were not compromised. To give such assurance, in 1989 a special *Annex on the Protection of Confidential Information* was included in the rolling text.[25] In this annex, general principles for the handling of confidential information are set down, such as criteria for classification, and more specific measures, such as limiting access of inspectors to confidential information, measures to protect sensitive installations and procedures in case of breaches or alleged breaches of confidentiality.

Challenge Inspections

The draft convention that then-Vice President George Bush introduced in the Conference on Disarmament on April 18, 1984, mainly reflected well-known ideas that were shared by most of the Western countries. One article, Article X, was disturbingly new—disturbingly new because it was so radical that many delegations feared that it could never be acceptable for the Soviet Union and would, therefore, kill any prospect of agreement on a convention. The essence of Article X was that parties would be obliged to accept international inspections on short notice without a right of refusal.[26] Bush recognized that his proposal was unprecedented and would come at a price. But, as he stated, "an effective ban on chemical weapons requires this kind of 'open invitation' inspections. . . . We, our President, the United States Government, are willing to pay the price of such openness. The enormous value of an effective ban warrants our doing so."[27]

Then the tables were turned. The Soviet Union completely accepted the essence of the American proposal of 1984 and most, if not all, other countries seemed to be willing to do the same. The big question then was whether the United States would accept its own proposal. The outcome of the review of the American position, which began after the inauguration of President Bush, was still eagerly awaited at the start of 1990.

The crux of the matter is that any exception to the rule that everything should be open for challenge inspections creates a perfect loophole for violations. Up to 1984 nobody had dared to draw the logical conclusion that even—or especially—high security interests should not form an exception on this rule. The United States did have the courage to draw such a conclusion, although it should be added that nobody expected that the Soviet Union would accept it.

During 1989 the ad hoc committee made slow but substantial progress in developing a regime for challenge inspections. The leading thought is that these inspections can be requested anytime, anywhere, and can never be denied, but that measures could be taken to prevent their use for collecting sensitive information that has no relation to chemical weapons. Several types of measures are being considered. Such measures are included in the long inspection protocol that will regulate the conduct of inspections. One safeguard is the previous acceptance of international inspectors by the country to be inspected. The main answer to the question of improper use of challenge inspections, however, will probably not be found in setting general rules but in finding concrete solutions to individual problems.

Trial challenge inspections show that most military secrets are, upon close scrutiny, either not so secret or sensitive after all or can be easily exempted from inspection. An inspection team, for example, does not have to study a small electronic device very closely to make sure it is not a chemical weapon. Such a "managed conduct" of an inspection can, in the majority of cases, bring about an agreement on the conduct of a challenge inspection that is acceptable both for the inspection team and the challenged party. It is, however, impossible to preclude a situation in which the inspection team considers it necessary to see more than the challenged party likes to show. In such cases it is the inspection team that should have the final say. As indicated earlier, it is not yet certain whether the United States is willing to accept this position. Another point of debate is the role of the observer of the challenging party during the inspection. Should the observer have a decisive say in the conduct of the inspection and be allowed to get the same information as the inspection team (as the United States would probably like), or should the role be more limited? A more limited role would lessen the risk that a country would request a challenge inspection for espionage.

Prospects for Concluding the Negotiations

Most of the members of the delegations in Geneva agree that a successful conclusion is possible within two years' time. Although this has been said for at least six years, a more credible estimate is not available. As of summer 1990, it would seem that to reach the final goal of the negotiations four hurdles will have to be taken. The lowest hurdle might be the finalization of the text of the convention. This task should not be underestimated, but in view of the progress made so far it would seem possible to finalize the text within two years. Illustrative of the progress made since the summer of 1983[28] is the number of pages of the rolling text. This number ranged from 21[29] in 1983 to 135 in the beginning of 1990.

Conclusion of the negotiations is, however, not possible until the United States makes up its mind whether it really wants a convention[30] and is prepared to pay the necessary price. In view of the clear commitment of

President Bush, it could be expected that this hurdle might be taken in 1990. However, as soon as the United States delegation really starts pushing the negotiations forward, it has to be expected that other delegations will raise their voices. It is, for example, still not clear whether all other delegations will accept a regime of short-notice challenge inspections without right of refusal. Thanks to the position of the United States, some delegations could until now afford themselves the luxury of keeping silent.

When the text of the convention is agreed upon and finalized, the convention will still await its greatest challenge: Will all nations become party? Even without making the success of the convention formally dependent on the accession of the very last CW-capable state, it is clear that the goal will not be reached until countries such as Egypt, Israel, and Syria join the convention.

Notes

A note on sources:

The verbatim records of the *Conference on Disarmament* (CD) (numbered CD/PV...) and the documents submitted to the Conference (numbered CD/...) are published and distributed to specialized libraries all over the world. Both types of documents are included in the yearly report of the CD to the General Assembly of the United Nations, which is also distributed to major libraries.

The ad hoc Committee on Chemical Weapons does not keep records. The working papers submitted to it (identified as CD/CW/WP . . .) are generally not distributed. However, the Canadian Ministry for Foreign Affairs publishes a yearly compendium of both the verbatim records and documents of the CD on chemical weapons, and all the working papers of the ad hoc Committee.

The papers of the working groups of the ad hoc Committee are only distributed in the conference room. Most of them are only of interest to the diplomats involved and research scholars. Their numbering changes from year to year. During the 1988 session the documents of working group A were identified as CW/GA . . .

1. The proposal for the conference was probably also the result of the desire of the administration to deflect congressional pressure for sanctions against Iraq for its use of chemical weapons.
2. Paragraph 4 of the Declaration of the Paris Conference (published in *Arms Control Reporter*, p. 704. B.338.2).
3. Paragraph 3 of the Declaration of the Paris Conference (*Arms Control Reporter*, p. 704. B.338.2).
4. Until then, Iran had prevented consensus on the admission of Iraq as an obser-

ver. Iraq was admitted together with about twenty-five other states at the start of the 1989 spring session.

5. Admission of Israel was complicated because Israel did not request admission together with other states directly after the Paris Conference but a few months later. General agreement on the individual admission of Israel was difficult to obtain; Israel was finally admitted at the start of the 1990 spring session together with a large number of other observers.

6. Details are given in the final record of the Conference published by the Australian government.

7. Washington was in fact embarrassed by this commitment when chemical companies refused to sell the US government the precursor thionylchloride for its production of binary weapons (*Los Angeles Times*, March 28, 1990).

8. The Geneva-based Conference on Disarmament in all its manifestations should be clearly distinguished from the New York-based United Nations Disarmament Commission (UNDC). The UNDC comprises all member-states of the United Nations but does not have a mandate to negotiate arms control agreements.

9. The Conference on Disarmament has evolved from the Eighteen-Nation Committee on Disarmament (ENDC), which in 1961 was instituted as a replacement of the short-lived Ten-Nation Committee on Disarmament. The ENDC was composed of five (in practice four, because France chose not to take part) Western and five Eastern European delegations (like the Ten-Nation committee on Disarmament) plus eight neutral and nonaligned countries. The ENDC was in successive stages expanded to the current membership of forty countries (nine Western, nine Eastern, twenty-one neutral and nonaligned and China) and also renamed several times. In 1969 it became the Conference of the Committee on Disarmament, (CCD), in 1978 Committee on Disarmament (CD), and in 1984 Conference on Disarmament (CD).

10. This way of organizing its work is not only unique, but also inefficient, because few if any delegations are able to negotiate fruitfully for three consecutive months without any time for reflection and consultation at home. Furthermore, the period from August to February is not used efficiently.

11. The Soviet Union has declared that it possesses not more than 50,000 agent tons. The size of the US stockpile is estimated to be around 32,000 agent tons. No other countries have officially declared their chemical weapons, but no doubt exists that Iraq possesses them. It seems likely, however, that the United States and the Soviet Union account for more than 90 percent of current world stocks.

12. This definition should not be confused with the definition of chemicals whose production and use will be monitored on the basis of Article VI. The definition in Article II is based on the (subjective) intent and could therefore, at least in theory, relate to almost any existing chemical. The lists of chemicals in the Chemical Annex, on the other hand, are objectively defined on the basis of the potential use of a chemical for chemical warfare purposes.

13. Nevertheless, the amount of the most relevant super-toxic lethal chemicals that a party is allowed to produce for protective purposes is limited, as these chemicals are listed on schedule 1.

14. The rolling text is the draft-text of the convention that is updated every few months.

15. No generally agreed definition exists of a CW-capable state, but it seems reasonable to assume that every state with a civil chemical industry is capable, if it wants to, of producing one or more chemical warfare agents. The larger and more sophisticated the civil chemical industry, the easier it is to do so. The amount of time and money required to build up a militarily relevant quantity of chemical weapons should, however, not be underestimated. It has taken Iraq many years and large amounts of money to produce chemical weapons.

16. Abandoning the option to produce chemical weapons after the entry into force was, however, made conditional on the willingness of the Soviet Union to agree to the proposals President Bush presented at the General Assembly of the United Nations in September 1989.

17. Such limitations will only apply for the production of super-toxic lethal chemicals on list 1, not for those on list 2.

18. Hydrogen cyanide (HCN) and phosgene ($COCl_2$) are both used in very large quantities as precursors for civil products such as plastics. Both chemicals have, however, also been used as warfare agents. They are, therefore, both included in list 3.

19. Although some experts maintain that the word "key precursor" should be given a precisely circumscribed meaning, it generally does not mean more than an important precursor of chemical weapons.

20. Binary chemical weapons contain two canisters with the precursors of a warfare agent. The warfare agent is only formed when, during the trajectory of the weapon, the two precursors are brought together and react. The main advantage of binary weapons is that the risks involved in transport and storage are much smaller, because the lethal compound is not yet present.

21. Whether facility means a single production unit or a complete plant is still not completely clear.

22. This proposal was published as a document of the Conference of Disarmament, CD/791. A revised version was published on September 6, 1988 (CD/869).

23. In 1988 three working groups existed. Working group A dealt with the problem of verification of nonproduction. The proposal on ad hoc checks was introduced on March 21 as document CW/GA/6. It was revised on April 11 (CW/GA/6/rev.1).

24. According to the official position of the United States this right would even be limited to the five members of the Fact Finding Panel. It is, however, generally believed that the United States will eventually drop this position as few countries would be willing to allow the United States and the Soviet Union (who would both be permanent members of the panel) a right that they themselves would seldom have.

25. See the rolling text of CD/961, pp. 57-62.

26. Bush limited the scope in his speech to "military or government-owned or government-controlled facilities." This limitation lead to some misunderstandings. In fact, however, every possible relevant facility or location would fall within the scope of the open invitation.

27. See the verbatim records of the Conference on Disarmament of April 18, 1984, CD/PV.260.

28. Annex I of the Report of the Ad Hoc Working Group on Chemical Weapons to the Committee on Disarmament (CD/416 of August 22, 1983).

29. In reality the progress was even greater than appears, as the number 21 is

enhanced by the fact that it contains many alternative formulations and suggested additions. In latter editions of the rolling text such alternatives were normally no longer recorded.

30. No doubts exist about the sincerity of the commitment of President Bush to the accomplishment of a Chemical Weapons Convention. But within the US administration not everybody seems convinced that a worldwide ban on chemical weapons would be in the American interest. These doubts surface for example in the discussion about challenge inspections: On the one hand, it is claimed that the verification regime of the convention will not be sufficient, while, on the other hand, the challenge inspection regime proposed by then-Vice President Bush is claimed to be too intrusive. Another example is the US proposal to keep a security stock of chemical weapons until every CW-capable state has become party. This implies that the United States would like to be the last country to destroy its chemical weapons. This position has lead to allegations that the United States does not really want to do away with its chemical weapons.

8

International Negotiations on Environmental Issues: The Year Ahead

Andrew D. Sens

As A NEW DECADE BEGINS, international efforts to protect the global environment are at the forefront of the diplomatic agenda. Governments around the world increasingly recognize that responses are needed to a number of potentially serious environmental concerns. Governments also are aware that although national measures are essential, coordination and matching commitments from one's neighbors are important as well where regional or global issues are concerned.

Most of the negotiations are taking place in one of several multilateral environmental forums. Among these, the United Nations Environment Program (UNEP), headquartered in Nairobi, and the Economic Commission for Europe (ECE) in Geneva are very active, but other institutions are also closely involved with environmental matters. In addition, bilateral agreements can serve as models for others seeking to resolve similar problems.

Climate Change

The most dramatic new issue on the international scene is climate change. In 1988, representatives of the governments of nearly forty developed and developing countries met in Geneva to address this concern under the auspices of the UNEP and the World Meteorological Organization. An ad hoc working group, the Intergovernmental Panel on Climate Change (IPCC), was created with a mandate to prepare an interim report that would consider the science uncertainties, assess the likely economic and social impacts of climate change, and propose response strategies with which to moderate or ameliorate its effects. The costs and benefits ratio of the various strategies was also to be considered.

The IPCC process is now well advanced under a Swedish chairman. Three working groups—science questions chaired by the United Kingdom, effects headed by the Soviet Union, and response strategies led by the United States—were expected to submit a consolidated report to the Second World Climate Conference in Stockholm in October 1990. Although the IPCC report will not itself be a treaty, which is often the product of an international negotiation, it will be a policy statement that almost certainly will help shape national response strategies and stimulate the political will to take effective action.

The IPCC process has already contributed in this regard. Progress in the IPCC led President George Bush to announce in May 1989 that he would support negotiations leading to a framework convention[1] on climate change following completion of the IPCC report in September 1990. In December 1989 at the US-Soviet summit in Malta, the president proposed that the United States host the opening round of those talks. In accordance with another proposal of the president's, a meeting of senior officials was held in Washington in the spring of 1990 to review science and economic aspects of the climate issue.

Other Atmospheric Pollution Issues

On the subject of ozone-depleting substances, an interim science assessment panel convening in 1989 recommended that controls be tightened worldwide on emissions of ozone-depleting substances. The Montreal Protocol initially called for a 50-percent reduction in consumption and use of ozone-depleting chlorofluorocarbons (CFCs) by 1998; the IPCC recommended a complete phaseout. Negotiations among more than forty developed and developing countries produced amendments to the protocol to phase out most ozone-depleting substances by agreed dates. The United States took the lead in calling for a phaseout of CFCs by the year 2000 where safe substitutes are available and extension of the protocol's coverage to such other substances as halons, carbon tetrachloride, and methylchloroform. These negotiations also addressed how best to assist developing countries to limit their ozone-depleting emissions without constraining their economic development.

Acid rain negotiations between the United States and Canada were scheduled to begin in mid-1990 as soon as the US Congress passed amendments to the clean air act. The Canadians have for some time sought an air quality accord that would commit the United States to reduce acid rain precursor emissions by 50 percent, as Canada is doing. The acid rain element of the president's proposed package of amendments to the Clean Air Act, submitted to the Congress in July 1989, calls for a ten-million ton reduction in SO_2 emissions by the year 2000. In addition, by this same date, those industrial boilers amenable to cost-effective retrofit with low NO_x burners would be required to install such devices. Such a program would reduce NO_x emissions by two million tons.[2]

Negotiations are also under way or will begin soon on several other atmospheric pollution issues in the context of the Long-Range Transboundary Airborne Pollution Convention (LRTAP). The LRTAP Convention was concluded in 1979 under the auspices of the ECE, a body that includes Eastern and Western European governments in addition to the United States and Canada. Some of the more prominent of these atmospheric pollution issues to be addressed in the ECE include:

- *Volatile Organic Compounds (VOCs):*[3] Preparatory work by an ECE Working Group is intended to lead to a new protocol to the LRTAP to control emissions of VOCs. Formal negotiations began in Geneva in January 1990. They were expected to continue through 1991. Some delegations were seeking a percentage reduction in VOC emissions; others were urging a commitment to adopt economically feasible "best available control technologies." Others argue for controls based on limits on "loadings" that the environment can safely accept.

- *An Updated SO_2 Protocol:* A 1986 Protocol to the LRTAP commits parties to reduce sulphur dioxide emissions—a precursor to acid rain—by 30 percent by 1995. Several European members of the ECE believe a follow-on SO_2 protocol, perhaps with even stricter emissions limits, should be negotiated. Discussions of a new or renewed SO_2 protocol were expected to begin in Geneva in the fall of 1990 and to last at least eighteen months. The United States did not become a party to the 1986 protocol as it did not allow credit for prior actions to limit emissions. The differences between delegations in this case may be even more marked than with respect to VOCs.

Marine Pollution Concerns

The oceans produce important elements of the world's food supply. They also have an important effect on world climate, absorbing and recycling the products of atmospheric and terrestrial processes, particularly CO_2, the most important "greenhouse gas." A major regional agreement dealing with marine pollution issues is the Convention for the Protection of the Marine Environment signed in 1983 in Cartagena, Colombia, by most of the Caribbean countries and also by the United States. At the conclusion of the negotiations, participants adopted resolutions urging parties to the new convention to develop protocols establishing specially protected areas for wildlife and measures to regulate land-based sources of pollution. Steps are now under way to realize both objectives:

- *Specially Protected Areas for Wildlife:* Meetings of experts in St. Croix and Kingston in 1987 and 1988 produced a draft protocol text with relatively few brackets (i.e., disputed provisions.) A plenipotentiaries meeting concluded a final protocol for Kingston in January 1990. The United States has played an active role in developing this protocol.

- *Land-based Sources (LBS) of Pollution:* Informal discussions of experts have identified areas for further work, but a decision to begin formal meetings to negotiate an LBS protocol has not yet been taken. Given the importance to the health of coastal areas and the oceans of controlling LBS, there is considerable pressure from environmentalists and industry to move this process along in the near future. Two workshops hosted by the EPA are scheduled on this problem for late 1990.

Transboundary Movements of Hazardous Wastes

After two years of negotiations, a Convention to Control Transboundary Movements of Hazardous Wastes was opened for signature in Basel, Switzerland, on March 22, 1989. The United States signed the convention on March 22, 1990. Forty-six countries and the Commission of the European Community so far have signed the convention. UNEP's executive director predicts the necessary twenty ratifications to bring the convention into force will be achieved within two years.

Diplomatic representatives at the plenipotentiary conference that concluded the negotiations adopted two resolutions calling for further negotiations. The executive director was urged to establish an ad hoc working group to develop elements of a protocol to the convention on liability and compensation for damage resulting from the transboundary movement and disposal of hazardous and other wastes. This working group began its meetings in July 1990. The director was also asked to establish a technical working group to prepare draft guidelines on the environmentally sound management of wastes subject to the convention. The economic implications and technical complexity of both issues will require careful—and probably extensive—reviews. The guidelines are to be considered for adoption by the parties to the convention at their first meeting after the convention enters into force.

Maintaining Biological Diversity

The destruction of the world's forests in the interest of economic development threaten to reduce further the diversity of species on which much of agriculture, medicine, and industry depends. The loss of forests also contributes to the climate change problem. The United States and others have recently urged that the UNEP address the need for guidelines to prevent further erosion of the world's biological diversity. The International Union for the Conservation of Nature has taken a first step in preparing a draft text for governments' legal and policy experts to review. Meetings began in 1990 to review basic issues and explore elements of an agreement.

Economic Summits

The seven industrialized countries whose leaders meet annually at the Economic Summit (Canada, France, Great Britain, Italy, Japan, the United States, and West Germany) will be key players in the effort to respond to the environmental challenges of the 1990s and beyond. The seven account for a significant share of the polluting emissions that threaten the atmosphere, the runoff that threatens the oceans, and the hazardous wastes that pollute soil and ground waters if not managed in an environmentally sound manner. The Economic Seven also lead in producing the technologies and processes that can be applied to resolve many environmental problems. They can, as well, assist others with fewer resources to meet their obligations to the environment.

At the economic summits in Paris in July 1989 and at Houston in July 1990, a substantial part of the text of the final "Economic Declaration" dealt with environmental matters. Issues addressed range from climate change and ozone depletion to hazardous wastes, from the preservation of tropical forests and the maintenance of ample biological diversity to oil spill clean-up and controls on marine pollution.

The Economic Seven meeting in Houston gave particular focus to environmental issues of global concern and impetus to the process of developing balanced response strategies. In addition to a discussion of climate, ozone depletion, and the role of developing countries in protecting the environment, the participants indicated their willingness to begin negotiations on a global forest convention and called for a comprehensive strategy to address land-based sources of pollution.

The 1991 summit will again be preceded by important negotiations among "sherpas" who prepare their respective leaders for these meetings and seek to narrow, as much as possible, the inevitable differences in approaches to these issues. Each declaration is a significant indication of how much political will exists in each of the industrialized countries to deal with environmental challenges.

The 1992 Review Conference

The next major conference concentrating solely on environmental issues will be held in Brazil in 1992, twenty years after the first Conference on Environment and Development, which took place in Stockholm in 1972. Maurice Strong, former director of the UNEP, heads a thirty-nine-nation steering committee, and Tommy Koh, former ambassador of Singapore to the United States and the United Nations, heads a preparatory committee. An organizing meeting of the preparatory committee took place in New York in April 1990. A preparatory meeting was held in Nairobi in August 1990, and a further such meeting will take place in Geneva in spring 1991.

Other Activities

The UN General Assembly will discuss environmental issues at its fall 1990 session and review progress in organizing a major world conference on environment and development scheduled for 1992. The UNEP, the Organization for Economic Cooperation and Development, the International Maritime Organization, the Food and Agricultural Organization, and a number of other international agencies and organizations also are engaged actively in efforts to protect the environment. In working groups, experts meetings, and a variety of informal exchanges policies are reviewed, programs are harmonized, and commitments are proposed and accepted. These international negotiating sessions do not always produce dramatic new mechanisms or initiatives. They do, however, make an important contribution to our understanding of the environmental problems we face and our search for effective responses.

Comment

Global environmental issues may have risen to the top of the international agenda, but much work remains to be done. On many issues, additional scientific research and economic analysis are needed before response strategies can be chosen. Before such strategies can be implemented, hard decisions about resource trade-offs must be made. Developing effective solutions to global environmental concerns is going to be a time-consuming, difficult, and possibly costly challenge. Deferring decisions and ignoring the challenge risks unacceptable damage to the environment.

Notes

1. A framework convention is one that sets out general principles of cooperation and creates a mechanism for moving forward, possibly establishing commitments to exchange information, research, and coordinated action. In the case of climate changes, it would not normally set timetables or targets for reduced greenhouse gas emissions but leave those decisions to subsequent protocols to be concluded when justified by the science and effects research programs and cost/benefit analyses now under way. The 1986 Vienna Convention for the Protection of the Ozone Layer is an example of a framework convention. The 1987 Montreal Protocol on Substances that Deplete the

Ozone Layer is an example of an implementing protocol imposing specific obligations on parties to control emissions.

2. For an account of US-Canadian discussions on this sensitive issue, see William A. Nitze, "Acid Rain: A U.S. Policy Perspective," in Daniel McGraw, ed., *International Law and Pollution*, University of Pennsylvania Press (forthcoming).

3. Ground-level ozone, the major component of urban smog, is formed when volatile organic compounds mix with NO_x in the presence of sunlight. The major sources of VOCs are motor vehicles, large point sources—e.g., petroleum refineries—and small point sources such as bakeries, dry cleaners, and processes that use solvents. Urban smog is a contributor to public health problems.

9

Ozone Diplomacy

Richard Elliot Benedick

ON SEPTEMBER 16, 1987, representatives of countries from every region of the world reached an agreement unique in the annals of international diplomacy. In the Montreal Protocol on Substances that deplete the Ozone Layer, nations agreed to significantly reduce production of chemicals that can destroy the stratospheric ozone layer that protects life on earth from harmful ultraviolet radiation and can also change global climate.

The protocol was not a response to an environmental disaster such as Chernobyl, but rather preventative action on a global scale. That action, based at the time not on measurable evidence of ozone depletion or increased radiation but rather on scientific hypotheses, required an unprecedented amount of foresight. The links between causes and effects were not obvious: A perfume spray in Paris helps to destroy an invisible gas six to thirty miles above the earth, and thereby contributes to deaths from skin cancer and extinction of species half a world and several generations away.

The ozone protocol was only possible through an intimate collaboration between scientists and policymakers. Based as it was on continually evolving theories of atmospheric processes, on state-of-the-art computer models simulating the results of intricate chemical and physical reactions for decades into the future, and on satellite-, land- and rocket-based monitoring of remote gases measured in parts per trillion, the ozone treaty could not have occurred at an earlier point in human history.

Reprinted with permission from *Issues in Science and Technology*, Vol. 6, No. 1 (Fall 1989); copyright © 1989 by the National Academy of Sciences, Washington, DC.

Another noteworthy aspect of the Montreal Protocol was the negotiators' decision not to take the timid path of controlling through "best available technology"—the traditional accommodation to economic interests. Instead, the treaty boldly established firm target dates for emissions reductions, even though the technologies for accomplishing these goals did not yet exist.

The ozone protocol sounded a death knell for an important part of the international chemical industry, with implications for billions of dollars in investment and hundreds of thousands of jobs in related industries such as food, transportation, plastics, electronics, cosmetics, and health care. Here, as in many other areas, international economic competition clashed with the need for international environmental cooperation, but in this case concerns about the environment eventually carried the day.

Similar conflicts between economic and environmental imperatives are bound to arise in the future, as more and more environmental problems cross national boundaries and require international solutions. Furthermore, there will be a growing number of threats to the environment that, although not obvious or immediate, pose serious long-term dangers. So it is worth considering what factors contributed to the Montreal Protocol's success, and what lessons the negotiations might hold for future attempts to deal with similar situations.

Environmental Bombshells

In 1974, two theories were advanced that suggested potentially grave damage to the ozone layer. According to the first, chlorine in the atmosphere could continually destroy ozone for a period of decades: A single chlorine atom was capable, through a catalytic chain reaction, of eliminating tens of thousands of ozone molecules. The other theory postulated that man-made chlorofluorocarbons (CFCs) would break down in the presence of radiation in the stratosphere and release dangerously large quantities of chlorine.

These hypotheses were environmental bombshells. Production of CFCs had soared from 150,000 metric tons in 1960 to more than 800,000 metric tons in 1974, reflecting their broad usefulness: CFCs are chemically stable and vaporize at low temperatures, which make them excellent coolants in refrigerators and air conditioners and ideal as propellant gases in spray cans; they are good insulators; they are standard ingredients in the manufacture of such ubiquitous materials as styrofoam; and they are generally inexpensive to produce. The stability of CFCs means that, unlike other man-made gases, they are not chemically destroyed or rained out quickly in the lower atmosphere. Rather, they migrate slowly upward, remaining intact for decades. The halons, a related family of chemicals used in fire protection, were found to have similar properties.

Theories about the relationship between the ozone layer, chlorine, and CFCs stimulated tremendous activity in scientific and industrial circles. Although the chemical industry vigorously denied the validity of any linkage between the state of the ozone layer and their growing sales of CFCs, the US scientific community mounted a major research campaign that confirmed the fundamental validity of the chlorine-ozone hypotheses.

Although the theory was sound, making precise measurements of effects was not so easy—especially since growing concentrations of carbon dioxide and methane (originating at least in part from human activities) could greatly offset the projected chlorine impact, and nitrogen compounds could influence the reaction in either direction. Thus, in the years following the initial hypotheses, there were wide fluctuations in the predicted results of CFC emissions. Theoretical-model projections of global average ozone depletion fifty to one hundred years in the future began at about 13 percent in 1974, increased to 19 percent in 1979, and dropped to less than 5 percent in 1982-1983. For a time, these swings tended to diminish public concern over the urgency of the problem.

But consensus was soon to develop. In 1986, an assessment spearheaded by the US National Aeronautics and Space Administration (NASA) and sponsored by the United Nations Environment Programme, the World Meteorological Organization, and other agencies concluded that continued CFC emissions at the 1980 rate would reduce global average ozone by about 9 percent by the latter half of the next century, with much larger seasonal and latitudinal decreases. New measurements also indicated that accumulations of CFCs in the atmosphere had nearly doubled between 1975 and 1985, even though production of these chemicals had stagnated over the same period, illustrating the potential long-term danger from these substances.

On the basis of these figures and of projections of continuing, though moderate, CFC emissions, the US Environmental Protection Agency (EPA) estimated that in the United States alone there could be more than 150 million new cases of skin cancer among people currently alive and born by the year 2075, resulting in more than 3 million deaths. EPA also projected 18 million additional eye cataract cases in the United States for the same population. Other possible results of CFC emissions included damage to the human immune system, serious impacts on agriculture and fisheries, increased formation of urban smog, and warming of the global climate.

The Great Atlantic Divide

As scientists analyzed the effects of CFCs on the ozone layer and the resultant implications for human health and the environment, the United States and the European Community (EC)—comprising twelve sovereign nations—emerged as the principal protagonists in the diplomatic process that culminated in the Montreal Protocol. Despite their shared political, economic, and environmental orientations, the United States and the EC, which together accounted for 84 percent of world CFC output in 1974, differed over almost every issue at every step along the route to Montreal.

The US Congress held formal hearings on the ozone layer soon after the theories were published, which led in 1977 to ozone protection legislation that banned use of CFCs as aerosol propellants in all but essential applications. This affected nearly $3 billion worth of sales in a wide range of household and cosmetic products and rapidly reduced US production of CFCs for aerosols by 95 percent. The US action was paralleled by Canada (a small producer), Denmark, Finland, Norway, and Sweden (all nonproducing, importing countries).

In contrast, European parliaments (except for the German Bundestag) showed scant interest in CFCs. The EC delayed until 1980 and then enacted a 30-percent cutback in CFC aerosol use from 1976 levels and announced a decision not to increase production capacity.

These EC actions, however, were feeble compared to the US regulation. With respect to the 30-percent aerosol reduction, European sales of CFCs for this purpose had, by 1980, already declined by more than 28 percent from the 1976 peak year. Moreover, the EC two years later defined "production capacity" in a manner that would enable current output to increase by more than 60 percent. The capacity cap was therefore a painless move, supported by European industry, which gave the appearance of control while in reality permitting undiminished rates of expansion for at least two more decades.

Relative to the gross national product, EC production of CFCs was more than 50 percent higher than that of the United States. Aerosols, which had virtually disappeared in the United States, still comprised during the 1980s more than half of CFC sales within the European Community. The EC was also the CFC supplier to the rest of the world, particularly the growing markets in developing countries. EC exports rose by 43 percent from 1976 to 1985 and averaged almost one-third of its production, whereas the United States consumed virtually all it produced.

These developments were reflected in growing differences in attitude between the chemical industries on the two sides of the Atlantic. Shaken by the force of public reaction in the 1970s over the threat to the ozone layer, American producers had quickly developed substitutes for CFCs in spray cans. US chemical companies were also constantly aware of their vulnerability in the environmentally charged domestic atmosphere. In their public pronouncements, industry spokespersons took the ozone problem with growing seriousness and appeared increasingly concerned about its effect on companies' reputations. The threat of a patchwork of state laws—legislation against CFCs was actually introduced or passed by California, Michigan, Minnesota, New York, Oregon, and others—made US industry not only resigned to but even publicly in favor of federal controls, which would at least be uniform and therefore less disruptive.

There was also resentment among American producers that their European rivals had escaped meaningful controls. A constant theme in the US chemical industry during the 1980s was the need to have a "level playing field"—to avoid recurrence of unilateral US regulatory action that was not followed by the other major producers.

In September 1986, the Alliance for Responsible CFC Policy, a coalition of about 500 US producer and user companies, issued a pivotal statement. Following the obligatory reiteration of industry's position that CFCs posed no immediate threat to human health or the environment, the Alliance spokesman declared that "large future increases in . . . CFCs . . . would be unacceptable to future generations," and that it would be "inconsistent with [industry] goals . . . to ignore the potential for risk to those future generations." Thus, only three months before the protocol negotiations began, US industry announced its support for new international controls on CFCs.

This unexpected policy change, which came after much soul-searching within US industry, aroused consternation in Europe. The British and French had been suspicious all along that the United States was using an environmental scare to cloak commercial motivations. Now, some Europeans surmised (incorrectly) that the United States wanted CFC controls because they had substitute products on the shelf with which to enter the profitable EC export markets.

For its part, EC industry's primary objective was to preserve its dominance and to avoid the costs of switching to alternative products for as long as possible. Taking advantage of public indifference and political skepticism, European industrial leaders were able to persuade most EC governments that substitutes for CFCs were neither feasible nor necessary—despite the demonstrated US success in marketing alternative spray propellants. Industry statements were echoed in official EC pronouncements that continually stressed the scientific uncertainties, the impossibility of finding effective substitutes, and the adverse effects of regulations on European living standards.

Self-serving Positions

Although the United States and the EC were the major CFC producers, the ozone problem threatened the entire world and therefore could be solved only through international agreement. Filling a catalytic role for such an agreement became the mission of a small and hitherto little-publicized United Nations agency, the UN Environment Programme (UNEP). Under the dynamic leadership of its executive director, Mostafa Tolba, an Egyptian scientist, UNEP soon made ozone protection a top priority. The agency worked to inform governments and world public opinion about the danger to the ozone layer, it provided a nonpoliticized international forum for the negotiations, and it was a driving force behind the consensus that was eventually reached.

In January 1982, representatives of twenty-four countries met in Stockholm under UNEP auspices to decide on a "Global Framework Convention for the Protection of the Ozone Layer." The following year a group of countries, including Canada, the Nordic nations, Switzerland, and the United States, proposed a worldwide ban on "nonessential" uses of CFCs in spray cans, pointing out that the United States and others had already demonstrated that alternatives to CFC sprays were technically and economically feasible. In late 1984, the EC countered with a proposal for alternative controls that would prohibit new additions to CFC production capacity.

Each side was backing a protocol that would require no new controls for itself, but considerable adjustment for the other. The United States had already imposed a ban on nonessential uses of CFCs, but US chemical companies were operating at close to their capacity and thus would suffer under a production cap. Their European counterparts, on the other hand, had substantial underutilized capacity and could expand CFC production at current rates for another twenty years before hitting the cap.

Despite these disagreements, by March 1985 the negotiators had drafted all elements of a protocol for CFC reductions except the crucial control provisions. Meeting in Vienna, all major producers except Japan signed an interim agreement—the Vienna Convention on Protection of the Ozone Layer—which promoted international monitoring, research, and exchange of data and provided the framework for eventual protocols to control ozone-modifying substances. Over strong objections from European industry representatives, the Vienna Conference passed a separate resolution that called upon UNEP to continue work on a CFC protocol with a target for adoption in 1987.

As formal negotiations began in December 1986, governments were divided into three camps. Despite growing internal strains, the EC followed the European industry line and mirrored the views of Italy, France, and the UK. The EC continued to advocate the kind of production capacity cap it had favored during the meetings leading up to the Vienna Convention. Because the scientific models showed there would be at least two decades before any significant ozone depletion would occur, EC negotiators felt there was time to delay production cuts and wait for more evidence. This perspective was initially shared by Japan and the Soviet Union.

Opposing this view were Canada, Finland, New Zealand, Norway, Sweden, Switzerland, and the United States, all favoring stronger new controls. They argued that action needed to be taken well before critical levels of chlorine accumulated: The long atmospheric lifetimes of these compounds meant that future ozone depletion stemming from past and current production was inevitable, and the process could not suddenly be turned off like a faucet. These countries were concerned about the health and environmental risks of delay and maintained that postponing meaningful action could necessitate draconian and thus costlier measures later on.

A third group of active participants, including Australia, Austria, and a number of Third World countries, were initially uncommitted, but as the arguments developed they moved toward favoring more, rather than less, stringent regulations.

Complicating the entire process was the fact that the EC had to achieve internal consensus among its member countries before (and during) international negotiations, which tended to make it a difficult and inflexible negotiating partner. There were deep divisions within the EC on the ozone issue. Belgium, Denmark, Germany, and the Netherlands were increasingly disposed toward strong CFC controls; but of these, only Germany was a major producer. The UK, supported by France and Italy—all large producers—resisted every step of the way. Greece, Ireland, Luxembourg, Portugal, and Spain did not even participate in most of the negotiations.

Another key factor was the EC presidency, which automatically rotates every six months among the member countries. Progress in the protocol negotiations occurred only after Belgium replaced the UK in the presidency in January 1987. Britain remained in the EC "troika" (past, present, and future presidents), which participated in closed meetings of key delegation heads during the negotiations, but only until the presidency rotated in July 1987. At that point, the troika included Belgium, Denmark, and Germany, all favoring stringent controls, and it may well be that this constellation, in the right place at the right time, influenced ultimate EC acceptance of considerably stronger measures than it had originally endorsed.

Deep Cuts

One of the central disputes of the negotiations was whether restrictions would be placed on the production or consumption of the substances covered by the agreement. This issue, though seemingly arcane, was one of the most important and most difficult to resolve.

The EC pushed for controls on production, arguing that it was simpler to control output since there were only a small number of producing countries, whereas there were thousands of consuming industries and countless points of consumption. But Canada, the United States, and others who favored a consumption-related formula pointed out that controlling production would confer unusual advantages on the EC while particularly prejudicing importing nations, including the developing countries. Since about a third of EC output was exported and there were no other exporters in the picture, a production limit essentially locked in the EC export markets. The only way the United States or others could supply those markets would be to decrease their domestic consumption.

The EC, with no viable competitors, would thus have a virtual monopoly. If European domestic consumption should rise, the EC could cut back its exports, leaving the current importing countries, with no recourse to other suppliers, to bear the brunt of CFC reductions. Because of this vulnerability, there would be incentives for importing countries to remain outside the treaty and build their own CFC facilities.

To meet the valid EC argument about controlling multiple consumption points, the United States and its allies came up with an ingenious solution: A limit would be placed on production *plus* imports *minus* exports to other Montreal Protocol signatories. This "adjusted production" formula eliminated any monopoly based on current export positions, in that producing countries could raise production for exports to protocol parties without having to cut their own domestic consumption. Only exports to nonparties would have to come out of domestic consumption, and this would be an added incentive for importing countries to join the protocol, lest they lose access to supplies. Additionally, an importing signatory whose traditional supplier raised prices excessively or refused to export could either produce on its own or turn to another producer country.

The single most contentious issue was the timing and extent of reductions. Again, the EC and the United States were the principal opponents. The United States originally called for a freeze to be followed by three phases of progressively more stringent reductions, all the way up to a possible 95-percent cut. But even late into the negotiations, the EC was reluctant to consider reductions beyond 10 to 20 percent.

The United States and others rejected this as inadequate. In fact, Germany, which had become increasingly concerned over the ozone problem, was already planning an independent 50-percent reduction, and early in 1987 it made urgent appeals to the other EC members also to accept deep reductions. Meanwhile, new scientific research was demonstrating that all of the control strategies under consideration would result in some degree of ozone depletion, the extent of which would depend on the stringency of international regulation. These developments helped garner support for deep cuts.

(An interesting sideshow during the negotiations was the attempt by some antiregulatory ideologues within the Reagan administration to overturn or weaken the US position by reopening basic questions about the science and possible impacts of ozone depletion. These efforts, which did not even have support from most of American industry, were effectively countered by the combined efforts of the Department of State, EPA, and the Council of Economic Advisors, among other agencies. The issue went for decision to the president, who reaffirmed the basic elements of the US drive for strong international regulation of CFCs and halons.)

The turning point in the negotiations came when Mostafa Tolba, head of UNEP, began to play a central role. He personally proposed a freeze by 1990, followed by successive 20-percent reductions every two years down to a complete phaseout, and he pressed for deep cuts during informal consultations with heads of key delegations.

Ultimately, even the most reluctant parties—the EC, Japan, and the Soviet Union—agreed to a 50-percent decrease. The treaty as signed stipulated an initial 20-percent reduction from the 1986 level of CFCs, followed by 30 percent. Halons were frozen at 1986 levels, pending further research. And one innovative provision—that these reductions were to be made on specific dates regardless of when the treaty should enter into force—removed any temptation to stall enactment of the protocol in the hopes of delaying cuts, and also provided industry with dates upon which to base its planning.

Negotiators at Montreal also faced the difficult task of encouraging developing countries to participate in the treaty. Per capita consumption of CFCs in those countries was tiny in comparison to that of the industrialized world, but their domestic consumption requirements—for refrigeration, for example—were growing, and CFC technology is relatively easy to obtain. The protocol thus had to meet their needs during a transition period while substitutes were being developed, and it had to discourage them from becoming major new sources of CFC emissions.

A formula was developed whereby developing countries would be permitted a ten-year grace period before they had to comply with the control provisions. During this time they could increase their consumption up to an annual level of 0.3 kilogram per capita—approximately one-third of the 1986 level prevailing in industrialized countries. It was felt that the realistic prospects of growth in CFC use to these levels in the developing countries was not great, as they would not want to invest in a technology that was environmentally detrimental and would soon be obsolete.

A Precedent-Setting Model

There was no single prime cause for the success at Montreal. Rather, it was a combination of key factors and events that made the agreement possible. Analysis of these elements offers insights into a possible methodology for dealing with other global issues, such as climate change, on an international level.

First, the ozone history demonstrates the importance of building scientific consensus by mobilizing the most knowledgeable scientists and the most advanced technological resources in a cooperative international effort. The development of a commonly accepted body of data and analysis, and the narrowing of the ranges of uncertainty, were instrumental in facilitating a political consensus among negotiating parties who were initially far apart in their positions.

In this process, close collaboration between scientists and government policymakers was crucial. This synergy contributed to the irresistible logic of the American position on ozone, and greatly strengthened the persuasiveness of US negotiators. The US government provided substantial financial resources for the necessary scientific research, and US policymakers paid attention to the results.

Second, public opinion must be adequately informed in order to mobilize the political will of nations. Here again, individual scientists and national academies have a substantial role, but their findings must be translated and disseminated. International organizations such as the United Nations Environment Programme (UNEP) and the World Meteorological Organization, through publications and other activities, undertook major educational efforts on the ozone issue. Individual governments—the United States, Canada, Germany, and the Nordic states—were also particularly active in informing their own and other countries' publics. Legislative hearings can be important for airing scientific opinion and analyzing policy alternatives: The US Congress held a number of public hearings on ozone and climate change during 1987 and 1988, and the German Bundestag convened a special commission on atmospheric issues that received well-publicized testimony from many scientists.

Third, it is useful to disaggregate a complex problem. Climate change, for example, has so many aspects that it is impossible to deal with everything at once. The concept of an initial framework agreement, similar to the 1985 Vienna Convention on the Protection of the Ozone Layer, is a useful model: It permits governments to agree in principle that a problem exists, and to launch coordinated scientific research to help guide policy. The next step—corresponding to the Montreal treaty—would be individual implementing protocols on specific aspects of the problem. It is worth noting that the ozone accord is itself an example of a partial solution to a global warming, since CFCs may contribute 20 percent or more of the heat-trapping effect.

Fourth, the mediating function of an international organization can be critical. UNEP's catalytic role in the events leading up to the ozone agreement has obvious implications for the future. In the information-gathering and consensus-building stages, and during the negotiations themselves, UNEP was indispensable—and it will undoubtedly be so again in the protocol implementation phase. A great deal of the credit for the treaty should go to the personal efforts of the executive director of UNEP, Dr. Mostafa Tolba, who was reelected in 1988 for another four-year term. Tolba's strong presence was a major factor, commanding respect from all sides for his commitment and his sensitivity to national interests.

It was UNEP, encouraging Third World governments that might otherwise have had little desire to participate in the process, that made the protocol truly global in scope. UNEP provided an objective international forum, free of irrelevant and time-consuming debates on extraneous political issues that have often marred the work of other UN bodies. It was, in short, the very model of how a UN agency should operate in a complex international negotiation.

Fifth, an individual country's commitment and policies can have a profound influence on the course of an international negotiation. The road to consensus in a democratic society is not always smooth, as the US experience illustrated. But US leadership in the ozone negotiations turned out to be a determining factor. The government's many scientific and diplomatic initiatives—reinforced by actions of the Congress, environmental groups, and industry—were crucial in achieving the Montreal accord. Within the European Community, the ascendancy of Germany toward the end of the process was a significant factor.

A sixth and final lesson from Montreal derives from the protocol itself—a dynamic and flexible instrument. Based on periodic scientific, economic, and technical assessments, the treaty can be adapted to evolving conditions. There are even provisions for emergency meetings of parties in case of unexpected and fast-breaking developments.

Many of the treaty's provisions represent creative resolutions of complicated equity and technical problems, which can point the way for future protocols: a trigger mechanism for entry into force, fixed target dates for the reductions, a process for reopening the timetable and reduction goals, transitional provisions for developing countries, two-stage voting to reflect large stakeholder's interests, and its use of trade restrictions as a disincentive to nonparties.

Montreal was not a radical treaty. It tried to distribute economic burdens fairly, and it was sensitive to special situations. Perhaps most important, the protocol was not a static solution; it is an ongoing process. For all of this, it should prove to be a lasting and precedent-setting model for international cooperation.

Basis for Optimism

Science is demonstrating that this planet is more vulnerable than had previously been thought. For example, the Antarctic ozone hole discovered in 1985 made it clear that the atmosphere, upon which all life depends, is capable of surprises: There is a potential for large and unexpected change. The international community can no longer pretend that nothing is happening, or that the planet will somehow automatically adjust itself to the billions of tons of man-made pollutants to which it is annually subjected.

But now there is some basis for optimism. In September 1987, twenty-four countries signed the Montreal Protocol on Substances that Deplete the Ozone Layer; many other countries added their signatures over the ensuing months. Six months later, in a rare display of unanimity, the US Senate approved the protocol by a vote of 83-0, and President Reagan promptly signed the ratification instrument, making the United States the second nation to ratify (after Mexico).

The treaty entered into force on January 1, 1989. By the time of the First Meeting of the Parties, held in Helsinki, May 2-5, 1989, thirty-six countries, accounting for about 85 percent of global consumption of CFCs and halons, had ratified it. Even now, under the farsighted process established by the negotiations, governments are actively considering whether to strengthen the protocol's control provisions on the basis of more recent scientific evidence concerning the impact of CFCs and halons on the ozone layer.

The Montreal Protocol stands as a landmark—a symbol both of fundamental changes in the kinds of problems facing the modern world and of the way the international community can address those problems. Mostafa Tolba has described it as "the beginning of a new era of environmental statesmanship." But the protocol may also have relevance for dealing with other common dangers, including national rivalries and war. The ozone treaty reflects a realization that nations must work together in the face of global threats, and that if some major actors do not participate, the efforts of others will be vitiated.

In the realm of international relations, there will always be uncertainties—political, economic, scientific, psychological. The protocol's greatest significance may be its demonstration that the international community is capable of undertaking complicated cooperative actions in the real world of ambiguity and imperfect knowledge. The Montreal Protocol can be a hopeful paradigm of an evolving global diplomacy, one wherein sovereign nations find ways to accept common responsibility for stewardship of the planet and for the security of generations to come.

Recommended Reading

Benedick, Richard E., *Ozone Diplomacy: New Directions in Safeguarding the Planet.* World Wildlife Fund/Conservation Foundation and the Institute for the Study of Diplomacy, Georgetown University. Cambridge, MA: Harvard University Press, 1991.

Miller, A.S., and I.M. Mintzer, *The Sky Is the Limit.* Washington, DC: World Resources Institute, 1986.

Rowland, F.S., "A Threat to Earth's Protective Shield," *EPA Journal* 12, No. 10 (December 1986).

Solomon, Susan, "The Mystery of the Ozone Hole," *Reviews of Geophysics* 26, No. 1 (February 1988).

United Nations Environment Programme, *The Ozone Layer.* UNEP/GEMS Environment Library No. 2, Nairobi, 1987.

Watson, R.J., F.S. Rowland, and J. Gille, *Ozone Trends Panel, Executive Summary.* Washington, DC: NASA, March 1988.

World Meteorological Organization, *Atmospheric Ozone 1985.* Geneva: WMO, 1986 (3 volumes).

10

Antarctic Treaty Diplomacy: Problems, Prospects, and Policy Implications

Christopher C. Joyner

MAJOR INTERNATIONAL DEVELOPMENTS affected the progress of Antarctic diplomacy during 1989. For one, the regime that had been painstakingly negotiated to regulate Antarctic mineral activities was scuttled by two of the very governments that had worked in good faith for six years to attain its promulgation. Second, the Fifteenth Antarctic Treaty Consultative Party Meeting convened in Paris in October to consider several factors relating to future environmental protection in Antarctica. Also, the Eighth Meeting of the Commission of the Convention for the Conservation of Antarctic Living Marine Resources, which met in Hobart, Tasmania, in November to deliberate and set conservation measures in the Southern Ocean, held direct policy relevance for the Antarctic.

This chapter assesses the legal, political, and policy implications of these developments for the course of diplomacy that governs activities in the Antarctic. At the outset, it is important to realize that the Antarctic region, which covers one-tenth of the earth's surface, is administered by a special series of international agreements. This arrangement of treaties, known as the Antarctic Treaty System, supplies the main conduits through which Antarctic diplomacy is channeled and policy for the region is formulated and set.

During 1989-1990, the author served as a guest investigator with the Marine Policy Center at the Woods Hole Oceanographic Institution. WHOI Contribution No. 7395.

The Antarctic Treaty System

Administration of the area south of 60° South Latitude during 1989 and 1990 continued under the legal framework set out by the 1959 Antarctic Treaty.[1] Since coming into force nearly three decades ago, the treaty has grown into a multifaceted international regime. By 1990 this regime, known as the Antarctic Treaty System, had evolved into five major components: the Antarctic Treaty itself, an agreement for conserving Antarctic fauna and flora, a convention for conserving Antarctic seals, a convention for conserving Antarctic living marine resources, and a convention for regulating development of Antarctic minerals. These special elements of the Antarctic Treaty System experienced important changes—and in some cases, serious stresses and strains—during the past year.

The Antarctic Treaty represents a hallmark achievement in modern diplomacy: An entire continent and its circumpolar waters are reserved for peaceful uses only; freedom of scientific investigation is guaranteed for the entire region. The preeminent purpose of the treaty is well expressed in its preamble: "It is in the interest of all mankind that Antarctica shall continue forever to be used exclusively for peaceful purposes and shall not become the scene or object of international discord." For thirty years, the Antarctic Treaty has successfully accomplished that chief ambition.

International diplomacy for the frozen south continues to be guided by provisions in the treaty. Article I provides for the peaceful use of Antarctica, with prohibitions placed on any activities of a military nature. Article II ensures the freedom of scientific investigation and international cooperation. In related fashion, Article III promotes the free exchange and availability of operations, plans, scientific results, and personnel. Article IV is critical for accommodating the politically sensitive question regarding national sovereignty and the lawfulness of claims to the continent.

Seven states—Argentina, Australia, Chile, France, New Zealand, Norway, and the United Kingdom—currently assert claims to parts of Antarctica. (See Figure 10.1.) Article IV of the treaty "freezes" the claims situation so that it will not obstruct cooperation within the treaty framework, especially with other states that do not recognize the legitimacy of those claims. This provision guarantees that prior claims, or rights to claims, are not renounced; simultaneously, Article IV prohibits any new claims or assertions of national activities during the treaty's duration from being made as a basis for substantiation of past or future claims. Article V prohibits nuclear explosions and the disposal of radioactive waste material in the Antarctic.

157

Figure 10.1 Antarctica: Claims and Jurisdictions in the Southern Ocean

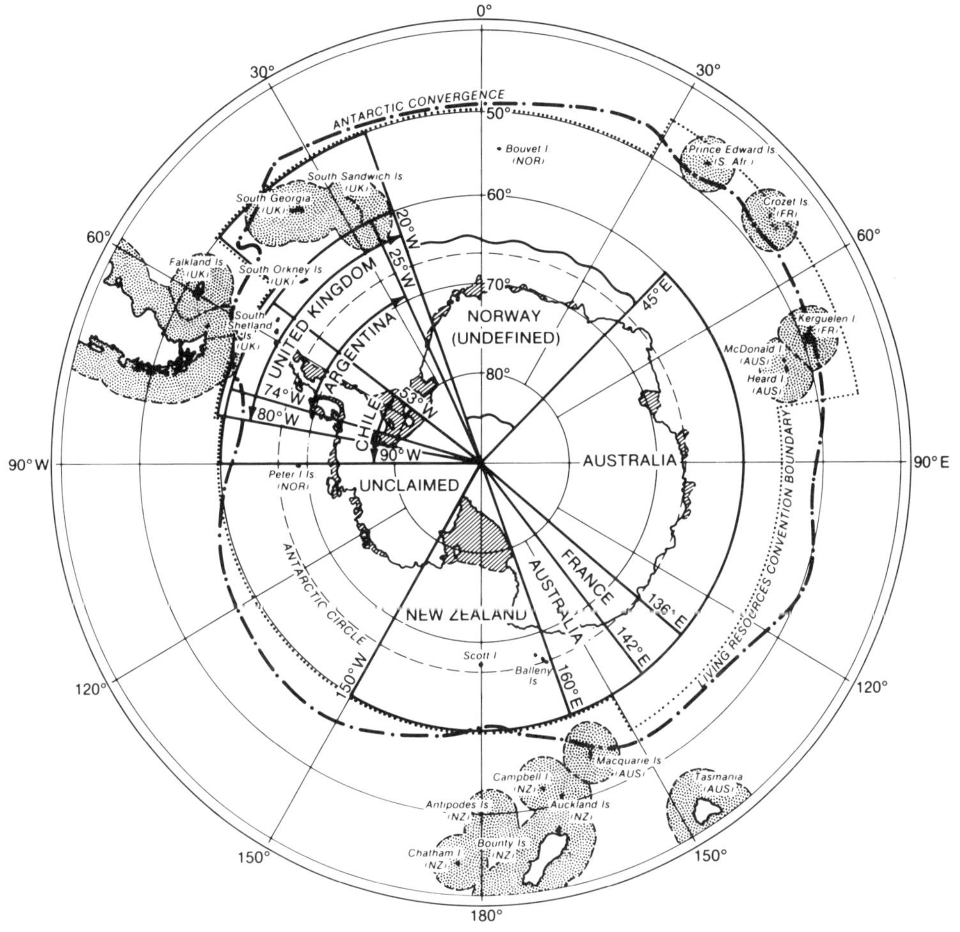

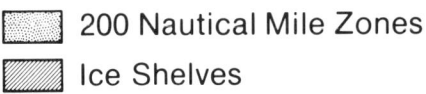

200 Nautical Mile Zones
Ice Shelves

© Christopher C. Joyner
Woods Hole Oceanographic Institution, 1987

Article VI establishes the treaty's jurisdictional application to all areas south of 60° South Latitude without prejudice to high-seas rights under international law. Article VII guarantees open, unannounced on-site inspection of any state's Antarctic operations by any other state party to the treaty. Article X mandates that each party should ensure that no one engages in any activities in the Antarctic that are contrary to the principles and purposes of the treaty. Finally, Article XI sets out dispute settlement procedures, including resort to the International Court of Justice.

A common misunderstanding is that the Antarctic Treaty expires in 1991. No termination date is set out in the treaty. What is stipulated, however, is of signal importance to the future of the Antarctic Treaty System.

As provided for in Article XII, paragraph 2, of the Antarctic Treaty, after the expiration of thirty years from the date that instrument entered into force—after June 23, 1991—any consultative party can request—and perforce require—the convening of a special review conference. Put simply, any of the current twenty-five Antarctic Treaty Consultative Parties (ATCPs) could require such a conference, not just one of the original twelve in 1959. Moreover, all contracting parties, not only those in the consultative group, would be permitted to participate in the conference. As set out in Article XII, this special review conference could amend the Antarctic Treaty by a simple majority of all parties present, including a majority of consultative parties at the conference. Entry into force of any proposed amendments would require the unanimous consent of all consultative parties. The critical concern at stake is that during such a review conference certain amendments might be proposed that could undo or derail the treaty's purposes or procedures that have worked so well for thirty years.

During the 1980s, concern about such a review conference centered on the new entrants into the consultative party group—especially India, the People's Republic of China, and Brazil—and the prospect that as leaders of the Third World they might seek to have Antarctica declared part of the common heritage of mankind. Over the past decade that apprehension has diminished. What makes the possibility of such a review conference particularly worrisome today is that for the first time since 1959 serious diplomatic tensions have surfaced within the ATCP membership. Contention centers on the minerals convention as an "either or" proposition: Either adopt the minerals regime or protect the environment. The key to resolving this situation will rest in constructing a comprehensive environmental protection regime that aims to conserve the Antarctic by placing a moratorium on minerals and hydrocarbons development, but retains the Wellington

Convention as a fail-safe mechanism should the moratorium break down.

In mid-1990, convention of a review conference for any reason by a consultative party does not appear in the offing. The national interests of consultative parties are still better served by the present system, in spite of new intragroup pressures and frictions. Even so, given the swing of recent Antarctic diplomatic events, the likelihood of convening such a conference should not be casually dismissed. The possibility for requiring a review conference does not expire with the end of 1991. After that year, it becomes a persistent contingency—one that the consultative parties cannot help but keep in mind throughout their intragroup negotiations in the future.

The group established by the Antarctic Treaty to make policy for the region, the ATCPs, has more than doubled in membership since the treaty came into force. Twelve states were original members of the treaty—Argentina, Australia, Belgium, Chile, France, Japan, New Zealand, Norway, South Africa, Soviet Union, United Kingdom, and the United States. Since the treaty's inception, thirteen new members have been granted ATCP status and participate as equals in decision-making by consensus: Poland in 1977, the Federal Republic of Germany in 1981, Brazil in 1983, India in 1983, the People's Republic of China in 1985, Uruguay in 1985, Italy in 1987, German Democratic Republic in 1987, Spain in 1988, Sweden in 1988, Finland in 1989, Peru in 1989, and the Republic of Korea in 1989. These states meet biennially to set recommended policy for activities within the Antarctic Treaty area for the membership. The consultative parties have also adopted nearly 200 policy "recommendations" (more accurately, rules) that pertain to activities in the Antarctic and cover a broad range of issues from the environment, meteorology, and agenda-setting to logistics, tourism, transportation, and telecommunications. In addition, there are fourteen states that are "nonconsultative" parties to the Antarctic Treaty. These states have acceded to and are obligated by the treaty, but have either not sought or yet attained consultative party status.[2]

The first instrument added to the Antarctic Treaty, the Agreed Measures on the Conservation of Antarctic Fauna and Flora, came in 1964 as Recommendation III-8.[3] The Agreed Measures are intended to protect native mammals, birds, and plant life on the continent, to prohibit the introduction of nonindigenous flora and fauna into the region, and to prevent marine pollution near the coast and ice shelves.

The Convention for the Conservation of Antarctic Seals is the second major instrument of the Antarctic Treaty System.[4] The seals convention, promulgated in 1972, entered into force in 1978 and strives to protect six specified species of Antarctic seals from unrestricted commercial exploitation.

The Convention on the Conservation of Antarctic Marine Living Resources (CCAMLR),[5] the third facet of the Antarctic Treaty System, was negotiated in 1980 and entered into force in 1982. The CCAMLR was negotiated to foster preservation of Antarctic marine living resources, including fish, crustaceans (krill, for example), creatures on the continental shelf, and bird life.

Though currently not in force, the Convention on the Regulation of Antarctic Mineral Resource Activities (CRAMRA) was also negotiated during the 1980s with the expectation that it would become part of the Antarctic Treaty System.[6] Opened for signature in November 1988, CRAMRA was designed to regulate minerals resource activities on and around the Antarctic continent. Progress toward entry into force of this convention, however, was stymied in 1989 by certain diplomatic developments. Just how much CRAMRA will eventually contribute to the Antarctic Treaty System has consequently been cast into serious doubt. Significantly, it is the minerals issue and conflicting national priorities within the consultative party group that has come to dominate considerations affecting Antarctic diplomacy during 1989 and into 1990.

The Antarctic Minerals Regime

The sensitive, salient issue of whether to develop mineral resources on the continent provoked a major development for Antarctic diplomacy in 1989. By way of background, from 1982 through 1988 the ATCPs convened in numerous negotiations aimed at producing a special regime to regulate the prospecting, exploration, and exploitation of mineral resources in the Antarctic, if ever these activities should occur there. Agreement came in June 1988 on the text for a new minerals treaty, and, in November 1988, the CRAMRA was opened for signature in Wellington, New Zealand.[7]

The Wellington Minerals Convention is an impressive document, containing sixty-seven articles and an annex for an arbitral tribunal. The convention is not a detailed mining code. Rather, it creates a regulatory framework for mineral activities. Four new institutions would comprise the CRAMRA regime:

- An Antarctic Minerals Commission would be the forum for making executive policy decisions. The commission would set rules and designate through consensus any areas to be opened for exploration and development.

- A special meeting of states' parties, open to all parties to the Antarctic Treaty, could give advice to the commission on any decision to open an area.

- An advisory committee would advise the commission and regulatory committees on matters requiring scientific, technical, and environmental expertise about Antarctic mineral activities. Although not a decision-making body with binding powers, the advisory committee was created to provide special opportunities for consultation and cooperation.

- Regulatory committees would be established for each geographic area designated by the commission for possible minerals exploration and development activities. These mechanisms are expected to play a central role in the regime.

CRAMRA allocates broad powers to the regulatory committees, including approval of applications for exploration and development permits, approval of management schemes—the contracts between operators and the convention's regulatory authority—as well as inspection and the power to suspend minerals activities in an area. Establishment of a secretariat for CRAMRA would also seem desirable to coordinate bureaucratic affairs for managing the regulation of minerals activities on the continent.[8]

Notwithstanding negotiation of CRAMRA in 1988, political circumstances pertaining to that agreement severely aggravated diplomatic relations among the ATCPs over the next year. On May 22, 1989, Prime Minister Robert Hawke of Australia announced that his government would not sign the Wellington Convention. The Hawke government instead declared its intention to negotiate a comprehensive environmental protection convention and establish Antarctica as an international wilderness preserve (or world park area), wherein all mining and oil drilling activities would be prohibited.[9] This decision effectively torpedoed the Wellington Minerals Convention because Article 62 of that instrument requires that all claimant states must be parties for it to enter into force. Australia, of course, is a claimant state and actually asserts the largest territorial claim in Antarctica.

Why did Australia abruptly decide to reverse course in its Antarctic minerals policy? That the Australian cabinet clearly was influenced by four reported environmental disasters that occurred in polar waters in 1989 is one explanation. On January 28, 1989, the Argentine supply ship *Bahia Paraiso* hit rocks offshore near the US Palmer Research Station on the Antarctic Peninsula. Some 250,000 gallons of diesel fuel leaked into the sea, killing thousands of krill, scores of penguins and other marine birds, and ruining several scientific projects along the coast.[10] On February 7, news of another Antarctic accident was reported. The British resupply ship *HMS Endurance* hit an iceberg four feet below its waterline near Deception Island. Photographic evidence by Argentine scientists of the vessel in Esperanza Bay shortly after the accident suggests that a spill likely occurred, although this was vehemently denied by the British Antarctic Survey. On February 28, the Peruvian research vessel *BIC Humboldt* ran aground and began leaking oil in Fildes Bay off King George Island. Although only a minor oil spill resulted, the Humboldt incident became the third ecological threat to the region in less than a month.[11] These three episodes in the Antarctic were vastly overshadowed on March 24 by the Arctic disaster that resulted when the tanker *Exxon Valdez* struck a reef off Prince William Sound, Alaska. Some 11 million barrels of crude oil spilled into the frigid waters and killed thousands of otters, birds, and fish as it washed ashore along a 45-mile-long pollution zone. Paradoxically, the *Exxon Valdez* tragedy may be the best thing ever to have happened for Antarctic environmentalists. It graphically demonstrated the high costs and real liabilities of transporting crude oil in frigid waters. Clearly, the pervasive international publicity generated by this ecocatastrophe figured into Australia's decision to oppose the minerals treaty.

The Hawke government was also motivated by increasing domestic awareness of environmental issues among the general public. Of special concern in Australia was publicity about the widening ozone hole over Antarctica and reported increases in skin cancer warnings for Australians.

Policy perceptions by the Hawke government were also obviously influenced by the ascendant political power of the environmental movement in local Australian elections. Earlier in May, "Green" Independents won five legislative seats in the Australian state of Tasmania, a number sufficient enough to control the balance of power in that local parliament. Realization that twenty environmental groups had formed a political coalition to make environment issues prominent in the March 1990 federal election were also factors in Australia's anti-minerals treaty position.

Another prominent consideration influencing the Australian government hinged on the negative implications that CRAMRA would pose for the status of Australia's territorial claim to Antarctica. Establishment of a multinational minerals regime was perceived by some as undermining the legal validity of Australia's claim to sovereign title to the continent. By agreeing that a treaty-based minerals arrangement on the continent was necessary and proper, Australia would be admitting that its claim to sovereignty was soft and could be compromised. No less important for Paul Keating, the Hawke government's head of the Exchequer, was that CRAMRA failed to provide any royalties to claimant states for other states' exploration or exploitation activities in claimed sectors. This premeditated failure to compensate claimant states with privileged payments for mining operations in claimed sectors could be read as tacit admission that claimant states were willing to give up full administrative control over *their* territory. Notwithstanding the popular appeal of environmental motivations, the sacrifice-of-sovereignty argument apparently carried compelling sway to push the Australian government's decision not to sign the Wellington Convention.

France, another claimant, declared in June 1989 that it would join Australia in not signing the minerals convention. In August, the prime ministers of Australia and France announced a joint initiative to promote the protection of the Antarctic environment.[12] International commitment to CRAMRA began to unravel rapidly as other ATCPs indicated that they, too, were having second thoughts about the purposes and implications of putting a minerals treaty in place. By the end of 1989, Belgium, Italy, India, and the People's Republic of China had all signaled doubts about going forward with the Wellington Convention. By March 1990, reports from New Zealand suggested that government's possible shift away from the minerals treaty as well. CRAMRA had stopped dead in its diplomatic waters.

Although nonratification by either Australia or France would preclude the Wellington Convention in its present form from coming into force, it would not ensure that a world park concept would replace the derailed minerals agreement. This raises the ominous possibility that no agreement at all might be forthcoming on the minerals question—in effect, leaving a legal vacuum.

Central to the debate that surfaced in 1989 over CRAMRA is the question of whether a minerals regime will be likely to encourage or discourage exploratory and developmental pursuits by private corporations in Antarctica. Treaty advocates, such as the United States, United Kingdom, Japan, and the Soviet Union, argue that the Wellington Convention supplies an on-site regulatory regime that was negotiated to consider the possibility of undertaking and, if agreed upon, to manage minerals activities in Antarctica. The premise undergirding the position of treaty proponents is that if no rules are put in place to regulate minerals activities in the frozen south, an unregulated scramble for minerals resources could occur there. The regulations in CRAMRA would place legal strictures on potential miners, impose an orderly process for decision-making, operate to ensure environmental protection, and preclude Antarctica from becoming, in the words of the preamble to the Antarctic Treaty, the "scene or object of international discord."

The argument put forward by environmentalists against setting up a minerals regime pivots on their hope of maintaining the status quo of the continent as provided for in the 1959 Antarctic Treaty: a peaceful, nonmilitarized area of the world reserved for scientific research only. Environmentalists contend that an unregulated free-for-all for Antarctic minerals is not likely to occur in the absence of investment security and acknowledged property rights. By stabilizing such guarantees for security and property rights, however, the Wellington Convention would actually encourage mining. Environmentalists also allege that mining in Antarctica could inject rivalry over strategic resources. If so, this situation not only could put Antarctica's environment at risk, but also provoke destabilization of the treaty and undermine the nonmilitarized status of the region.

In the view of environmentalists, CRAMRA is gravely flawed in its primary purpose. The agreement is not really designed to preserve and protect the environment. Rather, environmentalists argue that its principal rationale is to provide opportunities and guarantees for mining to go forward and to facilitate political accommodation between various groups of ATCPs; by its very character mining cannot take place without damaging the environment. If there exists a real aspiration to protect the Antarctic environment, the consultative parties must not permit any areas to be opened for mineral exploitation. Moreover, if mineral development goes forward in the Antarctic, not only will the physical environment suffer, but so also will the quality of vital scientific research on the continent. Scientific research and international cooperation—the hallmarks and founding purposes of the Antarctic Treaty—could become victimized by the priorities of commercial exploitation. Preoccupation with the search for commercial resources would diminish scientific cooperation and breed competition over prospecting activities at the expense of pure scientific research.

The Wellington Convention does not purport to offer full resolution of all problems associated with mineral resource activities in Antarctica. Some provisions are left incomplete and vague. How should "significant effects" in Article 4, for example, be defined for gauging environmental impacts in CRAMRA? What constitutes "adequate information" and "informed judgments" in Article 4 for making informed decisions about possible environmental impacts arising from minerals activities? In terms of operator liability in Article 8, how can the surface of Antarctica possibly be restored to the *status quo ante* after mineral activities have taken place? In addition, some critical issues are sidestepped—for example, resolution of the thorny problem of sovereignty claims and designating what precisely will happen to revenues derived from mineral activities in Antarctica. Still, other issues are put off until later—most expressly, the liability requirements found in Article 8(7) that are to be developed in a future liability protocol.

Critics and advocates aside, the fact remains that CRAMRA does establish a legal and institutional framework for regulating mineral resource activities in Antarctica. CRAMRA provides for inspection, monitoring, reporting, compulsory settlement of disputes, access to courts, and suspension of activities causing unacceptable damage to the environment. Enforcement, however, is left to individual governments. Each party to the Wellington Convention would be expected to elaborate and fix its own definition and regulation of environmental integrity, according to its own national rules and standards.

The Wellington Convention supplies an impressive first step in filling the need for a minerals regime in the Antarctic Treaty System. It is a dynamic agreement providing for an on-site regulatory regime that could be made operational in the event that mineral activities in Antarctica become a possibility.

The diplomatic imbroglio that Australia and France touched off does not have to become a flashpoint for fraying relations among the consultative parties. There is no urgency to put the Wellington Convention in place, because mining in Antarctica is several decades away at the earliest. These developments in 1989, however, crystallized the issue of environmentalism versus regulation of mineral activities in Antarctica and sharpened the international debate over the continent. The Australian-French action also linked CRAMRA's fate with the issue of comprehensive environmental protection—a notion initially proposed in May 1989 by Chile at the preparatory consultative party meeting in Paris. Not surprisingly, the issue of comprehensive measures figured prominently in the regularly scheduled meeting of the ATCPs that convened later in October.

The Fifteenth Antarctic Consultative Treaty Meeting

The ATCPs convened for their fifteenth regular meeting in Paris from October 9-20, 1989. Following the plenary session, the meeting broke into two working groups, one to consider environmental matters and the second to deal with other items on the agenda.

Although the meeting did not deal formally with the question of the minerals convention, clearly the most visible item on the agenda was consideration of the comprehensive measures for protection of the Antarctic environment and dependent and associated ecosystems. Even so, neither that issue nor the related sensitive question of the minerals regime diverted attention from the main purpose of the session. The Fifteenth Antarctic Consultative Treaty Meeting (XVth ATCM) adopted twenty-two recommendations and one declaration, an especially impressive accomplishment because that was the second largest number of recommendations ever approved at a single treaty meeting. Significantly, nearly all of these recommendations directly or indirectly concern environmental protection of the Antarctic.

Regarding comprehensive measures, recommendations were adopted to convene two extraordinary meetings in 1990. One gathering will discuss comprehensive environmental protection and will be designated a special Antarctic Treaty Consultative Party Meeting. The mandate for this session aims to develop further principles of environmental protection under the Antarctic Treaty System, review existing protection measures and determine how best to improve them, clarify more precisely the nature of legal obligations vis-à-vis the environment, and promote scientific research and greater information that would allow for more effective monitoring of protection measures. Because no specific agenda was set for this meeting, the basis of these discussion will likely focus on five papers prepared earlier, one jointly by France and Australia, and the others by Chile, New Zealand, and the United States, with a general overview assessment by Sweden. As provided for in Recommendation XV-2, the second meeting in 1990 will "explore and discuss all proposals relating to Article 8(7)," meaning to initiate negotiations on elaborating a protocol on liability for mineral resource activities. Chile offered to host both meetings.[13]

The XVth ATCM also approved a substantial revision of the waste disposal provisions in the 1975 Code of Conduct for Antarctic Expeditions and Station Activities (Recommendation VIII-11). The revised provisions transform "recommended procedures" in the code into binding obligations with which governments are required to ensure compliance not only for their national programs, but also for private operators working under their jurisdiction. The clear intent here is to reduce environmental degradation that has resulted from disposal of wastes produced by normal operations of scientific stations and bases in the Antarctic. One problem with the new code is its reliance on the incineration of combustible wastes, a process that merely recycles pollutants from the land and sea to the air and back again. Also left untreated in the new code is the need to minimize air pollution from energy generation, particularly that produced by diesel generators.

Based on proposals by the United States, the XVth ATCM also produced a policy statement that addressed the problem of marine pollution. Recommendation XV-4 requires states to take measures within their competence to ensure compliance by vessels supporting or engaged in national Antarctic operations with six prominent international anti-pollution agreements: the 1972 Convention on the Prevention of Marine Pollution by Dumping of Wastes and Other Matter (the London Dumping Convention);[14] the 1973 International Convention for the Prevention of Pollution from Ships, and the 1978 Protocol Relating Thereto, with annexes I, II, III and V (MARPOL 73/78);[15] the 1974 International Convention for the Safety of Life at Sea and the Protocol of 1978 Relating Thereto (SOLAS);[16] the 1978 International Convention on Standards of Training, Certification and Watchkeeping for Seafarers with Annex;[17] the 1966 International Convention on Load Lines;[18] and the 1972 Convention on the International Regulations for Preventing Collisions at Sea (COLREGS).[19] Taken in train, the relevant provisions of these agreements would ban discharge of oil and disposal of plastics and garbage within the Antarctic Treaty area and of sewage within twelve nautical miles of land. Warships, naval auxiliaries, and other state-owned vessels, however, were left exempt from these restrictions on grounds of state immunity, although "every effort" should be made "to ensure that vessels with [such] sovereign immunity... should act in a manner consistent with these provisions."[20]

Regarding preventive measures, another XVth ATCM recommendation calls upon nonconsultative parties to formulate environmental impact assessments in the event that they establish new stations or facilities in the Antarctic. In addition, two new categories of protected areas were adopted. Recommendation XV-10 provides that "Special Reserved Areas" will be set aside to protect "areas of outstanding geological, glaciological, geomorphical, aesthetic, scenic, or wilderness value."[21] The second, "Multiple-Use Planning Areas," will be designated to facilitate cooperative planning and coordinated management in areas where various activities may interfere with one another or contribute to negative cumulative environmental impacts. In the spirit of preservation, the XVth ATCM also approved setting aside three new Sites of Special Scientific Interest at Ablation Point, Avian Island, and Mount Flora and redesignating a fourth, at Cape Shirreff. Two new historic monuments were also approved for Richard E. Byrd at McMurdo Station and the buildings and artifacts at the US East Base on Stonington Island.

Recommendation XV-21 dealing with the use of Antarctic ice recognized the benefits of discouraging commercial efforts to exploit ice in the Antarctic prior to further study and consideration by the ATCPs. Given that 90 percent of the world's ice, containing 70 percent of the world's fresh water, is locked up in Antarctic ice, the importance of this recommendation is strong and clear.

Several recommendations approved at the XVth ATCM pertain to scientific research in Antarctica. One problem of increasing concern is the concentration of stations in certain ice-free areas of the continent, a tendency that has compounded adverse pressures on the local environment and created interference between research and logistics facilities. Recommendation XV-17 calls for increased consultation among proximate stations with the concomitant need to assess the environmental impact and any possible cumulative effects. Five other recommendations advocate increased cooperation to enhance scientific productivity from research programs, including those monitoring programs of global significance. Ways to promote the exchange and integration of Antarctic data with that gathered from elsewhere were a particular concern. Development of a research program on ozone depletion is called for and will be carried out in cooperation with the Scientific Committee for Antarctic Research. Recommendation XV-14, crafted as a declaration, reaffirms commitments to cooperative scientific research of global significance in Antarctica and acknowledges the need to take into account the significance of Antarctica in monitoring global change. It is also intended to ensure that all activities in Antarctica are based on adequate information that will permit informed judgments about environmental consequences. Two other related documents addressed the importance of Antarctic scientific research in monitoring ozone depletion (Declaration on the Ozone Layer and Climate Change) and the need to establish an Antarctic Scientific and Environmental Data System (Recommendation XV-16).

The *Bahia Paraiso* oil spill underscored the need for additional measures to avoid accidents by vessels in the Antarctic, especially by enhancing the quality of navigational charts for circumpolar waters. Prompted by proposals from Spain and the United Kingdom, a recommendation was adopted that called for cooperation in hydrographic survey and charting and urged states to coordinate national activities with the International Hydrographic Organization and Scientific Committee on Antarctic Research. A Soviet initiative also led to adopting a recommendation that would improve the accuracy and availability of information on Antarctic weather and sea ice. It requests the World Meteorological Organization to review and recommend action on the development of an operational marine meteorological and informational service for the Antarctic Treaty area.

The recent expansion in national research programs and tourism in Antarctica has resulted in expanded use of aircraft around the continent. Still another recommendation was passed at the XVth ATCM to increase cooperation in air safety, specifically by encouraging the exchange of information on air operations, flight schedules, and communications frequencies within the Antarctic Treaty area.

Other items discussed, but not acted upon, at the XVth ATCM underlined the need for consideration of such concerns as the need for a secretariat to facilitate information exchange, communications, and documentation among ATCPs as well as relevant institutions in the Antarctic Treaty System. Argentina—and, to a lesser degree, India and the German Democratic Republic—strongly oppose creation of a secretariat. Argentina argues that more flexible, government-to-government dealings are more efficient, less costly, and less institutionalized than an internationalized bureaucratic servicing center. However, given the pronounced growth of states as members of the treaty system, the expanded complexity of rules and regulations created as new problems are addressed, and the declassification of documents to accommodate enhanced public availability of information, it is understandable that the question of a secretariat will be reconsidered at the XVIth consultative meeting in 1991. It may be raised even earlier at the special meeting in November 1990 called to discuss comprehensive environmental measures. Another issue to be considered at the meeting pertains to the increase of international tourism to Antarctica and the need for appropriate measures to deal with potential adverse implications for the environment, scientific research, safety, search and rescue, and liability.

Prior to commencement of the XVth ATCM, a special consultative meeting was convened on October 9 to consider nominations for new consultative parties. Five states had submitted their nominations—Finland, the Republic of Korea, Peru, Ecuador, and the Netherlands. Finland, the Republic of Korea, and Peru were accepted as full consultative parties. Membership for Ecuador and the Netherlands, however, was deferred until further research activities by these states can be evaluated to determine if they fully meet the requirement of "substantial scientific activity" in Article IX(2) of the Antarctic Treaty.

The results of the XVth ATCM make clear that consensus among the Antarctic consultative parties will be difficult to achieve at the 1990 meeting concerning comprehensive measures. Even the form of the negotiated product is at issue. Australia and France strongly support negotiation by the ATCPs of a comprehensive framework convention to secure broad environmental protection in Antarctica. Chile, as set out in its national paper, leans more in favor of an Agreed Measures type of format.

The core question that surfaced in 1989 turns on the fundamental relationship between a new comprehensive environmental regime and the recently negotiated Wellington Convention on minerals. The Australian proposal advocated creation of a "Wilderness Park" that would permit scientific research and some tourist activities but preclude mineral activities. On the other hand, the joint Australian-French proposal of August 1989 calls for creation of a wilderness reserve, but does not specifically address the permissibility of mineral development. In either case, it is going to be difficult for Australia and France to reconcile their views with the need for negotiating a liability protocol, a necessary ingredient to effect compliance with regulations in the Wellington Convention. Similarly, the notion of a wilderness reserve or world park that carries connotations of excluding mineral activities in Antarctica will render it difficult for other countries—particularly, the United States, Japan, United Kingdom, and Soviet Union—to accept such a mandate for negotiating a binding set of new comprehensive measures.[22]

In late 1989, the United Nations added its official position to the mix of views on Antarctic environmental priorities. At its annual debate on the Question of Antarctica, the General Assembly on November 22 adopted a resolution sponsored by the Non-Aligned Movement that advocated establishment of an Antarctic world park. In its operative provisions, the resolution

> 5. *Urges* all members of the international community to support all efforts to ban prospecting and mining in and around Antarctica and to ensure that all activities should be exclusively used for the purpose of peaceful scientific investigation and that all such activities should ensure the maintenance of international peace and security in Antarctica and the protection of its environment and should be for the benefit of all mankind;

6. *Expresses its conviction* that the establishment, through negotiations with the full participation of all members of the international community, of Antarctica as a nature reserve or a world park, would ensure the protection and conservation of its environment and its dependent and associated ecosystems for the benefit of all mankind.[23]

Environmentalists may applaud this support as a positive development indicating that the United Nations views Antarctica to be valued for more than its resource exploitation potential. Even so, this resolution stands out as fundamentally different from the Australian-French proposal. Whereas the resolution calls for the full participation of the international community in accomplishing this goals, Australia and France prefer to work within the ambit of the Antarctic Treaty System. In any event, this General Assembly resolution is not legally binding; absent any firm support by Antarctic Treaty states, it is merely a hortatory document politically embraced by developing countries.

In respect to comprehensive measures, the key would seem to be for the ATCPs to reach a compromise that allows for some combination of making Antarctica a world wilderness preserve and setting a moratorium on mining, while preserving the Wellington Convention as a safety device in case the moratorium should one day collapse and mineral activities begin. There is still plenty of time for such an arrangement to be negotiated. The critical ingredient now needed to explore this possibility is the political will by the consultative parties to do so. Attaining this political will to negotiate toward compromise is a major challenge for Antarctic diplomacy in 1990 and beyond.

The Eighth Meeting of the CCAMLR Commission

The Antarctic area's natural resource base—both real and imagined—generated much international interest in 1989. No living resources of any major consequence exists on land. The circumpolar waters, however, teem with biological bounty. Whales, seals, squid, fish, and birds are found in substantial quantities. Even so, the living resource currently thought to hold the greatest potential economic value is krill, a small shrimp-like crustacean that comprises more than half the zooplankton crop in the Southern Ocean.

The most comprehensive effort by the ATCPs to manage living resources in Antarctic seas is found in the Convention on the Conservation of Antarctic Marine Living Resources. CCAMLR emerged largely in response to concern over increased levels of krill being harvested in the Southern Ocean by certain states, especially the Soviet Union. CCAMLR primarily aims at managing the harvests of Antarctic living marine resources by fostering "conservation," defined in Article II as "rational use." The unique perspective here is that CCAMLR intends to incorporate an "ecosystemic ecological approach" in determining conservation standards for fishery stocks. This special approach involves a systematic assessment of the ecological interrelationships between species and their physical environment.

Two main institutions are created by CCAMLR; a Commission for the Conservation of Antarctic Marine Living Resources and a Scientific Committee for the Conservation of Antarctic Marine Living Marine Resources. The commission in 1989 had twenty members: Argentina, Australia, Belgium, Brazil, Chile, the European Community, Federal Republic of Germany, France, German Democratic Republic, India, Japan, New Zealand, Norway, Poland, Republic of Korea, South Africa, the Soviet Union, Spain, United Kingdom, and the United States. This commission, which serves as a forum for discussion by parties to the CCAMLR regime, deals with matters of administration as well as policy. Its responsibilities include facilitating the study and compilation of data on Antarctic marine living resources; ensuring the acquisition of catch and effort statistics; formulating, adopting, and revising conservation measures on the basis of the best information available; and establishing systems for observation and inspection.

The Scientific Committee operates largely through ad hoc working groups. By 1989, at least seven working groups had been set up to provide timely scientific advice to the commission regarding activities affecting living marine resources within the convention area.

The jurisdictional scope of CCAMLR includes the marine area south of the Antarctic Convergence, the biological boundary between 48° and 60° South Latitude that is formed as the cold Antarctic waters meet the warmer sub-Antarctic waters. CCAMLR defines the Antarctic marine ecosystem as lying south of this boundary and would apply to finfish, mollusks, crustaceans, and all other species of living organisms, including birds, within that area.

A critical feature of CCAMLR is the ecosystems approach taken toward conservation and management of living resources in circumpolar waters. The convention provides for a management regime dedicated to ensuring that harvesting Antarctic living resources is conducted so that proper consideration is accorded the ecological relationships among dependent and related species. The ecosystems approach should be distinguished from the single species approach. The single species strategy calls for examination only of features pertaining to target species and seeks to acquire adequate information on that stock's situation relative to man's interference. The ecosystemic approach not only examines features directly affecting target species, but also those that hold importance for maintaining ecological relationships.

The Eighth Meeting of the CCAMLR Commission (CAMLR VIII) met from November 6-17, 1989, at CCAMLR headquarters in Hobart, Tasmania, Australia. Several significant developments during that meeting highlight the status of Antarctic diplomacy during 1989-1990 in regard to living resources in the southern seas. For one, the system of observation and inspection adopted in 1988 was put into operation for the 1989-1990 season, and no alleged infractions were reported. Four member states have designated inspectors—Argentina, Chile, the Soviet Union, and the United States.[24]

The krill catch reported for the 1988-1989 season was 395,470 metric tonnes, up from 370,663 tonnes in 1987-1988 and 376,456 tonnes in 1986-1987. The Soviet Union and Japan were still the major harvesting countries, catching some 300,000 and 80,000 tonnes of krill, respectively. At CAMLR VIII, the Soviet Union indicated that substantial expansion of its krill harvests could be likely over the next decade, a possibility largely attributable to various processing problems being solved. Japan, on the other hand, revealed that it does not anticipate increasing its catches as there is little market interest in Japan for krill products. Chile, Poland, and the Republic of Korea also reported krill catches, each of which amounted to less than 10,000 tonnes.[25]

CCAMLR is entrusted with the responsibility of ensuring the long-term viability of krill stock. Article II of the convention makes state parties obligated to regulate harvesting activity to avoid infliction of irreversible damage to the Antarctic ecosystem. To this end, the CCAMLR Ecosystem Monitoring Program is intended to monitor changes in dependent species and to ascertain effects of harvesting on these populations.

Problems that encumbered quantification of krill abundance and determination of which factors influence their regional distribution persisted throughout 1989. Information remains essential for the success or failure of CCAMLR. Collection of commercial fishing data is a priority mission for the CCAMLR regime because it provides the only central depository of information available about the Antarctic marine ecosystem. Serious problems persist, however, in gathering commercial data, especially given the incomplete quality of the information and its frequently nonstandardized format.

Information in the past had been accumulated according to calendar years, not fishing seasons, and had been lumped together by various compilers into irregular categories.

It has been exceedingly difficult to achieve the objectives of the Living Resources Convention because data received by the CCAMLR regime has come principally from commercial sources and has not proven adequate to permit effective implementation of the convention's ecological approach. In fact, environmentalists point out that CCAMLR has even been used by Japan to justify what should be considered persistent unlawful whaling activities. Japan continues to kill 300 Minke whales each year, purportedly on grounds of "scientific activity" to learn more about the regional distribution of krill by examining the stomach contents of whales taken in the Southern Ocean. A more likely reason for taking these Minkes is to sustain Japan's domestic commercial whaling industry.

In regard to fishing operations, CAMLR VIII reported total finfish catches of 104,405 metric tonnes in the Antarctic for the 1988-1989 season. This marks a substantial increase compared to the 88,354 tonnes taken during 1987-1988 and 98,055 tonnes in 1986-1987. The Soviet Union was the preeminent fishing state, though France reported that its nationals also engaged in fishing activities in the Southern Ocean. During 1989, a new fishery, the lantern fish, was also harvested, and some 30,000 tonnes were taken.[26]

Studies in recent years have suggested that many finfish stocks in the Southern Ocean are seriously depleted. For example, the Fish Stock Assessment Working Group reported to CAMLR VIII that it had examined the status of *Chamosocephalus gunnari* (mackerel icefish) around South Georgia Island, only to find that fishery so small as to render an insufficient amount of detailed biological data available.[27] Most commission members consequently advocated setting very conservative total allowable catch numbers around South Georgia to provide greater protection for the younger fish. The Soviet Union demurred, however, contending that the lack of detailed historical and current biological data was not attributable to small numbers of samples taken, but rather stemmed from random locations of fishing vessels and the fact that management procedures had not been fully implemented. The Soviet Union also rejected a proposal to increase the mesh size of fishing nets, a recommendation that in fact had been derived from studies on mesh selectivity of creatures caught based on analyses conducted by the Polish, Soviet, and British scientists and adopted by the Scientific Committee. In its report, the CCAMLR Commission was clear and unambiguous.

Soviet intransigence plainly indicated that Moscow was unwilling to accept the advice of the Scientific Committee for determining conservation measures.[28] In sum, the Soviet Union's attitude at CAMLR VIII strongly suggested that its national priorities remained aimed at short-term resource aggrandizement, rather than at a long-term, rational-use approach to Antarctic fisheries.

Some meaningful results were accomplished at CAMLR VIII, however. For one, conservation measures were adopted by the commission to apply in the 1989-1990 season around South Georgia. A total catch limit of 8,000 tonnes was set for *Chamosocephalus gunnari*. Prohibitions of directed fishing were also fixed for *Notothenia gibberifrous, Chacnocephalus aceratus, Pseudochaenichthys georgianus*, and *Notothenia squamifrous*. Also, special interim prohibitions were set on fishing for *Chamosocephalus gunnari* from November 20, 1989, through January 15, 1990, and from April 1, 1990, through November 4, 1990. In addition, a catch limit of 12,000 tonnes was placed on *Patagonothen brevicauda guntheri*. No less significant, it was agreed that the commission would monitor conservation measures under a catch reporting system, with fishermen submitting reports every five days.[29]

An important development at CAMLR VIII concerned the implementation of a new system for observation and inspection that had been agreed to in principle in 1988. Article 24 of the CCAMLR agreement contains the requirement that a system of observation and inspection be implemented for vessels conducting scientific research or harvesting marine living resources within the convention area. Such an on-the-spot system will permit inspectors to check commercial harvesting activities and verify fishermen's compliance with closed areas and closed season restrictions and total allowable catch numbers.

This system entered into force during the 1989-1990 season, notwithstanding opposition from Japan. A total of fifteen observers have been authorized to carry out inspections. These will not be scientific observations; rather they involve inspectors boarding fishing vessels for three hours and exercising an inquiry procedure to determine if conservation measures are being adhered to. Clearly, fisheries inspection and observation will permit better opportunities to gather basic data necessary for proper fisheries management—for example, obtaining a better idea of who is fishing where, when, how, for what, and for how much. This strategy is also designed to deter infringements, rather than lead specifically to arrests. The fundamental aim is not to seize fishing vessels, but to promote compliance with the CCAMLR regulations in force.[30]

CAMLR VIII also considered the problems associated with mortality of incidental species caused by man-made marine debris. Several sightings of marine debris concentrations were reported, along with the number of creatures affected. Ingestion of plastics by Antarctic seabirds within the convention area is geographically widespread: Australia reported increases in the accumulation of debris on Heard and Macquarie Islands, much of which was plastics from ships' garbage and lost fishing gear. The United States also described sighting a large amount of plastic debris, and the United Kingdom reported that it had found 208 fur seals pups entangled in marine debris of human origin during the 1988-1989 season. Concern was also expressed over potential incidental mortality associated with the possible use of gill and drift nets in the Southern Ocean, although no member of the CCAMLR Commission currently is believed to be using them there and no member state has indicated any intentions to do so in the foreseeable future.[31]

The krill stock in the Southern Ocean has not yet suffered appreciably from commercial harvesting activities. Present catch levels of krill approximating a half-million metric tonnes annually pose no direct threat to the recovery of depleted whale numbers. Still, the need exists to improve assessments of annual krill production to help minimize adverse effects on whales and other natural predators of krill including seals, fish, penguins, and other marine birds. CCAMLR fish-stock studies clearly indicate that the finfishery in the Antarctic region is severely depleted. Even so, it remains politically unacceptable for some states to close that finfishery until its stocks have recovered.

The 1989 commission meeting revealed that although notable progress is being made, the full potential of the "ecosystem-as-a-whole" conservation approach of CCAMLR is not being reached. Consensus voting permits certain fishing states to retain the power to stymie adoption of broad conservation measures. At the same time, other governments in CCAMLR have not yet committed themselves to challenge the intransigence of those fishing states.

CCAMLR marks a major diplomatic step in the evolution of a more holistic approach to conservation and management of living marine resources in the Antarctic. It remains an important agreement as evidenced by its membership, which includes the principal fishing countries of the world, among them Chile, Japan, Poland, the Soviet Union, and the United States.

The lessons learned from CAMLR VIII are clear: When uncertainties exist over natural resource availability, such as the size of fish stocks, the benefit of doubt should be given to environmental considerations, not to parochial national interests. The overriding need is for preventive action, not belated reactive response. The Antarctic marine ecosystem stays in constant flux, and CCAMLR must be equally dynamic in setting policy if it is to attain the purposes for which it was created.

Conclusion

Political and legal developments pertaining to Antarctica during 1989 and 1990 stirred much unease among diplomats, environmentalists, and scientists. Antarctic environmentalism received a tremendous boost with the decision by Australia and France not to sign the Wellington Convention. It came at a cost, however: For the first time in its 30-year history, the Antarctic Treaty System experienced serious dissension among its member governments, a circumstance growing out of disagreements regarding the utility and implications of an Antarctic minerals accord. International conservation measures designed to protect Antarctic marine living resources were also thwarted by contrary policies held by some states.

On balance, however, a number of positive developments also occurred. The environmental protection regime for Antarctica was visibly strengthened as the ATCPs adopted several important recommendations. The potentially confrontational issue of mineral development was postponed, until at least the special consultative meeting set for Chile in November 1990. This delay supplied a cooling-off period and allowed for important interim opportunities for ATCPs to discuss, negotiate, and consider possible compromise solutions. The system for inspection and observation of commercial fishing vessels operating in circumpolar seas came into effect, and catch restrictions were placed on several species of indigenous finfish.

In sum, the past year figured significantly in the course of Antarctic diplomacy. Not only was international environmental consciousness pointedly raised about the wilderness value of Antarctica, but the critical need for international cooperation and diplomatic negotiation was also highlighted by anxieties that self-serving natural political priorities and private greed might begin to unravel the legal ties that bind the Antarctic Treaty states together in a symbiotic relationship. Any such collapse of the Antarctic Treaty System would be highly regrettable.

Relevant events affecting Antarctic diplomacy in 1990 do not suggest that disintegration of the Antarctic Treaty System is either inevitable or even likely. Developments over the past year do, however, raise the political stakes for future consultative party meetings and boldly underscore the need to engage in good-faith diplomatic negotiation aimed at political compromise and mutually beneficial solutions. Only in that spirit of cooperation can the ATCPs ensure that the Antarctic Treaty will continue to fulfill its cardinal purpose—to benefit all mankind without becoming the scene or object of international rivalry and discord. That will remain the major challenge for Antarctic diplomacy in the coming decade.

Notes

1. Antarctic Treaty, done December 1, 1959, entered into force June 23, 1961. 12 *United States Treaties and Other International Agreements* (UST), 794, *United States Treaties and Other International Acts Series* (TIAS), No. 4780, 402 *United Nations Treaty Series* (UNTS), 71.

2. The fourteen "nonconsultative" Antarctic Treaty parties include Austria, Bulgaria, Colombia, Cuba, Czechoslovakia, Denmark, Ecuador, Greece, Hungary, Democratic People's Republic of Korea, Netherlands, Papua New Guinea, and Romania.

3. Done at Brussels, June 2-13, 1964, 17 UST 996, 998, TIAS No. 6058, modified in 24 UST 1802, TIAS No. 7692 (1973).

4. Done at London, June 1, 1972, entered into force March 11, 1978. 27 UST 441, TIAS No. 8826.

5. Done at Canberra, May 20, 1980, entered into force April 7, 1982. 80 *United States Treaties at Large*, 271, TIAS No. 10240.

6. Done June 2, 1988, opened for signature November 25, 1988. Document AMR/SCM/88/78 (June 2, 1988), reprinted in *International Legal Materials* 27 (July 1988): 859-900.

7. For the progressive development of the minerals regime, see Christopher C. Joyner, "The Evolving Antarctic Minerals Regime," *Ocean Development & International Law* 19 (1988): 73-95, and Christopher C. Joyner, "The Antarctic Minerals Negotiating Process," *American Journal of International Law* 81 (October 1987): 888-905.

8. For comparative assessments of the mineral regime's operation, see Christopher C. Joyner, "1988 Antarctic Minerals Convention," *Marine Policy Reports* 1 (1989): 69-85, and Peter J. Beck, "Convention on the Regulation of Antarctic Mineral Resource Activities: a major addition to the Antarctic Treaty System," *Polar Record* 25(152) (1989): 19-32.

9. Press Release from the Prime Minister for Australia: Joint Statement with the Minister for Foreign Affairs and Trade, Senator Gareth Evans QC, and the Minister for Arts, Sport, the Environment, Tourism & Territories, Senator the Hon. Graham Richardson, May 22, 1989, (mimeograph). See David Scott, "Australia Advocates Wilderness Status for Antarctica," *Christian Science Monitor*, May 24, 1989, and Robert Cockburn and Andrew Morgan, "Australia Blocks Antarctic mining operation," *The Times*, London, May 23, 1989.

10. John Noble Wilford, "Sunken Ship's Oil Spill Held a Peril to Antarctic Wildlife," *New York Times*, February 9, 1989, p. A-7.

11. "New Shipwreck Causes Oil Slick in Antarctic," *New York Times*, March 1, 1989.

12. Joint Statement on International Environment Issues Agreed by Prime Ministers Robert Hawke and Rocard, Canberra, 18 August 1988. See Malcolm W. Browne, "France and Australia Kill Pact on Limited Antarctic Mining and Oil Drilling," *New York Times*, September 25, 1989, p. A-10.

13. Antarctic Treaty, *Final Report of the Fifteenth Antarctic Treaty Consultative Party Meeting*, Paris, October 9-20, 1989, p. 47.

14. Done at Washington, London, Mexico City, and Moscow, December 29, 1972, entered into force August 30, 1975. 2 UST 2403, TIAS No. 8165.

15. Done at London, November 2, 1973, IMCO Doc. MP/CONF/WP.35. Protocol of 1978 Relating to the International Convention for the Prevention of Pollution from Ships, done at London, February 17, 1978, entered into force October 2, 1983.

16. Done at London, November 1, 1974, entered into force May 25, 1980. TIAS No. 9700; Protocol of 1978 Relating to the Convention for the Safety of Life at Sea, done at London, February 17, 1978, entered into force May 1, 1981. 32 UST 5577, TIAS No. 10,009.

17. Done at London, July 7, 1978, entered into force April 28, 1984. United Kingdom Command Papers No. 7543, UK Miscellaneous Series 6 (1979).

18. Done at London, April 5, 1966, entered into force July 21, 1968. 18 UST 1857, TIAS No. 6331, UNTS 133.

19. Done at London, October 20, 1972, entered into force July 15, 1977. 28 UST 3459, TIAS No. 8587.

20. *Final Report of the Fifteenth Antarctic Treaty Consultative Party Meeting*, p. 21 (paragraph 91).

21. *Ibid.*, p. 82.

22. Part of the difficulty associated with the notion of Antarctica being made a "world park" is defining precisely what the concept entails, as well as legal, environmental, and institutional obligations. For the environmentalist perspective, see Greenpeace International, *The World Park Option for Antarctica; Background for a Fourth UN Debate*, London (November 17, 1986).

23. UN General Assembly Resolution A/C.1/44 L.59, General Assembly Official Records, 44th session, First Committee (November 20, 1989), p. 3 (mimeograph).

24. Commission for the Conservation of Antarctic Marine Living Resources, *Report of the Eighth Meeting of the Commission*, Hobart, Australia, November 6-17, 1989, p. 35. Also see "Report of the Standing Committee on Observation and Inspection (SCOI)" in *ibid.*, pp. 101-107.

25. Scientific Committee for the Conservation of Antarctic Marine Living Resources, *Report of the Eighth Meeting of the Scientific Committee*, Hobart, Australia, November 6-10, 1989, pp. 3, 6.

26. "Report of the Working Group on Fish Stock Assessment," in *ibid.*, pp. 184-185 (composite figure).

27. *Report of the Eighth Meeting of the Scientific Committee*, pp. 20-24.

28. As articulated in the Commission Report:

> The Commission noted that this contradiction [between "most Members" and the Soviet Union], which formed a fundamental obstruction to its management responsibilities, seemed likely to persist either until all available historical and current data were proved or it was accepted that, in the absence of data that can only be provided by fishing nations, precautionary measures become essential.

Report of the Eighth Meeting of the Commission, p. 29, at paragraph 120.

29. See, generally, *ibid.*, pp. 21-34, "Consideration of Conservation Measures."
30. *Ibid.*, p. 35 and "Committee Report on Observation and Inspection" in *ibid.*, pp. 103-107.
31. *Ibid.*, pp. 3-7.

Departments

Looking Ahead: Diplomatic Challenges of 1991

DESPITE THE DIPLOMATIC ACHIEVEMENTS of 1989 and early 1990, as *The Diplomatic Record* goes to press, significant international issues remain unresolved and the world has been plunged into a new crisis by the Iraqi invasion of Kuwait. The following issues are likely to continue to challenge diplomats well into 1990 and, in some cases, into years beyond. Where deep-seated antagonisms stubbornly reject conciliation, the task of the diplomat will be less to resolve issues than to prevent the outbreak of armed conflict.

Africa, the Mediterranean, and the Middle East

Issues in the Middle East—complicated and overshadowed in the summer of 1990 by the Iraqi invasion of Kuwait—remained deeply entwined in ancient regional, religious, and ethnic rivalries. Whatever the outcome of international efforts to meet the threats from Iraq, the likelihood remained that the deep antipathies between peoples, factions, and nations would continue to preoccupy the United Nations and the world community well into 1990 and beyond.

Cyprus. United Nations talks in February 1990 aimed at restoring in some form a unified Cyprus government were inconclusive, suggesting a continuation of the tension between the Turkish and Greek areas of the island. UN peacekeeping forces remain in place, and the UN secretary-general remains charged with mediating the dispute.

The Israeli-Palestinian Issue. If there is to be future progress, it will depend on ultimately resolving Israel's basic political instability, the internal Palestinian struggle (*intifada*), the future status of the Palestine Liberation Organization (PLO) in negotiations, the level of provocative infiltration into Israel from outside, and the status of the issue of settlements in the occupied territories. In a broader context, the level of the emigration of Soviet Jews to Israel and their place of settlement in the country, the attitude of the Soviet Union toward the peace process, and the impact of the regional proliferation of missiles and chemical weapons will also affect peace prospects. As of June 1990, active peace efforts were on hold. The United States suspended its dialogue with the PLO, and a narrowly based Likud government faced an uncertain future. The initial PLO support of the Iraqi action against Kuwait further aggravated anti-PLO attitudes in Israel and diminished the credibility of the Palestinian organization as a partner in the peace process.

North Africa. The military conflict between the Polisario, which seeks independence for the Western Sahara, and Morocco quieted after hit-and-run attacks on Moroccan forces in October-November 1989. Although Polisario proved it was still a viable force, its ability to continue sustained resistance to Moroccan claims in the area may have been lessened by reduced financial and military support from Algeria. In early 1990, the United Nations redoubled its efforts to get agreement on a referendum in the region through resolving remaining Moroccan-Polisario differences over the administration of the referendum.

The Americas

Central America.[1] The prospects for pacification and democratization in the region improved during the 1988-1990 period marked, particularly, by the election in Nicaragua and the subsequent demobilization of the "contras." Internal conflicts continued in Guatemala and El Salvador, and the situation in Panama remained fragile after the overthrow of President Manuel Noriega by US forces. Diplomatic initiatives can be expected in the region through the Permanent Mechanism of Consultation and Political Settlement.[2]

Mexican-US Relations. Meetings between presidents George Bush and Carlos Salinas de Gortari in November 1988, October 1989, and June 1990 set the stage for improvements in relations between Mexico and the United States that are expected to continue into the 1991 period. The presidential meetings were supplemented by meetings of parliamentarians in New Orleans in March 1988 and Ixtapa-Zihuatanejo in April 1989 and by the seventh meeting of the Binational Commission at the cabinet level in August 1989. Issues that will continue to dominate diplomacy between the two countries are external debt, the battle against drug trafficking, migration, and the possibilities of a broad US-Mexican free trade agreement.

Asia

Afghanistan. The stalemate between the government of President Mohammed Najibullah in Kabul, the Afghan Interim Government in Pakistan, and the various resistance factions within the country continued to frustrate outside efforts to bring peace to Afghanistan. Peace depends both on an understanding between the United States and the Soviet Union on arms flows into the country and finding a pattern—so far elusive—that will bring together the multiple factions in this divided country.

Cambodia. As of mid-September, following a meeting of all factions under Indonesian and French leadership in Jakarta, efforts to create a Supreme National Council for Cambodia were under way. The first meeting of the new body, conceived under an agreement by the five members of the United Nations Security Council, took place in Bangkok on September 17. Deep differences remained among the four factions over the chairmanship, the United Nations seat, and over the future role of the Council. These were likely to continue into 1991.

Kashmir. Friends of both India and Pakistan in mid-1990, through bilateral diplomacy and the United Nations Security Council, were making diplomatic overtures designed to lessen the renewed tension over the present and future status of Jammu and Kashmir. Barring a major break-through on the issue— even if another Indo-Pakistan war is avoided—the problem of this Indian state, with its Hindu leadership and Muslim majority, is likely to continue to prevent fully satisfactory relations between these two major South Asian states.

Korea. In the Korean peninsula, the question for 1991 will be how far trends toward more friendly relations between North and South are likely to proceed. In 1990, North Korea appeared more and more to feel its isolation as an old-style Marxist Leninist state, troubled by Mikhail Gorbachev's meeting in June with South Korean President Roh Tae Woo and by a growing trade between China and South Korea. As a result of overtures from the North to the South, the prime ministers of the two nations met on September 4, 1990, in Seoul. It was the highest-ranking delegation to visit the South in forty-five years. The two nations, while not resolving issues of trade, US troop withdrawal, and freeing of South Korean dissidents imprisoned for visiting the North, maintained civility and agreed to continue talking. Serious obstacles to a genuine reconciliation leading to reunification remained on both sides of the dividing line, but the meeting seems to have initiated the most hopeful discussion since separation.

Europe

Conference on Security and Cooperation in Europe (CSCE). A summit meeting of the thirty-five nations in the CSCE was tentatively set for November 17. Expectations at mid-year were that the committee of allied powers and the German states would announce an accord on German unification, and negotiators on the reduction of conventional forces in Europe (CFE) would report an agreement. A tentative program of meetings under the CSCE for 1991 included these dates:

JANUARY 1991	Valetta, Malta: meeting on the "peaceful settlement of disputes."
MAY 1991	Cracow, Poland: meeting on "cultural heritage."
SEPTEMBER 1991	Moscow, USSR: third monitoring conference on human rights.
MARCH 1992	Helsinki, Finland: opening of the Fourth Review conference of the Helsinki Final Act.

European Community. By mid-1990, 60 percent of the directives prepared by the European Commission under the Single Europe Act designed to eliminate border controls by 1992 had been approved by the European Parliament. European Community finance ministers were expected to meet in late 1990 to discuss recommendations for the establishment of a single currency. Western European diplomacy in 1991 is likely to be dominated by continuing efforts to resolve the remaining issues relating to taxation and the movement of labor in an economically united Europe.

Strategic Arms Limitation Agreement. Despite warming relations between the United States and the Soviet Union, major differences continued in the START talks; an agreement before the end of 1990 seemed unlikely. Negotiations will likely continue into the next year, primarily to resolve differences over aircraft limitations and the question of naval arms control.

Trade

The Uruguay Round. Conclusion of the latest multilateral trade discussions under the General Agreement on Tariffs and Trade (GATT) are expected before the end of 1990. At least three significant questions involving the inclusion of new elements in the agreement remained at mid-year: intellectual property, the service sector, and investment codes.

Notes

1. For the material on Latin America, the editor is indebted to Lic. Dr. Miguel Gonzalez Avelar, Director of the Matis Romero Institute of Diplomatic Studies of the Mexican Ministry of External Relations.
2. Also known as the Group of Eight or the Group of Rio, the group consists of Mexico, Panama, Colombia, Venezuela, Uruguay, Argentina, Brazil, and Peru.

The Governance of Diplomacy: Recent Developments

Harold E. Horan

GOVERNANCE OF DIPLOMACY, as used in *The Diplomatic Record*, means the regulation of privileges, immunities, and responsibilities of diplomatic and consular missions, personnel, and communications, of sending and receiving states, and of international organizations, personnel, and communications. Basic to the governance of diplomatic and consular relations are the Vienna Convention on Diplomatic Relations (1961)[1] and the Vienna Convention on Consular Relations (1963)[2] as well as rules of customary international law. Within the context of the Vienna conventions and customary international law, the separate sovereign states also adopt laws, rules, and regulations affecting diplomatic and consular practice.

A quite distinct but related subject is that of the privileges, immunities, and responsibilities of international organizations, personnel, and communications. These matters are regulated, inter alia, by the General Convention on the Privileges and Immunities of the United Nations, adopted by the UN General Assembly on February 13, 1946.[3] The United States, however, did not at first accede to the convention and instead negotiated the Headquarters of the United Nations Agreement, which has remained in force since November 21, 1947.[4]

The Diplomatic Record is intended to monitor annual developments in diplomatic governance; what follows are selected highlights from 1988-1989.

US Diplomatic Practice: Recent Developments

The Department of State has obtained legislation that adds a new category of ineligibility for visas and for admission to the United States of former foreign diplomatic and consular personnel. The new law states, in essence, that any alien who has committed a serious criminal offence in the United States and for whom immunity from criminal jurisdiction was exercised is not eligible to enter the United States. The law also states that a serious criminal offense includes any felony, any crime of violence, and any crime of reckless driving or driving while intoxicated or under the influence of alcohol or prohibited substance if personal injury to another is involved.[5]

In a communication to the diplomatic community in Washington in December 1988[6] the Department of State advises, in essence, that when diplomatic or consular personnel are found to be carrying firearms without requisite authorization, department policy calls for the department to request a waiver of immunity from prosecution. "If immunity is not waived," the communication concludes, "the Department would, absent extraordinary circumstances, require the departure of the offending person, and "where the offender is a dependent of a mission member, of the mission member."[7]

In a more recent communication to the Washington diplomatic community[8] the Department of State states that as a matter of general policy in cases involving allegations of criminal misconduct and serious offenses, where a waiver of immunity is refused, the US government normally will require the alleged offender to leave the country, "including, where necessary, in the case of such serious offense by family members, departure of the mission member from whom the family member's immunity derives."[9]

In June 1989 the Department of State presented its sixth annual report to Congress on the activities of the Office of Foreign Missions (OFM) under the Foreign Missions Act covering the calendar year 1988.[10] Under the act, the US government is committed to a policy that will ensure equitable and reciprocal allocation of privileges and immunities to US personnel abroad, consider US government security interests in issues concerning the scope of the activities of foreign missions in the United States, and protect the interest of US residents against unacceptable conduct by foreign missions and their staffs.[11]

Two items contained in the June 1988 report are particularly illustrative of accomplishments under the first of the above objectives—to promote and protect equal treatment of US government personnel abroad with regard to privileges and immunities.

- As the report notes, "Cumbersome travel procedures were developed and imposed on Soviet diplomats as a reciprocal measure for the delays US Embassy personnel were experiencing in Moscow in obtaining tickets and reservations for travel within the Soviet Union. These steps took effect in mid-October. Shortly thereafter, Moscow agreed to drop their procedures, which had been the Department's objective, resulting in the lifting of the reciprocal US procedures."[12]

- Regarding reciprocal tax questions, the report describes as "perhaps the most notable success" obtaining the benefit of the Value-Added Tax (VAT) reimbursement on the purchase of vehicles for US consular personnel in the Federal Republic of Germany (FRG). To obtain this benefit, which had been previously denied, the Office of Personnel Management imposed a surcharge on vehicles purchased by certain FRG consular personnel in the United States. In late 1987, subsequent to bilateral discussion of the matter, the FRG announced that, "effective January 1, 1989, VAT reimbursements would be made available to U.S. consulates and consular personnel in Germany."[13]

International Organizations' Diplomatic Practice: Recent Developments

The International Law Commission of the United Nations held its forty-first session in Geneva from May 2 to July 21, 1989. In a major development, the commission completed work, begun in 1976, on the status of the diplomatic courier and the diplomatic bag not accompanied by diplomatic courier. The commission adopted a set of thirty-two draft articles on the subject, recommending to the General Assembly that it convene an international conference to conclude a convention on couriers and pouches. The commission also added two draft optional protocols to cover, respectively, the status of couriers and bags of special missions and international organizations of a universal character. The purpose of the draft articles is to establish a comprehensive and uniform regime for all kinds of couriers and bags.[14]

Notes

1. *United Nations Treaty Series* (UNTS), vol. 500, pp. 95-127. US Department of State, *United States Treaties and Other International Agreements* (UST), *United States Treaties*

and Other International Acts Series (TIAS) 7502. Ratifications, accessions, and successions from *Multilateral Treaties Deposited with the Secretary General*, Status December 31, 1985 (New York: United Nations, 1986), pp. 52-53.

2. UNTS, Vol. 596; ratifications, accessions, and succession from *Multilateral Treaties*, pp. 70-71.

3. TIAS 6900; 1 UNTS 16; text in *American Journal of International Law*, Vol. 43 (1949), Supplement, pp. 1-7. A corresponding convention covering the UN Specialized Agencies was adopted in 1947.

4. *Ibid.*, pp. 8-17. The Headquarters Agreement is divided into twenty-eight consecutively numbered sections, grouped under nine articles.

5. "Foreign Relations Authorization Act, Fiscal Years 1990 and 1991," Public Law (PL) 101-246, signed into law February 16, 1990. For full text of the new ineligibility provision see Section 131, pp. 38-39.

6. United States Department of State Circular Diplomatic Note, December 19, 1988.

7. *Ibid.*, p.4.

8. United States Department of State Circular Diplomatic Note, November 15, 1989.

9. *Ibid.*, p. 6.

10. United States Department of State Annual Report on the Implementation of Foreign Missions Act of 1982, amended (PL 97-24).

11. *Ibid.*, p. 2.

12. *Ibid.*, p. 25.

13. *Ibid.*, p. 21.

14. See Chapter 11 of the Report of the International Law Commission on work of its forty-first session, 44 UN General Assembly Official Records Supplement (No. 10), UN Document A/44/10 (1989). For a more detailed discussion of the draft articles see the *American Journal of International Law*, January 1989, Vol. 83, pp. 937-940.

Diplomatic Chronology

(Arranged Topically)

DIPLOMATIC RELATIONS

1989

JANUARY 20	Viraj Mendis, a leader of the Communist Party in Sri Lanka, was deported from the United Kingdom where he had been an illegal alien for the past ten years. Fearing death at the hands of Sinhalese extremists if he returned home, Mendis sought sanctuary in an Anglican church but was forcibly removed and sent home.
JANUARY 21	As Soviet forces withdrew from Afghanistan, the Federal Republic of Germany removed the last three members of its embassy staff in Kabul because of heavy fighting between government and mujahidin forces near the city.
JANUARY 27	France, Italy, Japan, and the United Kingdom announced intentions to close their Kabul embassies.
JANUARY 30	The US embassy in Kabul closed as fighting near the capital increased.
FEBRUARY 1	The Republic of Korea and the Hungarian People's Republic established full diplomatic relations.
FEBRUARY 2	The Republic of Cyprus established diplomatic relations with the Islamic Republic of Iran.
FEBRUARY 20	The nations of the European Community (EC) recalled their ambassadors to Iran following that nation's death threat to Salman Rushdie, whom many Moslems alleged had slandered their faith in his book *The Satanic Verses*.
FEBRUARY 25	The Republic of Indonesia and the People's Republic of China agreed to restore full diplomatic relations severed in the wake of the 1965 Indonesian failed communist coup attempt.

MARCH 7	Iran broke off diplomatic relations with the United Kingdom amid the acrimony surrounding the death threat to Rushdie.
MARCH 8	The United Kingdom expelled nine Iranian embassy staffers (who did not possess diplomatic immunity) from London in retaliation.
MARCH 9	The United States expelled Lt. Col. Yuri Pakhtusov, an assistant military attache at the Soviet embassy in Washington, for attempting to obtain classified documents from a US government computer system.
MARCH 15	The Soviet Union expelled US assistant military attache Lt. Col. Francis Van Grundy in retaliation for the US action of March 9.
MARCH 20	The EC agreed that its members may return their ambassadors to Tehran after having recalled them on February 20 following the Ayatollah Ruhollah Khomeini's call for the death of British author Salman Rushdie.
MARCH 23	The United States expelled Sergei Malinin, a Soviet trade official in New York, but did not accuse him of espionage.
MARCH 30	Canadian Minister of Exterior Affairs Joe Clark announced an end to Canada's ban on high-level government contacts with the Palestine Liberation Organization. Israel condemned the move.
APRIL 5	The Federal Republic of Germany recalled its ambassador to Bucharest to protest Romanian human rights abuses.
	Romania recalled its ambassador to London to protest British support for Romanian dissidents.
APRIL 12	The Republic of Seychelles established diplomatic relations with the Democratic Republic of Madagascar.
APRIL 19	The Republic of Seychelles established diplomatic relations with Ivory Coast.
APRIL 28	France expelled South African diplomat Daniel Storm and two others from that country's Paris embassy for their role in attempting to supply Blowpipe missile parts to representatives of a protestant Northern Irish paramilitary organization.
MAY	Chile engaged in a flurry of diplomatic activity by restoring consular relations with Poland and Hungary and hosting the opening of the Finnish embassy in Santiago.
MAY 4	Costa Rica recalled its ambassador to Managua after the Nicaraguan government accused him of participating in opposition activities.

MAY 5	The United Kingdom expelled two South African diplomats from London in a follow-up to the Daniel Storm affair of April 28.
MAY 9	The Palestine Liberation Organization applied for membership to the United Nations Educational, Scientific, and Cultural Organization (UNESCO).
MAY 15	The US ambassador to Panama, Arthur Davis, was recalled to Washington for consultations following the tensions surrounding the fraudulent Panamanian elections of May 7.
MAY 19	The United Kingdom expelled eight Soviet diplomats and embassy staff and three journalists for "activities incompatible with their status." Additionally, three other Soviet diplomats, then out of the country, were not allowed to return.
MAY 20	The Soviet Union took identical action against the British in Moscow.
MAY 25	The United Kingdom expelled four Czech diplomats from London for "activities incompatible with their status."
	Nicaragua expelled two U.S. diplomats for allegedly fomenting labor unrest in Managua.
MAY 31	The United States expelled two Nicaraguan diplomats in retaliation for similar Nicaraguan action five days earlier.
JUNE 11	Two Chinese diplomats stationed in San Francisco asked for asylum in the United States following their government's crushing of the pro-democracy movement in Beijing.
JUNE 28	The People's Republic of China recalled all ambassadors stationed abroad for consultations after the Tienanmen Square suppression.
JULY 17	Poland and the Vatican restored full diplomatic relations severed in 1945.
	Austria formally applied for admission to the EC.
AUGUST	Party-to-party relations were restored between the Lao People's Revolutionary Party and the Chinese Communist Party.
AUGUST 16-17	The United Kingdom and Argentina began talks in New York aimed at paving the way for the establishment of diplomatic relations severed at the time of the South Atlantic conflict. Further talks are to be held in Madrid on October 17-18.
AUGUST 21	The Republic of Senegal broke off diplomatic relations with the Islamic Republic of Mauritania.

	The Mauritanian government declared the ambassador of Senegal persona non grata.
AUGUST 22	Turkey announced it would close its border with Bulgaria in order to stem the flood of ethnic Turks to its territory.
SEPTEMBER 6	The US embassy in Beirut was closed and the staff was evacuated following violent demonstrations by Lebanese Christians protesting American "complicity" with Syrian forces battling Gen. Michel Aoun's Christian Lebanese army.
SEPTEMBER 18	Israel and Hungary reestablished diplomatic relations severed in 1967.
OCTOBER 19	Following three days of talks in Madrid, Argentina and the United Kingdom announced resumption of consular ties severed in 1982.
NOVEMBER 3	The State of Israel and Socialist Ethiopia established diplomatic relations.
NOVEMBER 26	El Salvador announced that it will sever all diplomatic ties with Nicaragua after two Nicaraguan aircraft alleged to have been carrying weapons to the Farabundo Marti National Liberation Front (FMLN) guerrillas, crashed in El Salvador.
DECEMBER 1	Following the meeting of Soviet leader Mikhail Gorbachev and Pope John Paul II in Rome, it was announced that the Vatican and the Soviet Union would work to establish diplomatic relations.
DECEMBER 8	The Soviet Union and South Korea announced plans to exchange consular missions in each other's capitals.
DECEMBER 20	The US State Department announced that the incomplete US embassy facility in Moscow would be razed. Construction on the building had been halted in 1985 after sophisticated eavesdropping devices were discovered throughout its structure.
DECEMBER 27	Egypt and Syria restored full diplomatic relations, severed for ten years following the Camp David accords.
DECEMBER 30	The Nicaraguan government expelled twenty US diplomats and cut the embassy support staff from 320 to 100 following the search of the residence of the Nicaraguan ambassador in Panama by US soldiers on December 29.

1990

JANUARY 3-4	South African Foreign Minister Roelof F. Botha visited Hungary to work toward establishing diplomatic relations between the two

Diplomatic Chronology

countries.

JANUARY 9 — France reopened its embassy in Afghanistan nearly a year after it had closed its mission because of security fears stemming from the withdrawal of Soviet troops in early 1989.

JANUARY 10 — The Soviet Union announced that it would allow the PLO's mission in Moscow to be upgraded into the "embassy of the state of Palestine in the Soviet Union." The Soviet representative to the PLO's government-in-exile in Tunis would in turn be considered an ambassador.

Israel and the Soviet Union agreed to upgrade Soviet representation in Israel from a consular delegation to a legation, a step closer to full embassy status.

FEBRUARY 9 — Hungary reestablished diplomatic relations with the Vatican.

Czechoslovakia restored diplomatic relations with Israel.

FEBRUARY 15 — Great Britain and Argentina restored diplomatic relations, which had been broken during 1982.

FEBRUARY 27 — Poland resumed full diplomatic relations with Israel.

MARCH 15 — The Vatican and the Soviet Union reestablished limited diplomatic ties that had been broken in 1923.

MARCH 22 — Panama announced the expulsion of Cuban Ambassador Lazaro Mora Secades because Cuba had refused to recognize the government of President Guillermo Endara.

MARCH 30 — South Korean officials announced that President Roh Tae Woo and Soviet President Mikhail Gorbachev had agreed to make efforts to normalize relations between their countries.

APRIL 19 — Diplomatic relations between the Vatican and Czechoslovakia were restored.

APRIL 24 — British Foreign Minister William Waldegrave said that restoration of British relations with Syria and Iran depended on positive moves from those two governments.

APRIL 30 — China lifted martial law in Tibet.

MAY 10 — China released dissidents in an effort to influence United States policy on trade relations with China.

The United States temporarily recalled Ambassador Alan Green, Jr., from Romania as a protest over reported irregularities in the Romanian electoral campaign.

Environmental Diplomacy

1989

MARCH	One hundred and sixteen nations, meeting in Basel, Switzerland, concluded the Convention to Control Transboundary Movements of Hazardous Wastes. Fifty-three nations, including the United States, have signed the agreement.
MARCH 11	An "environmental summit" was held in The Hague and issued a declaration calling for a supranational organization with special enforcement powers to protect the earth's atmosphere. Neither the United States nor the Soviet Union was invited to attend.
MAY 12	President Bush announced he would support negotiations leading to a framework convention on climate changes.
MAY 25	In a speech to environmentalists, British Prime Minister Margaret Thatcher called for stabilization of UK carbon dioxide emissions at 1990 levels by 2005.
JULY 11	Japanese Prime Minister Uno announced a $43-billion package of grants and loans to Third World countries to improve the global environment.
JULY 16	The Group of Seven—the leading industrial nations—devoted one-third of the final communiqué from their Paris summit to environmental concerns, such as controlling carbon dioxide emissions.
JULY 21	President George Bush submitted his proposed update of the Clean Air Act to Congress.
OCTOBER 2	EC environmental ministers agreed to impose emission standards for new small cars in 1992.
NOVEMBER 6	At a sixty-eight nation conference on global warming in the Netherlands, several nations called for a commitment to strong measures aimed at curbing carbon dioxide emissions.
DECEMBER 22	The UN General Assembly agreed to draw up a treaty on stabilizing world climate and to convene a world environmental conference in Brazil in 1992.

Before the Environmental Diplomacy section:

MAY 14 — Philippine and US negotiators opened talks on extending US leases of bases in the Philippines.

1990

JANUARY 9 — Soviet and US officials recommended the creation of an international park along the Bering Sea.

JANUARY 15 — Delegates from eighty-three nations met in Moscow for the Global Forum of Spiritual and Parliamentary Leaders on Human Survival.

In Kingston a meeting was held to conclude the final protocol on Specially Protected Areas for Wildlife.

JANUARY 29 — Formal negotiations began in Geneva on controlling emissions of volatile organic compounds.

APRIL 17-18 — President Bush issued a cautious call for more research on global warming at a White House conference on the subject. Foreign delegates criticized the statement for not proposing enough action.

MAY 2 — World Bank President Barber Conable said he would ask members to establish an environmental fund.

An international conference of legislators meeting in Washington called for a global "Marshall Plan" to provide aid to developing countries to cope with environmental problems.

MAY 9 — The United States announced its opposition to a UN plan to provide direct aid to Third World countries to reduce use of chlorofluorocarbons.

JUNE 29 — Review meeting of signatories to Montreal Protocol on Ozone opened in London.

Passage of Clean Air Act.

AUGUST 6-31 — The preparatory committee meeting on the next UN conference on Environment and Development (Brazil 1992) was held in Nairobi.

INTERNATIONAL ORGANIZATIONS

1989

SEPTEMBER 4-7 — The 102-member Non-Aligned Movement held its ninth summit in Belgrade. A more moderate, less anti-American final communiqué is issued at its conclusion than in years past.

SEPTEMBER 21	The forty-fourth annual session of the UN General Assembly opened in New York. Joseph Namvan Garba of Nigeria was elected president.
SEPTEMBER 26-28	The International Monetary Fund and World Bank met in Washington.
OCTOBER 18	Cuba, Ivory Coast, Romania, South Yemen, and Zaire were elected nonpermanent members of the UN Security Council for a term of two years.
OCTOBER 18-24	The forty-nine-member Commonwealth (formerly the British Commonwealth) held its annual meeting in Malaysia. The topic of sanctions against South Africa dominated the conference, with Great Britain dissenting against the majority's opinion that sanctions should be leveled and enforced.
OCTOBER 26	The UN High Commissioner for Refugees resigned over alleged misuse of funds.
OCTOBER 30	The US Congress cut $123 million from the administration's proposal for contributions to the UN and its agencies.

1990

JANUARY 4	The union of UN civil servants asked Secretary-General Javier Perez de Cuellar to extend the contracts of Chinese workers at the Secretariat to protect them from Chinese government pressure.
FEBRUARY 2	Cuban UN delegate Ricardo Alarcon de Quesada assumed presidency of the Security Council, the first Cuban to hold this post since 1957.
FEBRUARY 3	President Bush presented a budget plan that would pay off US debts to the UN over five years.
FEBRUARY 20	In an address to the UN General Assembly, James Baker called on that body to adopt a global antinarcotics program.

INTERNATIONAL TRADE AND ECONOMICS

1989

JANUARY 1	The US-EC trade dispute erupted over the refusal of the EC to allow imports of US beef treated with growth hormones. The US

Diplomatic Chronology 201

responded by placing a 100-percent tariff on the first $100 million of imported EC foodstuffs.

The US-Canada Trade Pact of 1988 became operative.

FEBRUARY 2-3   The finance ministers of the Group of Seven—Canada, Federal Republic of Germany, France, Italy, Japan, United Kingdom, and the United States—met in Washington and reaffirmed their commitment to stable exchange rates and economic coordination.

FEBRUARY 7   The US Congress approved a measure for $42 million in emergency aid to Panama.

FEBRUARY 19   The United States and the European Community called a truce in their trade dispute for seventy-five days after US Special Trade Representative (USTR) Carla Hills and EC External Affairs Commissioner Frans Andriessen met.

MARCH 10   US Treasury Secretary Nicholas F. Brady announced the "Brady Plan" for the Third World debt crisis calling for a degree of voluntary debt forgiveness by commercial banks and the aid of the International Monetary Fund (IMF) and World Bank in financing debt relief.

APRIL 3-4   The World Bank and IMF convened in Washington and endorsed the Brady Plan.

APRIL 8   The General Agreement on Tariffs and Trade (GATT) cleared the way to resume the stalled Uruguay Round of trade negotiations by resolving disputes in four areas: agriculture, textiles, intellectual property, and import safeguards.

MAY 25   Bush formally accused Brazil, India, and Japan of unfair trading practices in the first use of the so-called "Super 301" provision of the 1988 Omnibus Trade Act. He called for special bilateral trade negotiations with each nation to abolish the inequalities.

JUNE 21   At its semiannual meeting in Geneva, the GATT criticized the US unilateral denunciation of Brazilian, Indian, and Japanese trade practices.

JULY 4-5   Nineteen Western and Asian nations and seven international financial organizations met in Tokyo to unveil a massive multilateral aid package for the Philippines.

JULY 14-16   The economic summit of the Group of Seven industrial democracies was held in Paris.

Bush visited Paris for the Group of Seven economic summit.

SEPTEMBER 23   The finance ministers of the Group of Seven met in Washington.

SEPTEMBER 27	The Organization of Petroleum Exporting Countries (OPEC) concluded its meeting in Geneva. No agreement was reached establishing production quotas for member states.
OCTOBER 3	President Bush and Mexican President Carlos Salinas de Gortari signed a new US-Mexican trade agreement in Washington.
NOVEMBER 6-7	The Asian-Pacific Economic Cooperation Conference was held in Canberra. A permanent organization of twelve Pacific Rim nations, plus the United States and Canada, was formed to promote trade liberalization and economic cooperation in the region.
NOVEMBER 28	OPEC ministers convened in Vienna to sign an agreement establishing oil production quotas for the member states.
DECEMBER 7	The EC and the six-member European Free Trade Association—Austria, Finland, Iceland, Norway, Sweden, Switzerland—agreed to ease restrictions on economic transactions among the blocs.
DECEMBER 8-9	An EC summit in Strasbourg set the date for a conference on the European Economic and Monetary Union (EMU) for December 1990. Britain eased its position against such a conference.
DECEMBER 18	The EC blocked the application of Turkey to the organization.

1990

JANUARY 1	Fifteen industrial nations established a $1-billion fund to help stabilize the Polish *zloty* and make it fully convertible with Western currencies.
JANUARY 9	Suzuki Motor Co. Ltd. of Japan announced plans for a joint venture in Hungary to build that country's first automobile plant.
	Romania asked the United States to consider reviving Romania's Most Favored Nation trade status, which Nicolae Ceausescu renounced in 1988.
JANUARY 9-15	During a whirlwind tour of Europe, Japanese Premier Toshiki Kaifu announced a total of $1 billion in aid to Poland and Hungary.
JANUARY 10	The Council for Mutual Economic Assistance (COMECON) agreed to gradually adopt a free-market approach in their trading policies.
JANUARY 11	French Foreign Minister Roland Dumas visited Bucharest and announced a package of economic assistance for Romania.

JANUARY 17	Japan's Ministry of International Trade and Industry announced that the voluntary export quota of 2.3-million cars to the United States per year would also be used in 1990. China and Hong Kong announced that they will not obey a global ban on ivory trading.
JANUARY 24	International Business Machines (IBM) and Siemens AG of West Germany agreed to join together in the research and development of a new generation of semiconductor chips.
JANUARY 25	President Bush proposed a $1-billion aid package to Panama.
JANUARY 31	McDonald's (fast food restaurant) opened its first outlet in the Soviet Union in Moscow.
FEBRUARY 4	Mexico signed a new debt-reduction pact with its leading creditor banks.
FEBRUARY 5	The IMF approved $723 million in standby credit for Poland.
FEBRUARY 6	The World Bank approved $360 million to Poland.
FEBRUARY 7	The US Congress approved a measure for $42 million in emergency aid to Panama.
FEBRUARY 16	The Club of Paris group of creditor nations agreed to reschedule the payment of $9.4 billion of Poland's debt to Western governments. The G-24 nations—a group of twenty-four leading industrial nations—reaffirmed commitments to aid the Polish and Hungarian economies with financial and humanitarian assistance.
FEBRUARY 20	American and South Korean negotiators resolved some key disputes over the opening of the South Korean telecommunications market to US companies.
FEBRUARY 22	USTR Carla Hills said the United States would fight any attempt by Europeans to close their markets to Japanese cars manufactured in US "transplant" factories.
FEBRUARY 26	US and Canadian trade officials signed a fee export agreement for meat products.
FEBRUARY 27	The United States and the European Community reached agreement on holding regular summit meetings between their respective leaders.
MARCH 2-3	Prime Minister Kaifu and President Bush met in Palm Springs, California to talk about the long-standing trade imbalance between the United States and Japan.

MARCH 14	The IMF approved the first installment of $206 million in standby credit for Hungary.
MARCH 22	US and Soviet negotiators in Vienna reached a five-year grain agreement.
MARCH 23	The United States and Japan announced an agreement that would make Japanese markets more open to US-made supercomputers.
MARCH 23-25	As part of the Structural Impediments Initiative (SII), US and Japanese negotiators exchanged lists of detailed suggestions on improving each other's economies.
MARCH 27	Preliminary talks began on a free trade pact between the United States and Mexico.
MARCH 29	Mexico announced that it will resume a program of swapping debt for equity that was suspended in 1987.
MARCH 30	The US government released a foreign trade report that cited thirty-five countries and two regional trading blocs with barriers to US exports.
APRIL 1	EC finance ministers met in Galway, Ireland, to discuss economic and monetary union.
	The IMF reported that the United States was the world's largest exporter in 1989.
APRIL 5	The United States and Japan pledge to move toward eliminating major structural barriers to free trade.
APRIL 7	Economics ministers of the Group of Seven meeting in Paris discussed the fall of the yen and German unification.
APRIL 9	Forty-two industrial nations agreed at a meeting in Paris to create a special bank to aid the economies of Eastern Europe.
APRIL 12	Czechoslovakia signed a trade agreement with the United States.
APRIL 24	West German Chancellor Helmut Kohl and East German Premier Lothar de Maiziere agreed on instituting a currency union at the beginning of July.
APRIL 25	President Bush restored Nicaragua's eligibility for credits and loan guarantees from the US Export-Import Bank.
MAY 5	Costa Rican President Oscar Arias Sanchez signed a debt buy-back agreement with commercial bank creditors.
MAY 6	Finance officials from the Group of Seven meeting in Washington agreed to increase the lending resources of the IMF by 50 percent

Diplomatic Chronology 205

	and to penalize nations in arrears on repayment of IMF loans.
MAY 7	Czechoslovakia signed a ten-year accord on trade and cooperation with the European Community.
MAY 13	Mexico's Chamber of Deputies approved a constitutional amendment returning control of the nation's banks to private hands.
MAY 16	President George Bush announced that he cannot offer Nicaragua the immediate $40-million loan requested by Nicaraguan President Violeta Barrias Chamorro.
	The GATT's top decision-making council unanimously agreed to grant the Soviet Union observer status.

REGIONAL DIPLOMACY

Africa

1989

JANUARY 4-5	King Hassan II of Morocco held the first direct talks with leaders of the Polisario Front with whom Moroccan forces had been at war in the Western Sahara for thirteen years.
JANUARY 27	Kenya and Sudan quarreled over Sudan's assertion of territorial right to Kenya's northern Elemi Triangle region.
JUNE 22	President Mobuto Sese Seko of Zaire called a meeting of twenty African leaders in the Zairean town of Gbadolite that included Angolan President Eduard Dos Santos and Jonas Savimbi, leader of the Angolan antigovernment guerrilla organization, the Union for the Total Independence of Namibia (UNITA). The two agreed to a formal cease-fire in Angola on June 24 after thirteen years of civil war.
JULY 28-30	Peace talks between the government of Angola and UNITA began in Kinshasa, Zaire. Initial meetings end with little accomplished.
SEPTEMBER 7-19	The government of Ethiopia and representatives of the Eritrean People's Liberation Front held initial peace talks at the Carter Center in Atlanta, Georgia.
SEPTEMBER 18	President Mobuto called a meeting of the heads of state of Angola, the Congo, Gabon, Mozambique, Sao Tome and Principe, Zambia,

and Zimbabwe and tried unsuccessfully to mend the Angolan cease-fire, which had been broken since August. UNITA leader Savimbi declined to attend.

1990

JANUARY 5	Dissidents failed in a coup attempt to overthrow the regime of Liberian President Samuel K. Doe. The fighting destroyed several towns and sent thousands of people fleeing across the border into neighboring Ivory Coast.
JANUARY 8-FEBRUARY 24	To escape the civil war in Liberia, at least 70,000 refugees fled to the Ivory Coast and Guinea.
JANUARY 21	In a meeting in Zambia, the African National Congress (ANC) reaffirmed its readiness to engage in peaceful negotiations with the South African government.
JANUARY 25-FEBRUARY 1	Pope John Paul II visited Cape Verde, Guinea-Bissau, Mali, Burkina Faso, and Chad in his sixth trip to Africa.
FEBRUARY 2	The South African government lifted its thirty-year ban on the ANC.
FEBRUARY 11	South African black nationalist leader Nelson Mandela was freed after more than twenty-seven years in prison.
FEBRUARY 27	Mandela traveled to Zambia in his first trip outside of South Africa in twenty-seven years.
FEBRUARY 28	Zulu Chief Mangasuthu Gatsha Buthelezi met with President Bush in Washington, urging the lifting of economic sanctions against South Africa.
MARCH 1-2	The executive committee of the ANC formally named Mandela to be the organization's deputy president.
MARCH 12	Mandela met with Oliver Tambo, the ailing ANC president in Stockholm. It was their first meeting in twenty-eight years.
MARCH 21	Namibia became the world's newest independent nation, ending seventy-five years of South African rule.
MARCH 22	US Secretary of State James Baker met with South African President F. W. deKlerk in Cape Town to discuss potential reforms in South Africa.
MARCH 26-28	The foreign ministers of Libya and Chad met in Gabon to discuss the status of the Azouzou Strip.

APRIL 5	President deKlerk met with Mandela in Cape Town to prepare for future talks.
MAY 2-4	Representatives of the South African government and the African National Congress (ANC) held their first formal talks in Cape Town. A joint statement was issued, paving the way for further meetings.
August 25	African peacekeeping group landed in Liberia.

Asia and the Pacific

1989

JANUARY 16	North Korean Prime Minister Yon Hyong Muk agreed to a South Korean proposal to establish high-level talks between the governments of the two Koreas to be held in Seoul and Pyongyang.
JANUARY 16-19	Talks between senior representatives of the People's Republic of China and Vietnam were held for the first time in nine years. The question of Cambodia was discussed, with little result.
JANUARY 25	The US State Department announced that US and North Korean diplomats held meetings in Beijing during December 1988, the first such meetings since the United States eased restrictions on contacts with North Korea in October 1988.
FEBRUARY 1-4	Soviet Foreign Minister Eduard Shevardnadze visited the People's Republic of China to prepare the ground for the first Sino-Soviet summit since 1959 to be held in Beijing May 15-18.
FEBRUARY 5-6	Shevardnadze visited Pakistan to try to reach a settlement averting civil war in Afghanistan after the withdrawal of Soviet troops from that country. He asked Prime Minister Benazir Bhutto to cease arms shipments to the Afghan mujahiden.
FEBRUARY 8	Talks between the governments of North and South Korea, designed to pave the way for a foreign ministers meeting, broke down after only two hours.
FEBRUARY 11-13	Prime Minister Bhutto visited Beijing and signed a $225-million contract for the purchase of seventy-five F-7 fighter aircraft.
FEBRUARY 18-21	Peace talks between warring factions in Cambodia began under Indonesian auspices in Jakarta.

FEBRUARY 23-27	President Bush toured Asia, stopping first in Tokyo for the funeral of Emperor Hirohito and proceeding to the People's Republic of China and the Republic of Korea.
APRIL 9	Vietnam announced that it will remove all of its troops from Cambodia by the end of September.
MAY 15-18	Soviet President Mikhail Gorbachev visited the People's Republic of China, the first such visit by a Soviet leader in thirty years. Full normalization of diplomatic relations was established, and the issues of Cambodia and economic liberalization were discussed.
JUNE 13-14	A sixty-nation conference in Geneva adopted a Comprehensive Plan of Action designed to stanch the flow of refugees from Indochina.
JUNE 28	The United States and Vietnam signed an accord providing for the resettlement of former South Vietnamese government officials in the United States.
JULY 30-AUGUST 30	The nineteen-nation Peace Conference on Cambodia convened in Paris. All five factions striving for power in Cambodia were represented, and the conference was presided over by the Indonesian government.
SEPTEMBER 11	South Korean President Roh Tae Woo unveiled a comprehensive plan for the reunification of Korea. It was immediately dismissed by the North Korean government.
SEPTEMBER 28	North Korea offered to begin a new round of reunification talks with South Korea in early 1990.
OCTOBER 13	Radical South Korean students, opposed to US influence in their country, broke into the residence of US Ambassador Donald P. Gregg. Gregg and his wife escaped unharmed.
DECEMBER 9-10	The president's adviser on national security, General Brent Scowcroft, and Deputy Secretary of State Lawrence Eagleburger paid a surprise visit to Beijing where they held ten hours of talks with Chinese leaders in an attempt to stabilize Sino-American relations.
DECEMBER 12	The government of Hong Kong forcibly repatriated fifty-one Vietnamese refugees despite the criticism of the United States and Amnesty International.

1990

JANUARY 5	The first group of former political prisoners who had been tied to the American-backed regime in Saigon during the Vietnam War

	were allowed to emigrate to the United States.
JANUARY 6	India and Sri Lanka announced that they had reached agreement on the withdrawal of the final 25,000 Indian peacekeeping troops from Sri Lanka by March 31.
JANUARY 10	In Beijing, Li Peng announced the lifting of the eight-month-old martial law that had been imposed to stamp out democratic dissent.
JANUARY 13-16	British Foreign Secretary Douglas Hurd visited Hong Kong to assess plans for democratic reform here before its return to Chinese sovereignty in 1997.
JANUARY 16	The five permanent members of the UN Security Council issued a joint statement calling for a greater UN role in the settlement of Cambodia's eleven-year-old civil war.
JANUARY 20	China adopted a new twenty-two-point press code that expanded government control over foreign journalists.
JANUARY 21	The Indian government rejected a $470-million settlement agreement with US-based Union Carbide that was to compensate victims of a 1984 gas leak at the company's chemical plant in Bhopol, India.
JANUARY 21-23	The foreign ministers of Pakistan and India met in New Delhi to discuss the unrest in Kashmir.
JANUARY 23	Australian Foreign Minister Gareth Evans stated that Australia was ending its ban on visits to China by top government officials, but that proposed visits would have to be reviewed on an individual basis.
FEBRUARY 14-23	US Defense Secretary Richard Cheney toured South Korea, the Philippines, Hong Kong, and Japan. Although proposing some cuts in US forces in the area, he stressed that an American military presence was still critical for security purposes.
FEBRUARY 26-MARCH 1	The UN-sponsored Cambodian peace conference held at Jakarta ended with no conclusive agreement reached.
MARCH 24	India withdrew the last of its peacekeeping troops from Sri Lanka.
APRIL 1	The Chinese government sealed off most of Tiananmen Square to avert a repeat of last summer's massive demonstrations.
APRIL 10-15	Pakistan and Indian officials exchanged threats as fighting between Moslem separatists and the police continued in the Indian province of Jammu and Kashmir.
APRIL 30	China lifts martial law in Tibet.

May 10	China releases dissidents in an effort to influence US policy on trade relations with China.
May 14	Philippine and US negotiators open talks on extending US leases of bases in the Philippines.
August 28	Five permanent members of the United Nations Security Council agree on the main elements of a political settlement to end the Cambodian civil war. The agreement still required the compliance of the four competing military and political factions in Cambodia; they were scheduled to meet in Jakarta in October to discuss the plan.

Europe

1989

January 7-11	A 149-nation conference in Paris condemned the use of chemical weapons and reaffirmed the 1925 Geneva Protocol prohibiting the use of chemical weapons in war.
January 12	Relations between Greece and Turkey deteriorated after Greek and Turkish fighter aircraft sparred over the eastern Aegean. This followed closely the passage of a Turkish law of January 7 placing northern Cyprus and the eastern Aegean under Turkish air-sea rescue jurisdiction.
January 19	The Vienna Conference on Security and Cooperation in Europe (CSCE) Review Conference (the third such formal review) concluded. The Vienna Final Document reaffirmed and made more explicit the human rights provisions of the original Helsinki agreement.
February 7	The United Nations Conference on Disarmament (CD) convened in Geneva through April 27.
February 10-17	Secretary of State Baker toured NATO countries. The issue of allied short-range nuclear forces (SNF) predominated in his talks.
February 20	In a meeting in Dublin, EC foreign ministers gave their unanimous approval to German unity.
March 3	A British court sentenced a Czech national using a forged Dutch passport to ten years in prison for espionage.
March 6	The Conference on Conventional Forces in Europe (CFE) convened in Vienna, supplanting the Mutual and Balanced Force

	Reduction talks, which had begun in 1973. The twenty-three members of the North Atlantic Treaty Organization (NATO) and Warsaw Pact alliances negotiated directly within the framework of the larger CSCE process.
MARCH 7	The government of Poland formally accused the Soviet Union of having committed the Katyn Forest Massacre of 1940 in which 4,000 Polish military officers were executed in a wood outside Smolensk.
MARCH 9	The Conference on Confidence and Security Building Measures and Disarmament in Europe (CSE) convened in Vienna. All thirty-five members of the CSCE participated.
	The UN Commission on Human Rights voted 21 to 7 to investigate human rights abuses in Romania.
APRIL 5	The United States announced that it will issue 150,000 special visas over the next three years to Soviet citizens wishing to immigrate.
APRIL 5-7	President Gorbachev visited the United Kingdom during his return trip to Moscow from Havana, his first such visit since December 1987.
APRIL 11	The Warsaw Pact foreign ministers met in East Berlin and called for talks to abolish all short-range nuclear forces from Europe.
MAY 2	Hungary began dismantling the barbed wire partitions marking its border with neutral Austria.
MAY 4	A court in Scotland sentenced Yugoslav national Vizko Sinicic to fifteen years in prison for the attempted murder of Nikola Stedul, émigré leader of the Croatian Movement for Statehood.
MAY 5	Finland became the fortieth member of the Council of Europe.
	Round II of both the CFE and CSE commenced in Vienna and were scheduled to conclude July 13-14.
MAY 10-11	Baker visited Moscow to discuss arms control with Gorbachev and Shevardnadze.
MAY 22	Poland and the German Democratic Republic signed a treaty redefining their maritime boundary, which had been in dispute since the GDR's 1985 declaration extending its territorial waters to twelve miles.
MAY 26-JUNE 2	President Bush tours Western Europe, visiting Italy, West Germany, Belgium, and Britain. He participated in the NATO summit in Brussels, May 29-30.

MAY 29-30	The annual NATO summit in Brussels marked the fortieth anniversary of the alliance. Compromise is reached in the controversy surrounding the role of SNF in NATO arms control strategy.
JUNE 3	The Soviet ambassador to the United Kingdom, Leonid Zamyatin, issued a "vigorous protest" to the British government claiming that sixty electronic listening devices had been found in the Soviet trade delegation office and in the homes of Soviet diplomats and journalists in London.
JUNE 9	The United States granted asylum to a Soviet pilot who defected to Turkey on May 20 with his MiG-29 fighter aircraft.
JUNE 11-21	Chairman of the US Joint Chiefs of Staff Admiral William Crowe toured the Soviet Union, the first chairman of the Joint Chiefs to do so.
JUNE 12	The United States and Soviet Union signed an accord banning the use of military force in the event of accidental confrontation or misunderstanding.
JUNE 12-15	Gorbachev made his first state visit to the Federal Republic of Germany. He was enthusiastically welcomed by the West German public.
JUNE 13	The United Nations Conference on Disarmament in Geneva convened until August 31.
JUNE 19	Round XI of the Nuclear and Space Talks (NST) opened in Geneva after a seven-month recess.
JUNE 25-27	The EC summit was held in Madrid and leveled economic sanctions on the People's Republic of China following the crackdown on the pro-democracy movement in Beijing. Intention to proceed toward full economic union by 1992 was reaffirmed.
JULY 4-6	Gorbachev paid a state visit to France. On July 6 he addressed the Council of Europe at Strasbourg and concluded his visit by signing twenty-one separate accords with France concerning management training of Soviet executives in France, military exchanges between the two nations, and areas of agreement on the crisis in Lebanon.
JULY 7-8	The Warsaw Pact summit in Bucharest was marked by tension and some disunity over the scope and pace of political reforms in member countries.
JULY 8	Hungarian and Romanian diplomats met to discuss rising tensions caused by the mistreatment of ethnic Hungarians in Romania. The meeting was described as heated and unsuccessful by Hungarian foreign minister Gyula Horn.

Diplomatic Chronology

JULY 9-13	Bush visited Poland and Hungary and unveiled US aid packages for the two nations designed to expedite liberal reforms in those nations.
JULY 14-16	The seven Western industrial democracies held their annual summit in Paris and resolved to encourage liberal reform in Eastern Europe, cooperate to protect the earth's environment, and reduce Third World debt. The bicentennial of the French Revolution was also observed.
JULY 17	President Bush spoke in Leiden, the Netherlands, to endorse European political and economic integration.
AUGUST 24	The 108 East Germans encamped in the West German embassy in Budapest were allowed to immigrate to West Germany. By this day, 116 East Germans at Bonn's East Berlin mission and 150 at its Prague embassy had sought permission to immigrate. The previous day, Bonn was forced to close its Prague embassy to visitors because of the flood of East Germans.
SEPTEMBER 7-8	Round III of CFE and CSE convened in Vienna.
SEPTEMBER 20	West Germany closed its Warsaw embassy to visitors because of the flood of East Germans seeking asylum.
SEPTEMBER 22-23	Secretary Baker and Foreign Minister Eduard Shevardnadze met in Jackson Hole, Wyoming to discuss arms control matters.
SEPTEMBER 28	Round XII of the Strategic Arms Reduction Talks (START) began in Geneva.
SEPTEMBER 30-OCTOBER 4	More than 17,000 East Germans fled to West Germany via Prague and Warsaw.
OCTOBER 4	The eighteen East Germans encamped at the US embassy in East Berlin were promised permission to immigrate if they left the embassy compound.
OCTOBER 25-27	In his visit to Finland, Gorbachev declared that the Soviet Union will respect the sovereign authority of its neighbors to determine their own political systems. (Spokesman Gennadi Gerasimov declared that the Brezhnev Doctrine had been supplanted by the so-called Sinatra Doctrine allowing satellite nations to "do it their way.") Gorbachev also renewed his 1987 "Baltic Peace Initiative" designed to create a nuclear free zone in Scandinavia.
OCTOBER 26-27	The Warsaw Pact foreign ministers met in Warsaw. Shevardnadze advocated a shift in emphasis on Warsaw Pact from military to political alliance. He called for eventual phasing out of NATO and Warsaw Pact.

OCTOBER 30	Turkey and Bulgaria held talks in Kuwait designed to resolve their differences concerning the treatment of ethnic Turks in Bulgaria.
NOVEMBER 9	East Germany relaxed all restrictions on travel and immigration, virtually opening its borders.
NOVEMBER 9-10, 12-14	West German Chancellor Helmut Kohl visited Poland where he declared Germany's intent to honor the 1970 bilateral non-aggression treaty binding it to respect Poland's existing borders. No formal recognition of the territorial dispute could be extended, however, until a formal Polish-German peace treaty is signed. Kohl also announced a $1.9-billion aid package to Poland.
NOVEMBER 10	Round IV of CFE and CSE commenced in Vienna.
NOVEMBER 11	Kohl announced he will meet with the new East German leadership in December.
NOVEMBER 17	Romania closed its border with Hungary.
NOVEMBER 18	At the request of French President François Mitterrand, the EC held a special summit to discuss developments in Eastern Europe. It was agreed to increase economic aid to the countries making liberal reforms in the East Bloc and to avoid antagonizing the Soviet Union.
NOVEMBER 28	In an address to the Bundestag, Chancellor Kohl outlined a ten-point plan for the establishment of an East-West confederation of the two Germanies.
NOVEMBER 30	Czechoslovakia opened its border with Austria.
DECEMBER 2-3	Bush and Gorbachev held their first summit at Malta. Severe weather disrupts much of the summit, which was to have been held aboard Soviet and American warships off the coast. Talks were held instead aboard the Soviet ocean liner *Maxim Gorky* in Malta's harbor. Topics discussed included the upheaval in Eastern Europe, the pace of conventional and strategic nuclear arms talks, relaxation of US-Soviet trade restrictions, and the flow of Soviet-made arms into Central America. No major proposals were made.
DECEMBER 4	President Bush briefed NATO leaders in Brussels on the Malta summit. In the process, he reaffirmed the US commitment to the military defense of Europe and to its economic and political integration and called for the revitalization of the CSCE process to deal with the developments in Eastern Europe. He also outlined US policy on German reunification.
DECEMBER 7	In a telephone conference following up the Malta summit, Baker and Shevardnadze discussed methods of curbing the flow of Soviet-

made arms to Central America.

DECEMBER 11   The ambassadors of the four allied powers in Germany met in Berlin for the first time in eighteen years to discuss the need for stability "in and around" Berlin following the demise of the Berlin Wall.

DECEMBER 12   Secretary of State Baker, in Berlin, delivered a major speech detailing US policy toward Eastern Europe. Later he met with the new East German premier, Hans Modrow.

DECEMBER 16   President Bush and President Mitterrand met on the Caribbean island of St. Martin. The two agreed on the need for closer US political ties to the EC and an increased political role for NATO.

DECEMBER 18-19   Shevardnadze toured Western Europe, first signing a ten-year trade agreement with the EC and visiting NATO headquarters in Brussels and then addressing the European Parliament in Strasbourg.

DECEMBER 19   Chancellor Kohl and Premier Modrow met for the first time in Dresden. Later the two addressed a large gathering at the Berlin Wall.

1990

JANUARY 1   President Mitterrand called for a confederation of Eastern and Western Europe to ensure peace and security on the continent.

Diplomatic sources estimated that about 7,000 people died in the Romanian revolution of Dec. 1989.

The Romanian provisional government announced the formal disbanding of the Securitate, the Ceausescu regime's internal security apparatus.

JANUARY 2   Czechoslovakia's president, Vaclav Havel, paid official visits to both East and West Germany in his first official trip outside of Czechoslovakia.

JANUARY 6   Foreign Minister Shevardnadze visited Romania and vowed Kremlin support for any future form of political system that emerged in the country.

JANUARY 12   An ethnic crisis in Romania was eased, at least temporarily, by an accord that was reached by a special citizens' committee.

JANUARY 13   President Gorbachev expressed his willingness to accept a multi-party system in the Soviet Union.

JANUARY 15	The Bulgarian Parliament voted to revoke the constitutionally guaranteed dominant role of the Communist Party.
JANUARY 16	An unprecedented seminar on East-West military doctrine was held in Vienna for top military officials from thirty-five European and North American nations.
JANUARY 16-18	A three-day seminar in Vienna under the auspices of the CSCE focused on changes in military doctrine.
JANUARY 22	START resumed in Geneva with the signing of an agreement allowing both sides to inspect each other's nuclear warheads.
JANUARY 23	Yugoslavia's Communist Party voted to relinquish its constitutionally guaranteed political monopoly.
JANUARY 25-26	During official visits to Hungary and Poland, President Havel called for an informal liberal alliance between the three nations within the Eastern bloc.
JANUARY 27-29	The Polish Communist Party voted itself out of existence and reformed as the Social Democratic Party.
JANUARY 31	President Bush proposed the United States and the Soviet Union reduce their conventional forces in Central Europe to 195,000 troops on each side. He also proposed lowering ceilings on US and Soviet troops stationed in Central Europe.
FEBRUARY 1	West German Chancellor Kohl rejected East German Premier Modrow's plan for the eventual reunification of East and West Germany as a neutral nation.
FEBRUARY 2	Secretary of State Baker and German Foreign Minister Hans Dietrich Genscher met in Washington to discuss the prospects of the autumn CSCE meeting.
FEBRUARY 3	Kohl rejected calls for an international referendum on the question of German reunification.
FEBRUARY 6	The West German government promoted a plan to establish the West German mark as the single currency for East and West Germany.
FEBRUARY 6-11	Secretary Baker visited the Soviet Union, Czechoslovakia, Romania, and Bulgaria to confer with their leaders about changes in Eastern Europe, US aid, and disarmament.
FEBRUARY 7	The Soviet Communist Party Central Committee voted to renounce its constitutionally guaranteed monopoly on political power.

Diplomatic Chronology

FEBRUARY 7-10	Baker visited Moscow and discussed arms control issues with Shevardnadze and Gorbachev.
FEBRUARY 10	Kohl met with Gorbachev in Moscow, resulting in the Soviet agreement on the sole right of the German people to decide the issue of reunification.
FEBRUARY 11-13	NATO and Warsaw Pact foreign ministers meeting in Ottawa discussed "Open Skies," a proposal for more complete aerial verification procedures. They supported convening a CSCE summit in November.
FEBRUARY 13	The United States and the Soviet Union announced their intention to reduce the number of each of their nation's troops in Central Europe to 195,000, the ceiling proposed by President Bush in January.
	At an Ottawa conference of NATO and Warsaw Pact leaders, the 2-plus-4 formula for German reunification was established.
	Also at Ottawa, the Soviets and Americans agreed to specified reductions in their European force levels.
FEBRUARY 13-14	Kohl and Modrow met in Bonn to deal with the issues surrounding economic and monetary reunification.
FEBRUARY 15	Kohl met with Mitterrand in Paris to discuss the speed of EC political and economic union.
FEBRUARY 18-22	President Vaclav Havel visited the United States.
FEBRUARY 19	At Pisa, Kohl met Italian Premier Giulio Andreotti to discuss German reunification.
FEBRUARY 20	In a meeting in Dublin, Ireland, the European Community's twelve foreign ministers agreed to ease sanctions against South Africa when that country ended its repression of political dissent.
FEBRUARY 20-23	The United Kingdom unilaterally lifted its ban on new investments in South Africa without consulting with fellow European Community members.
FEBRUARY 21	Polish Prime Minister Tadeusz Mazowiecki declared that Soviet troops would remain in Poland until the "German problem" was resolved.
FEBRUARY 24	In the first true multiparty contest in the Soviet Union in seventy years, Lithuanian voters overwhelmingly backed non-Communist candidates for seats in the republic's parliament.

FEBRUARY 24-25	Kohl and Bush met at Camp David to discuss controversial aspects of German reunification.
FEBRUARY 26	In Moscow, Gorbachev and Havel signed an accord calling for the immediate commencement of a phased withdrawal of Soviet troops from Czechoslovakia to be completed by 1991.
FEBRUARY 28	The first round of lower-level NATO-Warsaw Pact negotiations on verification came to an end. A second round was set for April 23 in Budapest.
MARCH 1	Talks between USSR-Hungary on a complete withdrawal of Soviet forces from Hungary broke down.
MARCH 8	Kohl reassured NATO representatives in Brussels on the likely results of German reunification.
	Eight nations bordering on the North Sea reached an agreement to cut pollution there.
MARCH 11	Soviet forces began a complete withdrawal from Hungary.
	Lithuania's Parliament declared a restoration of the republic's independence from the Soviet Union.
MARCH 13-15	The Soviet Congress of People's Deputies, the national parliament, repealed the Communist Party's political monopoly and elected Gorbachev to a five-year term as executive president of the Soviet Union.
MARCH 14	The 2-plus-4 talks on German reunification opened in Bonn.
MARCH 15	The sixth round of CFE negotiations began.
MARCH 17	The Lithuanian Parliament formed a non-Communist coalition government.
MARCH 20	To discourage further immigration from East Germany, Kohl announced that his government would reduce aid to resettlers as of July 1.
MARCH 20-21	Polish Premier Mazowiecki held talks with President Bush in the United States.
MARCH 21-22	Havel visited Great Britain for talks with Prime Minister Thatcher and Queen Elizabeth II.
MARCH 23	In a speech before the seventeen EC commissioners in Brussels, Kohl said that German reunification would help speed EC integration.

Diplomatic Chronology 219

MARCH 27	The Soviet foreign ministry ordered all foreigners to leave Lithuania.
MARCH 29-30	Thatcher and Kohl held talks in London on current European issues.
MARCH 30	Estonia's Parliament adopted a resolution characterizing the republic as an "occupied" territory and proclaiming a "restoration" of Estonia's prewar status as a free nation.
MARCH 31	Gorbachev warned Lithuania to annul its declaration of independence or face grave consequences.
APRIL 2-3	Czechoslovak Foreign Minister Jiri Dienstbier proposed a new European security structure that included the members of both NATO and the Warsaw Pact.
APRIL 4-6	Shevardnadze met with Baker and Bush in Washington to discuss arms control and other issues. A summit meeting between Bush and Gorbachev was set for May 31-June 3.
APRIL 9	Officials from six nations of the "Adriatic-Danube group"—Austria, Czechoslovakia, Hungary, Italy, Poland, and Yugoslavia—met informally in the Czechsolovak city of Bratislava.
APRIL 21-22	Pope John Paul II visited Czechoslovakia and was greeted by huge crowds.
APRIL 24	Bush indefinitely delayed the imposition of US sanctions against the Soviet Union over the Lithuanian crisis.
APRIL 25	The United States and the Soviet Union concluded a tentative accord on chemical weapons. The agreement would set a ceiling of 5,000 tons for each nation.
APRIL 26	The sixth round of CFE talks in Vienna ended, with many major issues unresolved.
APRIL 28	Leaders of the twelve EC nations met in Dublin and agreed to move toward political union. France and Germany played the leading role, while Britain remained unconvinced.
APRIL 29	East German Premier Lothar de Maiziere visited Moscow and discussed a united Germany's role in NATO with Gorbachev.
MAY 3	Bush announced a decision to abandon plans to build a successor to the US Lance short-range nuclear missiles in West Germany. He also suggested the opening of negotiations with the Soviet Union over tactical nuclear weapons.

	Lithuanian Premier Kazimiera Prunskiene had a private visit with Bush in Washington.
May 4	The Latvian Republic voted in favor of independence from the Soviet Union.
May 5	Foreign ministers from East and West Germany and the four World War II allied powers met in Bonn to discuss German unification. The Soviets continued to oppose German membership in NATO.
May 15-18	Baker visited Moscow and met with Shevardnadze.
May 17	Gorbachev met with Lithuanian Premier Prunskiene in Moscow after the Lithuanian government agreed to suspend enforcement of laws passed since the Lithuanian declaration of independence.
May 31-June 3	Bush and Gorbachev met in Washington to discuss arms control and other issues.
August 23	The East German Paliament agrees to October 3 as the date for reunification. A pact was signed on August 2 in Bonn to hold elections on December 2, 1990.

Middle East

1989

February 16	Egypt, Iraq, Jordan, and North Yemen formed the Arab Cooperation Council. The event marks Egypt's further reintegration into the Arab political mainstream. *The London Observer* reported that the member states, all of whom aided Iraq during the Gulf war, may have signed a secret mutual defense pact.
February 17	Algeria, Libya, Mauritania, Morocco, and Tunisia created the Arab Mahgreb Union as a "means toward building comprehensive Arab unity and a springboard for wider union to include other Arab and African countries."
February 18-23	Shevardnadze toured the Middle East, visiting Syria, Jordan, and Egypt. On February 22 in Cairo, he met with Israeli Foreign Minister Moshe Arens.
February 23-27	Shevardnadze visited Iran.
February 26	Israel and Egypt signed an accord returning the Red Sea resort of Taba to Egyptian control by March 15.
March 13-16	The 18th Islamic Conference Organization foreign ministers'

	conference was held in Riyadh. The conference condemned Rushdie's book *Satanic Verses*, praises the Palestinian *intifada*, (popular uprisings), and hails the end of the Gulf war.
MARCH 28	Arab League General Secretary Chedli Kibi was unanimously reappointed for a third five-year term by the League's council in Tunis.
APRIL 17	A court in Afghanistan sentenced a Jordanian national to sixteen years in prison for espionage-related activities.
MAY 13	Egypt was readmitted to the Organization of Arab Petroleum Exporting States.
MAY 16	The Spanish ambassador to Lebanon, Pedro Manuel de Aristegui, was killed in Beirut when a mortar shell or rocket hit his residence.
MAY 23-26	The Arab League summit in Casablanca readmitted Egypt to the organization.
JUNE 8	France and Saudi Arabia signed an agreement for the Saudi purchase of French naval frigates and missiles.
JUNE 20-23	The visit of Iranian parliament speaker Ali Akbar Hashemi Rafsanjani to Moscow demonstrated a marked thaw of Soviet-Iranian relations.
SEPTEMBER 25-26	A summit meeting of the Arab Cooperation Council was held in Sana'a, Yemen Arab Republic.
OCTOBER 22	Christian and Moslem legislators in Lebanon concluded three weeks of Arab League sponsored negotiations designed to end Lebanon's civil war. They agreed in principle to a new national charter.
NOVEMBER 1	Mohammed Ali Marzouki, a Saudi Arabian diplomat in Beirut, was killed by gunmen purporting to be members of the Iranian-backed Islamic Jihad terrorist organization.
DECEMBER 6	The US State Department unveiled the "Baker Plan" for peace in the Middle East based on a US-Egyptian-Israeli conference in Washington, to be followed by an Israeli-Palestinian dialogue in Cairo to discuss Palestinian elections in the occupied territories.

1990

JANUARY 5	Iraqi President Saddam Hussein offered a three-point plan aimed at reviving the long-stalled effort to negotiate a permanent end to the Gulf war.

January 8	Iranian diplomats visited Moscow to deal with specific issues of Soviet-Iranian relations.
January 10	Both Iran and Iraq agreed to attend Soviet-chaired talks aimed at ending their Gulf war.
January 13	Turkey activated the Ataturk Dam on the Euphrates River in southwest Turkey, saying that it would take into account the needs and concerns of neighbors that used the river as well.
January 19	Israeli police arrested Faisal al-Husseini, one of the most prominent Palestinian nationalists in the Israeli-occupied West Bank. He was released three days later.
January 22	Soviets troops sealed the Iranian-Azerbaijanian border to prevent ethnic Azerbaijanis from supplying weapons to their Soviet counterparts.
January 23	Israel began accepting Azerbaijani Jews as refugees.
February 22–March 7	Iranian, Syrian, and US officials held diplomatic talks on the possible release of Western hostages in Lebanon.
March 8	Soviet Deputy Foreign Minister Vladimir Polyakov visited Saudi Arabia for talks on Jewish emigration from the Soviet Union to Israel.
March 11	Libyan leader Col. Muammar Qaddafi released Abu Nidal, the notorious Palestinian terrorist, from house arrest in Tripoli.
March 15	The Islamic Jihad publicly threatened to attack airlines carrying Soviet Jews to Israel.
March 16	Shamir's government lost a no-confidence vote in the Israeli Knesset after he refused to accept a US plan for beginning Israeli-Palestinian peace talks.
March 28	The United States and Britain uncovered an attempt by Iraq to obtain restricted US-made electronic devices used to trigger nuclear weapons.
April 10	A Libyan-backed terrorist group led by Abu Nidal freed three European hostages held in Beirut, Lebanon. The releases appeared to result from French-Libyan talks.
April 11	British customs officials impounded a shipment of parts for a giant artillery gun bound for Iraq.
April 12-27	An attempt by Jewish settlers to occupy a building next to the Church of the Holy Sepulchre in Jerusalem provoked protests by the US government and Christians around the world.

APRIL 22	Lebanese kidnappers freed American hostage Robert Polhill. Syria and Iraq were credited with helping to arrange the release.
APRIL 24	The US House of Representatives approved a nonbinding resolution recognizing a united Jerusalem as the capital of Israel.
APRIL 30	Lebanese kidnappers released American hostage Frank Reed. President Bush thanked Iran for its role.
MAY 4-17	Israeli and Iranian officials and Lebanese militants traded demands concerning the possible swap of Western hostages in Lebanon for Shiite prisoners held by pro-Israeli forces.
MAY 13	The United States and Iran signed an agreement settling small financial claims arising from the 1979 Iranian Revolution.
MAY 16	Iran and the European Community held their first high-level meeting in over a year, but no progress on the issues of hostages and Salman Rushdie's death sentence was reported.
MAY 20	A deranged Jewish gunman killed seven Palestinian laborers inside Israel, sparking a wave of riots in the Gaza Strip and West Bank.
MAY 22	North Yemen and South Yemen merged to form a unified Republic of Yemen.
AUGUST 2	The Iraqi invasion of Kuwait.
AUGUST 6	UN Security Council Resolution 661 placed sanctions against Iraq by a 13-0 vote with Cuba and Yemen abstaining.
AUGUST 25	UN Security Council resolution authorized "all appropriate measures" to enforce sanctions.

Western Hemisphere

1989

FEBRUARY 2	The presidents of Venezuela and Colombia met to establish a commission to settle border disputes between the two nations.
FEBRUARY 10	President Bush made his first official trip outside the United States to meet with Prime Minister Brian Mulroney in Ottawa.
FEBRUARY 14	A Central American summit of Costa Rica, El Salvador, Guatemala, Honduras, and Nicaragua held at Tesoro Beach, El Salvador, resulted in agreement to dismantle the bases of US-sponsored "contra" guerrillas in Honduras, repatriate the contras to Nicaragua, and hold free elections in Nicaragua by February 25, 1990.

APRIL 2-5	President Gorbachev visited Cuba and signed a new Treaty of Friendship and Economic Cooperation with President Fidel Castro in Havana. Gorbachev and Castro clashed over the merits of Soviet policies of *glasnost* and *perestroika*.
MAY 17	The Organization of American States (OAS) convened an emergency session in Washington to discuss the election in Panama and to urge a peaceful transfer of power in that country to a legitimately elected government.
JULY 21	The United Nations announced that it will monitor the Nicaraguan elections to be held February 25, 1990.
AUGUST 7	The presidents of the five Central American nations met in Tela, Honduras, to discuss the repatriation of the contra rebels to Nicaragua.
SEPTEMBER 13-15	Representatives of the government of El Salvador and the FMLN met in Mexico City and agreed to begin formal peace talks October 16-17 in Costa Rica.
SEPTEMBER 19	The Canadian Department of Exterior Affairs recommended that Canada join the OAS. Canada has held official observer status since 1972.
OCTOBER 16-18	The government of El Salvador and representatives of the FMLN held peace talks in San Jose, Costa Rica. Little progress was made, but monthly talks between the two sides were arranged.
OCTOBER 25	The United States extended trade sanctions against Nicaragua, which had been established in May 1985, claiming that Nicaragua had failed to live up to its pledge to cease supplying arms to FMLN guerrillas in El Salvador.
OCTOBER 27	Canadian Prime Minister Brian Mulroney announced that Canada would formally join the OAS in November.
OCTOBER 27-28	A summit of sixteen Western Hemisphere leaders was held in Costa Rica, the first such meeting since the 1967 Punta del Este conference. Originally held to discuss the "Six D's" (debt, deforestation, democracy, development, drugs, and disarmament), the meeting was instead dominated by Nicaraguan President Daniel Ortega's announcement that he intended to end his government's cease-fire with US-sponsored contra guerrillas. Extreme acrimony between Ortega and President Bush ensued.
NOVEMBER 9-21	The Nicaraguan government and representatives of the contra resistance opened peace talks in New York under the auspices of the OAS and the UN.

DECEMBER 10-12	A summit of five Central American leaders was held in San Jose, Costa Rica, and reached agreement on a new accord concerning regional peace.
DECEMBER 22	The OAS adopted a resolution "deeply deploring" the US intervention in Panama two days earlier.
DECEMBER 23	A UN Security Council resolution condemning the US invasion of Panama was vetoed by Britain, France, and the United States.
DECEMBER 24	Deposed Panamanian strongman General Manuel Antonio Noriega sought sanctuary in the Papal nunciature in Panama City, which, although unable to grant him political asylum, agreed to give him "temporary refuge."
DECEMBER 29	US troops forcibly searched the residence of the Nicaraguan ambassador in Panama City, Antenor Ferrey. The Bush administration apologized immediately for what the president termed a "screw-up."

1990

JANUARY 1	Under the Panama Canal Treaty (1977), the Panama Canal Commission was handed over to Panamanian control.
JANUARY 3	Col. Roberto Armijo stepped down as head of the new Panamanian Public Force (FPP) less than two weeks after assuming the position. He was replaced by his deputy, Lt. Col. Eduard Herrera Hassan, a nephew of the late Panamanian ruler, General Omar Torrijos.
	Ousted Panamanian dictator Noriega surrendered to US officials ten days after he had taken refuge in the Vatican's diplomatic mission in Panama City.
JANUARY 4	Noriega was arrested by US Drug Enforcement Agency agents and sent to a federal district court in Miami, where he was arraigned for outstanding indictments relating to drug trafficking.
JANUARY 5	The Bush administration offered to help fund the international commission responsible for helping the contra rebels relocate from Honduras to Nicaragua.
JANUARY 8	The OAS passed a resolution—19-0 with 7 abstentions—condemning a search of the Nicaraguan ambassador's residence by US troops in late December 1989.

	The US government called off plans for the US Navy to monitor airborne drug traffic off the coast of Colombia after the idea drew critical comments from Colombian leaders.
	US congressmen announced that future aid to El Salvador was dependent upon the bringing to justice of those involved in the November 1989 slayings of six Jesuit priests.
JANUARY 11	The FMLN accepted a proposal to ask the UN to mediate peace talks between it and the Guatemalan government.
JANUARY 17	The Medellin drug cartel signaled its willingness to end its campaign of terror in exchange for amnesty or pledges not to be extradited to the United States.
JANUARY 24–FEBRUARY 13	Brazilian president-elect Fernando Collor de Mello embarked on a world trip to gain support for his planned economic programs.
JANUARY 26	France suspended financial aid to Haiti to protest that country's recent state of siege and its accompanying bloody crackdown.
JANUARY 27–29	US Vice President Daniel Quayle visited Panama, Honduras, and Jamaica to reassure regional leaders about US policy in the Western Hemisphere in the aftermath of the December 1989 US invasion of Panama.
JANUARY 30–FEBRUARY 2	Salvadoran President Alfredo Cristiani visited the United States for talks on US aid and ways to deal with leftist rebels.
FEBRUARY 8	In rejecting the defendant's claim that he was a prisoner of war, a US federal district court judge ruled that Noriega must stand trial for drug trafficking in Miami.
FEBRUARY 9	Fulfilling a pledge under a Central American peace agreement, the Nicaraguan government freed all remaining political prisoners.
FEBRUARY 15	In Cartagena, the presidents of Bolivia, Colombia, Peru, and the United States signed an accord that pledged cooperation in the fight against illegal narcotics trafficking.
FEBRUARY 25	Violeta Chamorro of the National Opposition Union (UNO) defeated incumbent president Daniel Ortega in Nicaraguan national elections, ending the ten-year Sandinista rule.
MARCH 1–13	Panamanian President Endara staged a fast in Panama City to protest the lack of US aid to his shattered country.
MARCH 6	Representatives of President-Elect Chamorro opened talks with contra leaders in Honduras to deal with the proposed demobilization of rebel forces.
MARCH 13	Bush lifted all economic sanctions against Nicaragua.

Diplomatic Chronology

MARCH 15-20	Canadian Prime Minister Mulroney visited Mexico and Barbados to discuss issues of trade, economic aid, pollution, and drugs.
MARCH 23	The Nicaraguan contras agreed to dismantle their camps in Honduras, beginning no later than April 20.
MARCH 27-28	In Oslo, representatives from the Guatemalan government and leftist rebels held talks to end that country's civil war.
MARCH 28	Colombian president Virgilio Barco Vargas resumed extraditions of drug suspects to the United States.
APRIL 3	Five Central American presidents, meeting in Montelimar, Nicaragua, set April 25 as a deadline for full demobilization of Nicaragua's contra rebels.
APRIL 4	Salvadoran President Cristiani and the FMLN rebels agreed to renew talks on ending El Salvador's civil war.
APRIL 5	President Bush signed an executive order officially ending all US sanctions against Panama.
APRIL 8	In Peru, dark horse candidate Alberto Fujimori received enough votes in the presidential elections to challenge novelist Mario Vargas Llosa in a run-off.
APRIL 10	Venezuelan troops under UN command began arriving in Honduras to oversee demobilization of Nicaraguan rebels.
APRIL 18	Mexican Attorney General Enrique Alvarez del Castillo met with US Attorney General Richard Thornburgh and protested the abduction of a Mexican suspect in the slaying of an American drug agent.
APRIL 19	Representatives of the Sandinista army, the contras, and the incoming government signed a cease-fire agreement.
APRIL 20	The thirty-two nations of the OAS signed a twenty-point agreement on ways to combat illegal narcotics.
APRIL 20, 24	The United States approved sharp increases in funds to help the Bolivian and Peruvian militaries combat their domestic cocaine industries.
APRIL 25	Violeta Barrias de Chamorro was sworn in as president of Nicaragua. She announced an end to the draft and most government controls on the economy.
APRIL 30	Panamanian President Guillermo Endara and US president George Bush signed three agreements on fighting drug trafficking.

MAY 6-13	Pope John Paul II visited Mexico and met briefly with President Salinas de Gortari.
MAY 8	In a meeting with Bolivian President Jaime Paz Zamora, President Bush pledged to seek an increase in US aid to Bolivia to help cut Bolivian cocaine production.
MAY 12	Chile reached a tentative accord with the United States under which it would pay compensation to the United States for the 1976 killing of Chilean exile Orlando Letelier and an aide, Ronni K. Moffitt.

Note on Definitions

CFE	*Conventional Forces in Europe* talks. Convening on March 6, 1989 as the successor to the Mutual and Balanced Force Reduction (MBFR) talks, the CFE is the principle negotiating forum for conventional arms control in Europe. They are conducted by the members of the NATO and Warsaw Pact alliances within the larger framework of the CSCE.
CSCE	*Conference on Security and Cooperation in Europe.* Composed of the sixteen members of NATO, the seven members of the Warsaw Pact, and the twelve neutral and non-aligned countries of Europe, the CSCE, which began in 1973 and produced the 1975 Helsinki accords, is a forum for the discussion of political, economic, and human rights issues facing Europe.
CSE	*Conference on Confidence and Security Building Measures and Disarmament in Europe.* Begun on March 9, 1989 as the principle forum on operational arms control in Europe, the CSE succeeded the 1984-1986 Stockholm Conference on the same topic.

Sources

American Journal of International Law
The Economist
Facts on File
Foreign Broadcast Information Service news summaries
Keesing's Record of World Events
New York Times
Washington Post

Acronyms and Abbreviations

AIG	Afghan Interim Government
ANC	African National Congress
ATCP	Antarctic Treaty Consultative Party
BRC	Bilateral Review Commission
CAMLR-VIII	Eighth Meeting of the Convention on the Conservation of Antarctic Marine Living Resources Commission
CCAMLR	Convention on the Conservation of Antarctic Marine Living Resources
CD	Conference on Disarmament
CFC	chlorofluorocarbon
CFE	Conference on Conventional Forces in Europe
COMECON	Council for Mutual Economic Assistance
CRAMRA	Convention on the Regulation of Antarctic Mineral Resources Activities
CSCE	Conference on Security and Cooperation in Europe
CSE	Conference on Confidence and Security Building Measures in Europe
CTW	Cuban troop withdrawal
CW	chemical weapons
DRA	Democratic Republic of Afghanistan
D&S	defense and space
EC	European Community
ECE	Economic Commission for Europe

EMU	Economic and Monetary Union
ENDC	Eighteen-Nation Committee on Disarmament
EPA	Environmental Protection Agency
FAPLA	Angolan People's Liberation Army
FLS	front line states
FMLN	Farabundo Marti National Liberation Front
FPP	Panamanian Public Force
FRG	Federal Republic of Germany
FTOL	Follow-on-to-Lance
GATT	General Agreement on Tariffs and Trade
GLCM	ground-launched cruise missile
GNP	gross national product
ICRC	International Committee of the Red Cross
IMF	International Monetary Fund
INF	Intermediate Nuclear Forces
IPCC	Intergovernmental Panel on Climate Change
ISI	Interservices Intelligence Agency
LBS	land-based sources
LRTAP	Long-Range Transboundary Airborne Pollution Convention
MBFR	Mutual and Balanced Force Reductions
MPLA	Popular Movement for the Liberation of Angola
NATO	North Atlantic Treaty Organization
NST	Nuclear and Space Talks
OAS	Organization of American States
OAU	Organization of African Unity
OFM	Office of Foreign Missions
OIC	Organization of the Islamic Conference
OPEC	Organization of Petroleum Exporting Countries
PDPA	People's Democratic Party of Afghanistan
PIA	Pershing IA

PLO	Palestine Liberation Organization
SADF	South African Defense Force
SCOI	Standing Committee on Observation and Inspection
SDI	Strategic Defense Initiative
SNF	short-range nuclear forces
START	Strategic Arms Reduction Talks
SII	Structural Impediments Initiative
SWAPO	South-West Africa People's Organization
TIAS	*United States Treaties and Other International Acts Series*
UNAVEM	United Nations Verification Mission in Angola
UNDC	United Nations Disarmament Commission
UNEP	United Nations Environment Programme
UNESCO	United Nations Educational, Scientific, and Cultural Organization
UNGA	United Nations General Assembly
UNHCR	United Nations High Commissioner for Refugees
UNIIMOG	United Nations Iran-Iraq Military Observer Group
UNITA	National Union for the Total Independence of Angola
UNO	National Opposition Union
UNTAG	United Nations Transition Assistance Group
UNTS	*United Nations Treaty Series*
UST	*United States Treaties and Other International Agreements*
USTR	United States Special Trade Representative
VAT	value-added tax
VOC	volatile organic compound

Bibliography

Editor's Note: The bibliography of works on diplomacy published in 1989 and 1990 includes books published in the United States and benefits as well from submissions by members of the advisory committee in India and Mexico. It is hoped that in future issues this section may, by other submissions, be truly worldwide.

Al-Adoofi, Ibrahim S., *Struggle for Freedom: the United Nations, the Palestine Question, and the Superpowers*. Delhi: H.K. Publishers, 1990.

Asopa, Sheel K., *The Soviet Union and the Third World: From Dogmatic Marxism to Glasnost*. Jaipur: Printwell, 1990.

Boersner, Demetrio, *Relaciones Internacionales de América Latina Breve Historia*. Venezuela: Editorial Nueva Sociedad, 1989.

Brown, L. Carl, *Center Stage: American Diplomacy Since World War II*. New York: Holmes and Meier, 1989.

Bustamente, Jorge A., y Wayne A. Cornelius (Coordinador), *Flumos Migratorios Mexicanos Hacia Estados Unidos*. Serie Comisión sobre el futuro de las Relaciones México-Estados Unidos, Vol. 3, México: Fondo de Cultura Economica, 1989.

Chester, Edward, *The Scope & Variety of U.S. Diplomatic History, Vol. II.: Readings Since 1900*. New York: Prentice Hall, 1989.

Coatsworth, John H. y Carlos Rico (Coordinador), *Imágenes de México en Estados Unidos*. Serie Comision sobre el Futuro de las Relaciones México-Estados Unidos, Vol. I., Mexico: Fondo de Cultura Economica, 1989.

Cordova, Macías Ricardo y Manaut Raúl Benítez (Composition), *La Paz en Centroamérica: Expediente Documentos Fundamentales (1979-1989)*. México: Centro de Investigaciones Interdisciplinarias en Humanidades, Universidad Nacional Autonoma de Mexico, 1990.

Crabb, Cecil V., Jr., *American Diplomacy and the Pragmatic Tradition*. Baton Rouge: Louisiana State University Press, 1989.

Craig, Gordon A. and Alexander L. George, *Force and Statecraft: Diplomatic Problems of Our Times*. Second edition, New York: Oxford University Press, 1989.

Damodaran, A.K. and U.S. Bajpai, ed., *Indian Foreign Policy: The Indira Gandhi Years*. New Delhi: Radiant Publishers, 1990.

Ganjoo, Satish, *Afghanistan's Struggle for Resurgence*. Delhi: Akash-Deep, 1989.

Ghoble, T.R., *China's Foreign policy: Opening to the West*. New Delhi: Deep & Deep, 1990.

Ghosh, Partha S., *Cooperation and Conflict in South Asia*. New Delhi: Manohar, 1989.

Glade, E. William y Luiselli Cassio (Coordinador), *La economía de la interdependencia: México y Estados Unidos*. Serie Comisión sobre el Futuro de las Relaciones México-Estados Unidos, Vol. 2, Mexico: Fondo de Cultura Economica, 1989.

González, Guadalupe y Marta Tienda (Coordinador), *México y Estados Unidos en la Cadena Internacional del Narcotráfico*. Serie Comisión sobre el Futuro de las Relaciones México-Estados Unidos, Vol. 4, Mexico: Fondo de Cultura Economica, 1989.

Green, Rosario y Peter Smith (Coordinador), *La política Exterior y la Agenda México-Estados Unidos*. Serie Comisión sobre el Futuro de las Relaciones México-Estados Unidos, Vol. 5, México: Fondo de Cultura Economica, 1989.

Gupta, Rakesh, ed., *India's Security Problems in the Nineties*. New Delhi: Patriot, 1989.

Haas, Richard N., *Conflicts Unending: the United States and Regional Disputes*. New Haven: Yale University Press, 1990.

Haksar, P.N., *India's Foreign Policy and its Problems*. New Delhi: Patriot, 1989.

Holbraad, Carsten, *Las Potencias Medias en la Politica Internacional*. México: Fondo de Cultura Economica, 1990.

IMRED (Coord. y Comp.), en edición, *Apertura de México al Pacífico*. IMRED, SRE, México, 1990.

Instituto Matias Romero de Estudios Diplomaticos (Coordinador y Composition), en edition, *Apertura de México al Pacifico*. México: Instituto Matias de Estudios Diplomaticos, 1990.

Janitschek, Hans, *Oscar Arias en Busca de la Paz*. México: Editorial Diana, 1989.

Kesaven, K.V., ed., *Contemporary Japanese Politics and Foreign Policy*. New Delhi: Radiant, 1989.

Kinney, Douglas, *National Interest-National Honor: The Diplomacy of the Falklands Crisis*. New York: Praeger, 1989.

Kodikara, Shelton U., ed., *South Asian Strategic Issues: Sri Lankan Perspectives*. New Delhi: Vistaar, 1990.

Kremenyuk, Viktor, and others, *U.S. Policy Towards the Pacific*. New Delhi: Allied, 1989.

Lakos, Amos, *International Negotiations: Case Studies, a Bibliography*. Monticello, IL: Vance Biblios, 1989.

Lall, John, *Aksaichin and the Sino-Indian Conflict*. New Delhi: Allied, 1989.

Lowenthal, Abraham, *La Convivencia Imperfecta (Los Estados Unidos y América Latina)*. México: Editorial Nueva Imágen, 1989.

Mattox, H.E., *The Twilight of Amateur Diplomacy*. Kent, OH: Kent State University Press, 1989.

Mautner-Markhof, Frances, ed., *Processes of International Negotiations*. Boulder, CO: Westview Press, 1989.

McClanahan, Grant V., *Diplomatic Immunity: Principles, Practices, Problems*. New York: St. Martin's Press, 1989.

Meyer, Lorenzo y José Luis Reyna, *Los Sistemas Políticos en América Latina*. México: Editorial Siglo XXI, 1990.

Modern Law of Diplomacy: External Missions of States and International Organizations. New York: United Nations, 1989.

Newsom, David D., ed., *Diplomacy Under a Foreign Flag: When Nations Break Relations*. Washington, D.C.: Institute for the Study of Diplomacy, 1990.

Nicolson, Harold, *Diplomacy*. Third edition, Washington, D.C.: Institute for the Study of Diplomacy, 1989.

Olea, Flores Víctor (Coordinador), *Relación de Contadora*. México: Secretaria de Relaciones Exteriores y Fondo de Cultura Economica, 1989.

Prasad, Shashi Bhushan, *The China Factor in Indo-Nepalese Relations 1955-72: A Study of Linkage Phenomena*. New Delhi: Commonwealth, 1989.

Saaty, Thomas L. and Joyce M. Alexander, *A New Logic to Resolve Conflicts: The Analytic Hierarchy Process*. New York: Praeger, 1989.

Schulzinger, Robert D., *American Diplomacy in the Twentieth Century*. Second edition, New York: Oxford University Press, 1989.

Secretaría de Relaciones Exteriores, *El Problema del Narcotráfico/Visión Internacional*. México: Dirección General del Acervo Histórico Diplomático, Secretaria de Relaciones Exteriores, 1989.

Sen Gupta, Bhabani, *Studies in Violence, National Integration and Non-Alignment*. New Delhi: Commonwealth, 1989.

Serbin, Andres, *El Caribe: ¿Zona de Paz? Geopolítica, Integración y Seguiridad en el Caribe no Hispánico*. Venezuela: Editorial Nueva Sociedad, 1989.

Smith, Raymond F., *Negotiating with the Soviets*. Bloomington: Indiana University Press, 1989.

Stein, Janice Gross, ed., *Getting to the Table: The Process of International Prenegotiation*. Baltimore: Johns Hopkins University Press, 1989.

Talavera, Navarrete Ela, *Panamá ¿Invasión o Revolución?* México: Editorial Planeta, 1990.

Tinoco, Victor Hugo, *Conflicto y Paz El Proceso Negociador Centroamericano*. México: Editorial Mestiza, 1989.

Tuch, Hans, *Communicating with the World: U.S. Public Diplomacy Overseas*. Washington, D.C.: Institute for the Study of Diplomacy, 1990.

United States Advisory Commission on Public Diplomacy, *1989 Report*. Washington, D.C.: U.S. Government Printing Office, 1989.

Index

Ablation Point, 168
Abu Nidal, 222
Acid rain, 135
Acton (Lord), 87
Adriatic-Danube group, 219
Afghan Alliance, 48, 49, 51, 55(n8)
Afghan Interim Government (AIG), 53, 54, 185
Afghanistan, 3, 4, 5, 31, 184, 221
   anticommunists in. *See* Afghan Resistance
   border formulation, 46, 52
   diplomatic relations, 193, 197
   Geneva negotiations, 35-56
   internal rivalries, 7
   invasion of, 78, 79, 82
   Jallalabad offensive, 53
   Pakistani relations, 207
   self-determination, 40
   Soviet arms transfers to, 55
   Soviet withdrawal from, 35-56
   symmetry, 52-53, 55
Afghan Resistance, 38, 41, 45, 49, 53
   Iranian support for, 40, 53
   Pakistani support for, 39, 51
   US support for, 46
Africa. *See* Southern Africa; *individual countries*
African National Congress (ANC), 206, 207
African National Union, 12
Agreed Measures on the Conservation of Antarctic Fauna and Flora, 159

AIG. *See* Afghan Interim Government
Air pollution, 134-135, 140(n3), 141-154, 167, 198
Akhromeyev, Sergei, 74
Alarcon de Quesada, Ricardo, 200
Algeria, 184, 220
Alliance for Responsible CFC Policy, 145
Alvarez del Castillo, Enrique, 227
Amin, Hafizullah, 38
ANC. *See* African National Congress
Andreotti, Giulio, 217
Andriessen, Farns, 201
Andropov, Yuri, 42, 45
Angola, 3, 4, 205, 206
   Cuban intervention in, 9, 10, 12-13 16-18(table), 19-20, 21, 22, 24, 26, 31-33
   Cuban troop withdrawal (CTW) from, 9, 15, 16-18(table), 19-20, 24, 25, 26, 29-30, 31, 33
   instability of, 7
   -Namibia link, 9, 10, 12-14, 16-18(table), 19-20, 28, 29-30
   South Africa and, 12-13, 16-17(table), 22, 24-25
Annex on Chemicals, 124, 130(n12)
Annex on the Protection of Confidential Information, 126-127
Antarctica
   ecosystems approach to, 172-173, 176
   international secretariat for, 169
   jurisdictions, 156, 157(fig.)

marine resources, 171-177
minerals regime, 158, 160-165
Multiple-Use Planning Areas, 167-168
Soviet policies, 159, 163, 169, 170, 172, 173, 174-175, 176, 180(n28)
Special Reserved Areas, 167
Antarctic Consultative Treaty Meeting, 166-171
Antarctic Minerals Commission, 161
Antarctic Treaty Consultative Parties (ATCPs), 155, 158, 159, 160, 161, 163, 164, 165, 166-171, 177-178
Antarctic Treaty System, 155, 156, 158-165, 166, 177-178
Aoun, Michel, 196
Arab Cooperation Council, 220, 221
Arab League, 221
Arab Mahgreb Union, 220
Arab unity, 220
Arens, Moshe, 220
Argentina, 156, 159, 169, 172, 173, 187(n2), 195, 196, 197
Arias Sanchez, Oscar, 204
Armijo, Roberto, 225
Arms control, 5-6, 76, 187, 211, 216, 217, 219
   bilateral relations and, 77-88
   conventional, 75
   public opinion and, 69-70
   zero options, 61-62, 72-75
Arms transfers, 5, 30, 46, 55, 214-215
ASEAN. *See* Association of Southeast Asian Nations
Asian-Pacific Economic Cooperation Conference, 202
Association of Southeast Asian Nations (ASEAN), 6
Ataturk Dam, 222
ATCPs. *See* Antarctic Treaty Consultative Parties
Australia, 72, 118, 125, 147, 156, 161-163, 165, 166, 170, 171, 172, 177, 209
Austria, 147, 195, 202, 214, 219
Avian Island, 168
Azerbaijanis, 222
Aziz, Tariq, 91, 98-99, 107

Azouzou Strip, 206

Baaths, 92
Bahia Paraiso, 162, 168
Bahias, 92
Baker, James, 54, 200, 206, 210, 211, 213, 214, 215, 216, 217, 219, 220
Baker Plan, 221
Belgium, 62, 148, 159, 163, 172, 211
Bering Sea, 199
Berlin Wall, 215
Besharati, Ali Mohammad, 92
Bhutto, Benazir, 51, 54, 207
BIC Humboldt, 162
Bilateral Review Commission (BRC), 78
Biological diversity, 137
Biological weapons, 115
Bolivia, 227, 228
Botha, Roelof, F., 196
Brady, Nicholas F., 201
Brady Plan, 201
Brazil, 158, 159, 172, 187(n2), 201
Brazzaville Protocol, 15, 18(table)
BRC. *See* Bilateral Review Commission
Brezhnev, Leonid, 39, 42, 62, 82
Brezhnev Doctrine, 13, 213
Bulgaria, 178(n2), 196, 214, 216
Burkina Faso, 206
Bush, George, 15, 77, 208, 217, 218, 219, 227, 228
   arms control and, 216, 217, 219
   Canada relations and, 223
   chemical weapons policy, 115, 123, 127, 129, 131(nn 16, 26), 132(n30)
   environmental efforts and, 134, 198, 199
   foreign aid and, 213
   foreign relations and, 215
   Gorbachev summits, 214, 220
   INF treaty and, 59, 71
   Mexico and, 184
   NATO and, 211, 214
   Nicaragua and, 204, 205, 224, 225, 226
   Panama and, 203, 227
   trade relations and, 201, 202, 203
   United Nations and, 200

US-Soviet relations and, 79, 80-81, 83, 85
Buthelezi, Mangasuthu Gatsha, 206
Byrd, Richard E., 168
Byrd amendment, 80, 87(n3)

Cambodia, 185, 207, 208, 209, 210
Camp David accords, 7
Canada, 10, 27, 28, 137, 144, 146, 147, 148, 151, 194, 201, 202, 224
  environmental efforts and, 134-135
  Soviet relations, 83
  US relations, 203, 223
  US trade, 201
Cape Shirreff, 168
Cape Verde, 26, 27, 206
Cartagena accord, 226
Carter, Jimmy, 61
  Pakistan policy, 39
  Southern Africa policies, 10, 13
Castro, Fidel, 17(table), 20, 31, 224
CCAMLR, *See* Convention on the Conservation of Antarctic Marine Living Resources
CCD. *See* Conference of the Committee on Disarmament
CD. *See* Conference on Disarmament
Ceausescu, Nicolae, 202, 215
CFCs. *See* Chlorofluorocarbons
CFE. *See* Conventional forces in Europe
Chad, 206
Chamorro, Violeta Barrias de, 205, 226, 227
Chemical Annex. *See Annex on Chemicals*
Chemical industry
  ozone depletion and, 142, 145, 146-147
  weapons and, 118, 120-121, 125-126, 130(n7), 131(n15)
Chemical weapons (CW), 210
  ban, 115-132
  binary, 131(n20)
  Canberra conference, 117-118
  compound classification, 124, 125(table), 130
  Paris conference, 116-117, 118, 122, 130(n5)
  stocks, 122-123, 130(n11), 132(n30)
  US policy, 115, 123, 127, 129, 131(nn 16, 26), 132(n30)
Chemical weapons ban
  bilateral negotiations, 119-120
  challenge inspections, 126, 127-128
  "intention" concept, 120
  internal negotiations, 119
  outstanding issues, 121-122
  rolling text, 122, 124, 126, 128, 130(n14)
  Technical Secretariat, 121, 126
  verification regime, 115, 120-121, 123-128, 131(n24)
Chemical Weapons Convention, 119, 120-121
Cheney, Richard, 209
Chernobyl nuclear accident, 82, 85, 87-88(n4), 141
Cherov, Nikolai, 74
Chile, 156, 159, 165, 166, 170, 172, 173, 176, 194, 228
Chinese Communist Party, 195
Chlorofluorocarbons (CFCs), 134, 142-150, 151, 153, 199
Clark, Dick, 34(n4)
Clark, Joe, 194
Clark Amendment, 22
Clausewitz, Karl von, 110
Clean Air Act, 135, 198, 199
Climate change, 133-134, 139(n1), 151, 198
Club of Paris, 203
Code of Conduct for Antarctic Expeditions and Station Activities, 166-167
Colombia, 178(n2), 187(n2), 223, 226
COLREGS. *See* Convention on the International Regulations for Preventing Collisions at Sea
COMECON. *See* Council for Mutual Economic Assistance
Commonwealth, 200
Conable, Barber, 199
Conference of State Parties, 121
Conference of the Committee on Disar-

mament (CCD), 130(n9)
Conference on Confidence and Security Building Measures and Disarmament in Europe (CSE), 211, 213, 214, 228
Conference on Disarmament (CD), 115, 117, 119, 130(nn 8, 9), 210, 212
　Committee on Chemical Weapons, 118, 119
Conference on Environment and Development, 138
Conference on Security and Cooperation in Europe (CSCE), 86, 186, 210, 211, 214, 216, 217, 228
Conflict management, 14
Congo, 26, 205
"Contact Group," 10, 12, 13, 16(table), 20, 27, 29
Conventional force reductions, 66
Conventional forces in Europe (CFE), 186, 210-211, 213, 214, 218, 219, 228
Convention for the Conservation of Antarctic Seals, 159-160
Convention for the Protection of the Marine Environment, 136
Convention on the Conservation of Antarctic Marine Living Resources (CCAMLR), 155, 160, 171-177
　Commission for, 155, 172, 174-175
　Scientific Committee, 172, 174-175
Convention on the International Regulations for Preventing Collisions at Sea (COLREGS), 167
Convention on the Prevention of Marine Pollution by Dumping of Wastes and Other Matter, 167
Convention on the Regulation of Antarctic Mineral Resource Activities (CRAMRA), 160-165
Convention to Control Transboundary Movements of Hazardous Wastes, 136-137, 198
Cordovez, Diego, 41, 42-43, 44-49, 50, 52, 54
Costa Rica, 194, 223
Council for Mutual Economic Assistance (COMECON), 202
Council of Europe, 211
CRAMRA. *See* Convention on the Regulation of Antarctic Mineral Resource Activities
Cristiani, Alfredo, 226, 227
Croatian Movement for Statehood, 211
Crowe, William, 74, 212
CSCE. *See* Conference on Security and Cooperation in Europe
CSE. *See* Conference on Confidence and Security Building Measures and Disarmament in Europe
CTW. *See* Angola, Cuban troop withdrawal from
Cuba, 178(n2), 197, 200, 223
　Angola and, 9, 10, 12-13, 15, 16-18(table), 19-20, 21, 22, 24, 25, 26, 29-32
　France and, 28
　Soviet relations, 224
CW. *See* Chemical weapons
Cyprus. *See* Republic of Cyprus
Czechoslovakia, 126, 178(n2), 195, 197, 204, 205, 214, 219

D&S. *See* Defense and Space Talks
Daniloff, Nicholas, 78, 87(n1)
Daniloff affair, 78, 81, 82, 87(n1)
Davis, Arthur, 195
de Aristegni, Pedro Manuel, 221
Declaration on the Ozone Layer and Climate Change, 168
Defense and Space (D&S) Talks, 66, 71
deKlerk, F. W., 206-207
de Maiziere, Lothar, 204, 219
Democratic Republic of Afghanistan (DRA), 39
Denmark, 144, 148, 178(n2)
"Design USA" exhibit, 83
Dienstbier, Jiri, 219
Diplomacy
　defined, 3-4
　governance of, 189-192
　in 1989, 193-196
　in 1990, 196-198

Doe, Samuel K., 206
Dos Santos, Jose Eduardo, 31, 205
DRA. *See* Democratic Republic of Afghanistan
Drugs, 200. *See also* United States, drug war
Dumas, Roland, 202

Eagleburger, Lawrence, 44, 208
East-West relations. *See* Soviet Union, US relations
EC. *See* European Community
ECE. *See* Economic Commission for Europe
Economic Commission for Europe (ECE), 133, 135
Economic integration, 6
Economic Seven, 137-138. *See also* Group of Seven
Economic summits, 137-138
Ecuador, 169-170, 178(n2)
EEC. *See* European Economic Community
Egypt, 7, 26, 129, 196, 220, 221
Eighteen-Nation Committee on Disarmament (ENCD), 130(n9)
Elemi Triangle, 205
Eliasson, Jan, 93-94, 95, 102, 105, 107, 108, 110
El Salvador, 184, 196, 223, 224, 226, 227
Embassy bugging scandal, 82, 88(n6)
EMU. *See* European Economic and Monetary Union
ENCD. *See* Eighteen-Nation Committee on Disarmament
Endara, Guillermo, 197, 226, 227
Environmental efforts
 cooperative, 84-85
 international negotiations, 133-140
 model of, 150-152
 1989 diplomacy, 198
 1990 diplomacy, 199
Environmental Protection Agency (EPA), 143, 149
EPA. See Environmental Protection Agency

Eritrean People's Liberation Front, 205
Estonia, 219
Ethiopia, 10, 196, 205
Europe
 anti-nuclear movement in, 64
 nuclear forces in, 60-61, 64-65, 73
 public opinion in, 61, 64, 65-66, 67-68
European Community (EC), 38, 144, 145-146, 147-149, 172, 186, 193, 194, 195, 198, 203, 204, 205, 212, 217, 219
 East Bloc and, 214
 German reunification and, 210
 Iran and, 223
 trade relations, 202
 United States and, 215
 US trade dispute, 200-201
European Economic and Monetary Union (EMU), 202
European Economic Community (EEC), 6
European Free Trade Association, 202
European reunification, 215. *See also* German reunification
Evans, Gareth, 209
Export Import Bank Act, 80, 87(n3)
Exxon Valdez, 162

Falin, Valentin, 85
FAPLA. *See* Forces of the Angolan People's Liberation Army
Farabundo Marti National Liberation Front (FMLN), 196, 224, 226, 227
Federal Republic of Germany, 10, 137, 144, 148, 149, 151, 152, 191, 193, 194, 201, 211, 212, 213, 216
 Afghanistan and, 38
 Antarctica and, 159, 172
 chemical weapons ban and, 117-118, 125
 EC and, 219
 INF and, 62, 64, 73
 Soviet relations, 83
Ferdinand, Franz, 7
Ferrey, Antenor, 225
Finland, 144, 147, 159, 169-170, 202, 211

Fish Stock Assessment Working Group, 174
FLS. *See* Front line states
FMLN. *See* Farabundo Marti National Liberation Front
Food and Agricultural Organization, 139
Force modernization, 64-65
Forces of the Angolan People's Liberation Army (FAPLA), 31
Ford administration, 10
France, 10, 20, 27, 28, 137, 201, 225, 226
   Afghanistan and, 38
   Antarctica and, 156, 159, 163, 165, 166, 170, 171, 172, 174, 177
   arms transfers by, 221
   chemical weapons ban and, 122-123
   diplomatic relations, 193, 194, 197
   EC and, 219
   environmental efforts and, 145, 147, 148
   INF and, 63, 68
   Soviet relations, 83, 212
Front line states (FLS), 10, 12, 16-17(table), 27
Fujimori, Alberto, 227

Gabon, 27, 205
Garba, Joseph Namvan, 3, 200
GATT. *See* General Agreement on Tariffs and Trade
Gavrilov, Stanislav, 43
General Agreement on Tariffs and Trade (GATT), 187, 201, 205
General Convention on the Privileges and Immunities of the United Nations, 89
Geneva Protocol, 122
Genscher, Hans Dietrich, 216
Gerasimov, Gennadi, 213
German Democratic Republic, 159, 169, 172, 211, 214
German reunification, 186, 204, 210, 214, 216, 217, 218, 219, 220
Glasnost, 67, 69, 85, 224
Glitman, Maynard W., 57, 67, 74
Global Forum of Spiritual and Parliamentary Leaders on Human Survival, 199
"Global Framework Convention for the Protection of the Ozone Layer," 146
Global warming. *See* Climate change
Gorbachev, Mikhail, 30, 35, 76, 186, 196, 197, 208, 211, 212, 213, 215, 217, 218, 219
   Afghanistan accords and, 45, 46-48, 50, 54-55
   Bush summits, 214, 220
   Cuba and, 224
   INF treaty and, 57-58, 60, 67, 68, 69-70, 72-73, 74, 75
   power consolidation by, 69
   public diplomacy by, 59, 67-68
   Reagan and, 69, 72
   US-Soviet relations and, 80, 81, 83
Gorbachev, Raisa, 57
Government-Industry Conference against Chemical Weapons (1989), 117-118
Great Britain, 10, 26, 27, 28, 115, 137, 200, 201, 209, 210, 211, 222, 225
   Afghanistan and, 193
   Antarctica and, 156, 159, 163, 169, 170, 172
   chemical weapons ban and, 126
   diplomatic relations, 194, 195, 196, 197
   EC and, 219
   environmental efforts and, 134, 145, 147, 148, 198
   INF and, 62, 63, 64, 68
   South Africa policy, 217
   Soviet relations, 211, 212
Greece, 148, 178(n2), 210
Green, Alan, 197
Gregg, Donald P., 208
Gromyko, Andrei, 44, 62, 66
Group of Eight, 187(n2)
Group of Rio, 187(n2)
Group of Seven, 137-138, 198, 201, 204, 213. *See also* Economic Seven
G-24 nations, 203
Guatemala, 184, 223, 227
Guinea, 206

Guinea-Bissau, 206
Gulf, 35. *See also* Iran-Iraq war

Haig, Alexander, 61
Haiti, 226
Hammadi, Sa'dun, 101
Hammer, Armand, 50
Hassan, Eduard Herrera, 225
Hassan II (Moroccan king), 205
Havel, Vaclav, 215, 216, 217, 218
Hawke, Robert, 161, 162
Hazardous waste transport, 136-137
Headquarters of the United Nations Agreement, 189
Helsinki Final Act, 80
Hills, Carla, 201, 203
Hirohito (Japanese emperor), 208
HMS Endurance, 162
Honduras, 223
Hong Kong, 203, 208, 209
Horn, Gyula, 212
Human rights
 Bush policy, 81
 Reagan policy, 77, 79
 in Soviet Union, 77, 79, 81, 86-87
 US-Soviet relations and, 86-87
Hungary, 178(n2), 193, 194, 196-197, 202, 203, 204, 211, 212, 213, 214, 218, 219
Hurd, Douglas, 209
Hussein, Saddam, 89, 91, 100, 105, 107, 221
Husseini, al-, Faisal, 222

IBM. *See* International Business Machines
Iceland, 202
ICRC. *See* International Committee of the Red Cross
IMF. *See* International Monetary Fund
India, 158, 159, 163, 169, 172, 185, 201, 209
Indonesia, 193, 207, 208
INF. *See* Intermediate Nuclear Forces Treaty
Information exchanges, 85-86

"Information USA" exhibit, 83
Intergovernmental Panel on Climate Change (IPCC), 133-134
Intermediate Nuclear Forces (INF) Treaty, 57-76
 negotiations, 59
 verification of, 59
International Business Machines (IBM), 203
International Committee of the Red Cross (ICRC), 105, 110
International Convention for the Prevention of Pollution from Ships, 167
International Convention for the Safety of Life at Sea (SOLAS), 167
International Convention on Load Lines, 167
International Convention on Standards of Training, Certification and Watchkeeping for Seafarers, 167
International Court of Justice, 158
International Hydrographic Organization and Scientific Committee on Antarctic Research, 169
International Maritime Organization, 139
International Monetary Fund (IMF), 200, 201, 203, 204-205
International Union for the Conservation of Nature, 137
IPCC. *See* Intergovernmental Panel on Climate Change
Iran, 76(n4), 90, 116, 117, 129-130(n4), 222
 Afghanistan occupation and, 40, 41, 53, 55
 Afghan refugees in, 38
 Afghan Resistance and, 40, 53
 diplomatic relations, 193, 194, 197
 European Community and, 223
 hostages and, 223
 negotiating position, 99, 100, 102, 103, 105, 106, 108
 regional role of, 91
 security concerns, 91-93, 97, 99
 Soviet relations, 221, 222
Iran Air incident, 97, 98

Iran-contra affair, 71, 76(n4)
Iran-Iraq war, 3, 4, 5, 7
  Algiers accord, 101-103
  cease-fire, 7
  chemical weapons use in, 98, 115-116, 117, 122, 129(n1)
  face-saving and, 103
  peace negotiations, 101-109, 221, 222
  POWs, 105-106, 108-110
  pre-negotiation phase, 95-101
  UN mediation, 89-90, 92-95, 96, 98, 99-100, 102, 103, 110, 111-112
  war of the cities, 96
Iraq, 7, 116, 117, 220
  Baaths in, 92
  chemical weapons, 98, 115-116, 117, 122, 129(n1)
  hostages and, 223
  Kuwait invasion, 183, 184, 223
  negotiating position, 98-99, 100, 101-102, 105, 106, 108
  nuclear weapons, 222
  security concerns, 93
  UN sanctions, 223
Ireland, 148
ISI. *See* Pakistan, Interservices Intelligence Agency
Islamic Conference Organization, 220-221
Islamic Jihad, 221
Islamic Unity of Afghan Mujahidin. *See* Afghan Alliance
Israel, 7, 116, 117, 122, 129, 130(n5), 183-184, 194, 196, 197, 220, 221, 223
Italy, 62, 137, 147, 148, 159, 163, 193, 201, 211, 219
Ivory Coast, 27, 194, 200, 206

Jackson-Vanik amendment, 79, 80, 87(n2)
Japan, 72, 115, 137, 193, 201, 209
  Antarctica and, 147, 150, 159, 163, 170, 172, 173, 174, 175, 176
  environmental efforts and, 198
  Ministry of International Trade and Industry, 203
  trade relations, 201
Jews, 92
  Azerbaijani, 222
  Israeli settlers, 222
  Soviet, 81, 87, 184, 222
John Paul II (pope), 196, 206, 219, 228
Johnson Act, 80
Jordan, 220
Junejo, Mohammed Khan, 49, 51, 52

Kaifu, Toshiki, 202, 203
Kampelman, Max M., 67
Karmal, Babrak, 38, 47
Karpov, Viktor, 67, 74
Kashmir, 185
Katyn Forest Massacre, 211
Keating, Paul, 163
Kenya, 205
Kerensky, Aleksandr, 80
KGB, 88(n5)
Khamenei, Ali, 99, 101
Khomeini, Ruhollah (ayatollah), 97, 100, 107, 194
Kibi, Chedli, 221
Kishtmand, Ali, 43
Koh, Tommy, 138
Kohl, Helmut, 73, 204, 214, 215, 216, 217, 218, 219
Korean conflict, 7
Korniyenko, Georgi, 44
Kovalyev, Anatoly, 48
Kuwait, 5, 183, 184, 214, 223
Kvitsinsky, Yuli, 62, 63-64

Lancaster House settlement, 10
Lao People's Revolutionary Party, 195
Larijani, Mohammad Javad, 106
Latvia, 220
LBS. *See* Pollution, land-based sources
Lebanon, 196, 221, 222
Letelier, Orlando, 228
Libya, 116, 117-118, 206, 220
Li Peng, 209
Lithuania, 81, 217, 218, 219, 220
London Dumping Convention, 167
Lonetree, Clayton, 88(n5)

Long Term Grain Agreement of 1983, 79
Lusaka disengagement accord, 19, 25
Luxembourg, 148

McDonald's corporation, 203
McMurdo Station, 168
Madagascar, 194
Mahallati, Mohammad Ja'far, 106
Mali, 206
Malinin, Sergei, 194
Malta Summit, 214
Mandela, Nelson, 206, 207
Marine pollution, 136, 167
Marine spying scandal, 82, 88(n5)
Marzouki, Mohammed Ali, 221
Mauritania, 195-196, 220
Maxim Gorky, 214
Mazowiecki, Tadeusz, 217, 218
MBFR. *See* Mutual and Balanced Force Reductions
Medellin drug cartel, 226
Mello, Fernando Collor de, 226
Mendis, Viraj, 193
Mexico, 184-185, 187(n2), 202, 203, 204, 205
Mitterand, François, 116, 123, 214, 215, 217
Mobuto Sese Seko, 205
Modrow, Hans, 215, 216, 217
Moffitt, Ronni K., 228
Montreal Protocol on Substances that Deplete the Ozone Layer, 134, 139-140(n1), 141, 142, 144, 149, 150-152, 153, 199
Morocco, 27, 184, 205, 220
Mount Flora, 168
Mozambique, 10, 12, 27, 205
MPLA. *See* Popular Movement for the Liberation of Angola
Mugabe, Robert, 12
Mujahidin, 42, 46, 49, 53, 54, 55(n8)
Mulroney, Brian, 223, 224, 227
Multilateralism, 6, 37
Mutual and Balanced Force Reductions (MBFR), 75, 210-211, 228

Najibullah, Mohammed, 47, 48, 51, 53, 54, 185
Namibia, 3, 4, 5, 9, 10, 12-14, 16-18(table), 19-20, 28, 29-30, 35, 206
NASA. *See* National Aeronautics and Space Administration
National Aeronautics and Space Administration (NASA), 143
National Institutes of Health, 81
National interest, 3, 6
National Opposition Union (UNO), 198, 226
National Union for the Total Independence of Angola (UNITA), 16-18(table), 21, 22-23, 25, 27, 31, 32, 33, 34, 205, 206
NATO. *See* North Atlantic Treaty Organization
Netherlands, 62, 118, 124, 148, 169-170, 178(n2)
Neutral nations, 4. *See also* Non-Aligned Movement
New Zealand, 147, 156, 159, 163, 166, 172
Nicaragua, 7, 76(n4), 184, 194, 195, 196, 204, 205, 223, 224, 225, 226, 227
Nigeria, 27
Nitze, Paul, 62, 63-64, 67
Nixon, Richard, 82
Non-Aligned Movement, 30, 170-171, 199. *See also* Neutral nations
Noorani, Zain, 51
Noriega, Manuel Antonio, 184, 225, 226
North, Oliver 76(n4)
North Atlantic Treaty Organization (NATO), 27, 58, 62, 211, 212, 214, 215, 218, 219, 228
  disunity in, 65
  INF treaty and, 60
  "two-track" decision, 60-61
North Sea, 218
North Yemen, 220, 223
Norway, 144, 147, 156, 159, 172, 202
Novosti, 85, 88(n7)
NST. *See* Nuclear and Space Talks
Nuclear and Space Talks (NST), 67

Nuclear Regulatory Commission, 85
Nuclear weapons
  chemical weapons and, 122
  in Europe, 211

OAS. *See* Organization of American States
OAU. *See* Organization of African Unity
Obukhov, Alexei A., 57, 67
OECD. *See* Organization for Economic Cooperation and Development
OIC. *See* Organization of the Islamic Conference
OPEC. *See* Organization of Petroleum Exporting Countries
Open Skies proposal, 217
Organization of African Unity (OAU), 30
Organization for Economic Cooperation and Development (OECD), 139
Organization of American States (OAS), 224, 225, 227
Organization of Arab Petroleum Exporting States, 221
Organization of Petroleum Exporting Countries (OPEC), 202
Organization of the Islamic Conference (OIC), 38, 39, 40
Orlov, Yuriy, 86
Ortega, Daniel, 224, 226
Ozone-depletion, 134, 141-154, 168

Pakhtusov, Yuri, 194
Pakistan, 207
  -Afghanistan accords, 37, 41-55
  Afghan occupation and, 39, 40-41, 51
  Afghan refugees in, 38, 49
  India relations, 209
  Interservices Intelligence Agency (ISI), 49
  -US relations, 39
Palestine Liberation Organization (PLO), 184, 194, 195, 197
Palestinians, 7, 183-184, 221, 222, 223
Palme, Olav, 95
Panama, 184, 187(n2), 195, 196, 197, 201, 203, 224, 225, 226, 227
Panama Canal Treaty, 225
Papua New Guinea, 178(n2)
PDPA. *See* People's Democratic Party of Afghanistan
Peace Conference on Cambodia, 208
People's Democratic Party of Afghanistan (PDPA), 38, 39, 40, 48, 49, 50, 51, 54
People's Democratic Republic of Korea, 178(n2), 185-186, 207, 208
People's Republic of China, 72, 158, 159, 163, 193, 195, 197, 200, 203, 207, 209, 210, 212
Perestroika, 69, 224
Perez de Cuellar, Javier, 15, 20, 24, 40, 41, 42, 92, 95, 98, 99, 101, 103-104, 106-107, 108, 109, 110, 200
Perle, Richard, 74
Persian Gulf. *See* Gulf
Peru, 159, 169-170, 187(n2), 227
Peshawar parties, 48, 53
Philippines, 198, 201, 209, 210
PLO. *See* Palestine Liberation Organization
Poindexter, John, 76(n4)
Poland, 79, 159, 172, 173, 176, 194, 195, 197, 202, 203, 211, 213, 214, 216, 219
Polhill, Robert, 223
Polisario, 184, 205
Polish Communist Party, 216
Pollution
  air, 134-135, 140(n3), 141-154, 167, 198
  land-based sources (LBS), 136
  marine, 136, 167
Polyakov, Vladimir, 222
Popular Movement for the Liberation of Angola (MPLA), 17(table), 21, 23, 25, 27, 28, 30, 31, 32, 33, 34
Portugal, 10, 148
Powell, Colin, 74
Power projection, 6
Pre-negotiations, 14
Prunskiene, Kazimiera, 220
"Public diplomacy," 59, 62, 63, 64-66, 67-68

Qaddafi, Muammar, 222
Quayle, Daniel, 226

Radio Free Europe/Radio Liberty, 85
Rafsanjani, Ali Akbar Hashemi, 89, 98, 221
Reagan, Nancy, 57
Reagan, Ronald, 61, 66
 Afghanistan policy, 46
 arms control and, 61-62, 77-88
 chemical weapons policy, 116, 127
 East-West trade and, 78-81
 environmental policies, 149, 153
 Gorbachev and, 69, 72
 human rights policy, 86
 INF treaty and, 57-58, 60, 68, 70-72, 74, 75
 Southern Africa policies, 10, 12, 13-14
 Soviet relations and, 84
 "zero-zero" proposal, 61-62
Reagan doctrine, 23
Reed, Frank, 223
Refuseniks, 87. *See also* Jews, Soviet
Republic of Cyprus, 183, 193, 210
Republic of Korea, 159, 169-170, 172, 173, 186, 193, 196, 197, 203, 207, 208, 209
Reykjavik summit, 78
Rhodesia, 10. *See also* Zimbabwe
Roh Tae Woo, 186, 197, 208
Romania, 178(n2), 194, 197, 200, 202, 211, 212, 214, 215
Rushdie, Salman, 193, 194, 221, 223

SADF. *See* South African Defense Force
Sakharov, Andrey, 86
Salinas de Gortari, Carlos, 184, 202, 228
Sao Tome and Principe, 205
Satanic Verses, The (Rushdie), 193, 221. *See also* Rushdie, Salman
Saudi Arabia, 43, 53, 55, 221, 222
Saunders, Harold, 14
Savimbi, Jonas, 205, 206
Schmidt, Helmut, 60
Scowcroft, Brent, 208
SDI. *See* Strategic Defense Initiative

Secades, Lazaro Mora, 197
Senegal, 195-196
Seychelles, 194
Shahi, Agha, 40, 41
Shamir, Yitzhak, 222
Shatt al-Arab waterway, 89, 101-103, 104, 105, 108, 109
Shcharanskiy, Anatoliy, 86
Shevardnadze, Eduard, 5, 48, 50, 52, 74, 75, 78, 207, 211, 213, 214, 215, 217, 219, 220
Shiites, 92
Shultz, George P., 15, 44, 52, 66, 74, 77, 78, 79
Siemens AG., 203
SII. *See* Structural Impediments Initiative
Sinatra Doctrine, 213
Single Europe Act, 186
Sinicic, Vizko, 211
Smirnov, Vitaly S., 40
SOLAS. *See* International Convention for the Safety of Life at Sea
South Africa, 32, 33, 159, 172, 194, 195, 196-197, 200, 217
 Angola and, 12-13, 16-17(table), 22, 24-25
 apartheid, 13
 Mozambique and, 12
 Namibia and, 9, 12-13, 22
 power projection by, 10, 12
 UN and, 24, 25
South African Defense Force (SADF), 18(table), 21, 22, 25, 31, 32
South Atlantic Conflict, 195
Southern Africa
 external actors, 26-34. *See also* Cuba; Soviet Union; United States
 negotiations, 14-15, 16-18(table), 19-34
 Soviet policies, 9, 10, 12, 13, 22, 23, 29-34
 US initiative, 9, 10, 12-15, 16-18(table), 19-34
South-West African People's Organization (SWAPO), 12, 16-18(table), 21, 22, 25, 27, 29
South Yemen, 200, 223

Soviet Communist Party, 216, 218
Soviet Union, 203, 218
   Afghanistan and, 35-56, 185
   African policies, 9, 10, 12, 13, 22, 23, 29-34
   Antarctica and, 159, 163, 169, 170, 172, 173, 174-175, 176, 180(n28)
   arms transfers by, 30, 55
   Baltic Peace Initiative, 213
   British relations, 211, 212
   chemical weapons ban and, 115, 119-120, 124, 127
   debt, 80, 81
   diplomatic relations, 195, 196, 197
   disinformation campaigns, 85
   emigration from, 86-87
   environmental efforts and, 134, 147, 150, 198, 199
   foreign policy, 212
   French relations, 83, 212
   FRG relations, 83
   human rights in, 77, 79, 81, 86-87
   India-Pakistan mediation, 33
   INF negotiations, 57-76
   Iran-Iraq war and, 96-97
   Iran relations, 221, 222
   Lithuania policy, 218, 219, 220
   Poland and, 211
   PRC relations, 207, 208
   SS missile testing, 60
   US exchanges, 83-85
   US relations, 4-5, 58, 69, 77-88, 191, 194, 196, 204, 211, 212, 214-215, 217
   Vatican relations, 196
Spain, 148, 159, 169, 172
Specially Protected Areas for Wildlife, 199
Sri Lanka, 193, 209
START. *See* Strategic Arms Reduction Talks
Stedule, Nikola, 211
Stevenson amendment, 80, 87(n3)
Stonington Island, 168
Storm, Daniel, 194, 195
Strait of Hormuz, 104
Strategic Arms Limitation Agreement, 187
Strategic Arms Reduction Talks (START), 66, 67, 70, 71-72, 187, 213, 216
Strategic Defense Initiative (SDI), 66, 67, 70, 71
Structural Impediments Initiative (SII), 204
Sudan, 205
Sunnis, 92
Suzuki Motor Company, 202
SWAPO. *See* South-West African People's Organization
Sweden, 4, 93-94, 144, 147, 159, 166, 202
Switzerland, 26, 146, 147, 202
Syria, 116, 117, 129, 196, 197, 220, 222, 223

Tambo, Oliver, 206
Tanai, Shahnawaz, 54
Ten-Nation Committee on Disarmament, 130(n9)
Thatcher, Margaret, 198, 218, 219
Thornburgh, Richard, 227
Tibet, 197, 209
Tolba, Mostafa, 146, 149-150, 152, 153
Torrijos, Omar, 225
Trade, 78-81, 200-205
"Treaty Between the United States of America and the Union of Soviet Socialist Republics on the Elimination of Their Intermediate-Range and Shorter-Range Missiles." *See* Intermediate Nuclear Forces Treaty
Tunisia, 220
Turkey, 196, 202, 210, 214, 222

UNAVEM. *See* United Nations, Verification Mission in Angola
UNDC. *See* United Nations, Disarmament Commission
UNEP. *See* United Nations, Environment Program
UNESCO. *See* United Nations, Educational, Scientific, and Cultural Organization

UNHCR. *See* United Nations, High Commissioner for Refugees
UNIIMOG. *See* United Nations, Iran-Iraq Military Observer Group
UNITA. *See* National Union for the Total Independence of Angola
United Kingdom. *See* Great Britain
United Nations, 10, 200
  Afghanistan negotiations and, 35-55
  Antarctica and, 170-171
  Cambodia and, 185, 209, 210
  Conference on Environment and Development, 199
  Declaration on Inadmissibility of Interference in the Internal Affairs of States, 36(table), 42-43
  Disarmament Commission (UNDC), 130(n8)
  Educational, Scientific, and Cultural Organization (UNESCO), 195
  environmental efforts, 198, 199
  Environment Program (UNEP), 133, 136, 137, 138, 139, 143, 146, 147, 151-152
  High Commissioner for Refugees (UNHCR), 36(table)
  International Law Commission, 191
  Iran-Iraq Military Observer Group (UNIIMOG), 94-95
  Iran-Iraq resolutions, 89-90, 91, 92-95, 96, 97, 98-102, 103, 105-107, 109, 111-112
  Morocco and, 184
  Namibia-Angola accords and, 10, 12, 15, 16(table), 23-24, 30
  Nicaragua and, 224
  Security Council Resolution 435, 10, 12, 13, 15, 20, 23, 24, 25, 27, 28, 29, 31
  Transition Assistance Group (UNTAG), 16(table), 24
  Verification Mission in Angola (UNAVEM), 24
United States, 137, 201, 225
  Afghan arms transfer, 46
  Afghanistan occupation and, 39, 42, 44, 45, 46, 50-51, 52, 54, 185, 193
  Africa policies, 9, 10, 12-15, 16-18(table), 19-34
  Antarctica and, 159, 163, 166, 170, 172, 173, 176
  Canada relations, 203, 223
  chemical weapons and, 115, 116-117, 118, 119-120, 121, 123, 127, 128-129, 131(nn 16, 24, 26), 132(n30)
  Council of Economic Advisors, 149
  credibility, 23-24
  Cultural Affairs Bureau, 84
  diplomatic practice, 190-191
  drug war, 225, 226, 227, 228
  economic relations, 200-205
  EC trade dispute, 200-201
  environmental efforts and, 134-135, 136, 137, 144, 145, 147, 149, 151, 153, 198-199
  INF negotiations, 57-76
  Iran and, 223
  Iran-Iraq war and, 96-97, 98, 99
  Israel policies, 223
  Japan and, 203, 204
  Lebanon and, 196, 222
  Mexico relations, 184-185
  Nicaragua and, 195, 196, 223, 224
  North Korea and, 207
  Office of the President, 84
  Pakistan and, 39
  Palestinian issue and, 184
  Philippines and, 198
  People's Republic of China and, 197, 208, 210
  Soviet exchanges, 83-85
  Soviet relations, 4-5, 58, 69, 77-88, 191, 194, 196, 204, 211, 212, 214-215, 217
  State Department, 149, 190
  trade relations, 200-205
  UN and, 200
  Vietnam and, 208
United States Information Agency (USIA), 84, 85
UNO. *See* National Opposition Union
UNTAG. *See* United Nations, Transition Assistance Group

Uruguay, 159, 187(n2)
USIA. *See* United States Information Agency
US-Soviet Joint Commercial Commission, 79
US-USSR General Exchanges Agreement, 83

Value-Added Tax (VAT), 191
Van Grundy, Francis, 194
Vargas, Virgilio Barco, 227
Vargas Llosa, Mario, 227
VAT. *See* Value-Added Tax
Vatican, 195, 196, 197
Velayati, Ali Akbar, 91, 98, 105, 106, 107, 108
Venezuela, 187(n2), 223, 227
Verification
 of chemical weapons ban, 115, 120-121, 123-128, 131(n24)
 of INF treaty, 59
Verity, William, 79
Vienna Convention on Consular Relations (1963), 189
Vienna Convention on Diplomatic Relations (1961), 189
Vienna Convention on the Protection of the Ozone Layer, 139(n1), 151
Vietnam, 207, 208
Vietnam War, 208
VOCs. *See* Volatile Organic Compounds
Voice of America, 86
"Volga Germans," 81

Vorontsov, Yuli, 51
Volatile Organic Compounds (VOCs), 135

Wahhabis, 92
Waldegrave, William, 197
Waldheim, Kurt, 40
Warsaw Pact, 211, 212, 213, 218, 219, 228
Weinberger, Caspar, 61, 74
Wellington Minerals Convention, 158-159, 160, 163-164, 170, 171, 177
Wick, Charles, 85
Wildlife sanctuaries, 136
World Bank, 200, 201, 203
World Climate Conference, 134
World Meteorological Organization, 133, 143, 151, 169

Yaqub Khan, Sahabzada, 41, 43, 44, 48, 50
Yon Hyong Muk, 207
Yugoslavia, 216, 219

Zahir Shah, Mohammed, 49, 50, 54, 55(n8)
Zaire, 200, 205
Zakharov, Gennadi, 87(n1)
Zambia, 26, 27, 205, 206
Zamora, Jaime Paz, 228
Zamyatin, Leonid, 212
Zia ul Haq, Mohammed, 39, 42, 43, 49, 50-51
Zimbabwe, 10, 27, 206